CAMBODIAN WITNESS

CAMBODIAN WITNESS
The autobiography of
SOMETH MAY

edited and with
an introduction by
JAMES FENTON

faber and faber
LONDON · BOSTON

First published in 1986 by
Faber and Faber Limited
3 Queen Square London WC1N 3AU
This paperback edition
first published in 1988
Reprinted 1988

Typeset by Goodfellow & Egan, Cambridge
Printed in Great Britain by
Cox & Wyman Ltd, Reading, Berkshire
All rights reserved

British Library Cataloguing in Publication Data

May, Someth
Cambodian witness : the autobiography
of Someth May.
1. May, Someth 2. Cambodia—Biography
I. Title II. Fenton, James
959.6082′092′4 CT1648.M3/

ISBN 0-571-15104-3

To the memory of my father
to all the family members I have lost
and to all victims of the Khmer Rouge

Contents

Author's Acknowledgements

For help with my family: to James Fenton, John Crowley, Jim and Elizabeth Hoagland, Douglas and Bessie Williams, Eloise Achhammer, Liliane, Charles Pritchard, Nancy Evans and Nancy Schnell. For help with the book: to Colin Lynes and especially to Nicola Richards. Bill Buford and Leon Wieseltier published early versions of the material in *Granta* and *New Republic* respectively.

Introduction

Shortly before Christmas 1979, at a time when reports of famine in Cambodia were at their grimmest and the stations and underpasses of London were full of carol-singers collecting for the relief appeal, I received a letter forwarded from the Red Cross Tracing Agency in Bangkok to 'The News Stastesment, London WC1'. 'Dear Mr James Martin Fenton!' the letter began, 'I hardly say to you that I could be alive up to now.'

The author, Someth May, went on to enquire politely about the health of my family before telling me about the misfortunes of his own. His father, two of his sisters, three of his brothers and his brother-in-law had died under the Khmer Rouge regime. Now he was living in a refugee camp on the Thai–Cambodian border and wondering whether I could find him an office job. 'I'm free right now,' he wrote, 'and especially I'm very poor.'

The fact that this letter had found its way to me gave me profound satisfaction and relief. Any foreigner who had worked in Cambodia before the Khmer Rouge victory in 1975 would inevitably have formed friendships there. We followed the news reports from the area with a particular horror and helplessness. Then in 1979 the Vietnamese invaded the country and swiftly defeated – or appeared to defeat – the Khmer Rouge, and in the ensuing months a large number of those who had suffered most during the previous four and a half years decided to escape into exile.

However, it seemed to me highly unlikely that I would meet any of my Cambodian friends again. True, I had heard that Dith Pran (the hero of Roland Joffé's film *The Killing Fields*) had managed to contact his former employer, Sydney Schanberg of the *New York Times*. Though this was great news, it did not convince me that there was much hope for my friends. Pran, a most respected figure, was known to be the best operator in the Cambodian press corps. If anyone could survive the Khmer Rouge it would be him.

The pressmen who did not survive the new regime included one who, in the early days after victory, voluntarily confessed to having taken photographs for a Western agency. After he apologized, he was congratulated for his honesty and shot.

While the foreign press were in Cambodia, the men we employed as drivers, interpreters, photographers and assistants were, despite the dangers of their jobs, privileged people. They normally earned enough to maintain their large families. They received their wages in dollars. They were protected from service at the front line. And some of our special status rubbed off on them. But when Phnom Penh fell, the press card became a death certificate. Only by luck, secrecy and the avoidance of informers could our old friends and colleagues survive.

Some of the Cambodian pressmen who were later considered contaminated by their contacts with foreign organizations were offered the opportunity to leave before Phnom Penh fell. Not all of them took the offer up (in the same way, strikingly few of the Lon Nol cabinet or the High Command were willing to leave their country) and as far as I know no great pressure was put on them to get out. I myself have to admit that I discouraged one friend from leaving, in the belief that he could expect no decent future in a foreign country. The American evacuation of Phnom Penh was not like the mass panic in Saigon. Some people indeed foresaw utter disaster, but a large body of opinion held that the end of the war would be a relief. For one reason or another, many of us mourn friends whom we could well have saved.

The Cambodian press corps was an exceedingly friendly and eccentric operation during the period I am talking about – the 'Decent Interval' between the Paris Peace Agreement in 1973, which ended direct American military involvement, and the collapse of the client state in 1975. We met every morning and evening at the Groaning Table Restaurant and Cocktail Lounge, for what was called the Briefing. The Briefing was not like the more famous Five o'clock Follies in Saigon. In fact, if you didn't know where to look for it, you might miss it altogether. For the Briefing was simply a piece of paper which emanated from the offices of General Am Rong and was pinned to a noticeboard, detailing the views of the

État-Major, the High Command, as to what had happened in the previous twelve hours. One of Am Rong's favourite phrases was *aucun incident significatif*.

(There was much amusement at the general's name. I ought to mention, though, what one of his officers told me later in Saigon. Am Rong joined the refugees when the Khmer Rouge emptied Phnom Penh, yet after a while he decided there was no point in trying to survive incognito. He turned round and walked back to the city to give himself up. He could have left earlier with the Americans but he chose to stay.)

The Groaning Table Restaurant and Cocktail Lounge was one of the perks of Am Rong's job. A jaunty sign was nailed to a hut in the grounds of his office, where the kitchen produced free food and drink for the general and his assistant. There was a fine banyan tree. We journalists sat under awnings at a group of tables, calling out for *Croque Monsieur, oeufs sur plat au jambon* and iced coffee with evaporated milk. The central table was favoured by the Westerners, who spent an hour or so breakfasting, chatting and obsessively cleaning their cameras before setting out for the front. There was a quieter and more exclusive table for the Japanese, who included some fated characters. There was a dare-devil photographer who was determined to cross the lines and get to Angkor Wat. He was killed on the second attempt. There was the Japanese translator of Orwell, who also crossed the lines and who lived with the Khmer Rouge until he died of disease. The Japanese were unusual in having a Cambodian woman for their assistant. The records of her interrogation and torture were later found, quite accidentally, by Elizabeth Becker at the Tuol Sleng extermination centre. Finally, there were other more riotous tables for the Cambodian journalists, interpreters and drivers, and for Am Rong's officers.

In the evenings, before dinner, we returned to swap notes on the day's events. It was then that Someth, the author of this book, served me the most extraordinary gin and tonic in the world. It came in a pint-sized straight-sided glass into which a brick of ice was inserted. The gin (the local brand from a bottle labelled simply GIN) filled up the remaining space. The tonic water was electric blue and came in a separate bottle. So the first task of the drinker was to try and find some way of balancing just a little tonic on the meniscus and drinking that off before it dissipated into the clear threatening spirit. The first thirsty minutes of this operation, if rushed, knocked you out for the rest of the evening. And yet I remember that I often managed two of these gins. The Western pressmen were divided between the dope-or-opium set and the drinkers. We had to relax, after all.

When he was not serving the press corps, Someth was studying sciences, and in 1974, the last year of the Lon Nol regime, he began a medical course at the university. We struck up a deal – he would try to teach me Cambodian in return for which I would correct his English compositions. Working as a freelance, and living from hand to mouth, I could never afford a full-time interpreter, so this kind of informal arrangement was very useful to me. It lasted until April 1975, when the capital began to fall and I left with the Americans.

After Someth's first letter in 1979 we lost contact for a while until he turned up on the Thai side of the border, in Khao-i-Dang camp. It was there that I went to arrange for his transfer to the West. It goes without saying that the always smiling and obliging school-boy I had known had changed greatly in the intervening years. His front teeth had been smashed in (see chapter 22) and the lines of his face showed continual tension, worry and fear. The shelter in which he was living with his three remaining sisters, an open palm-leaf structure, was no place for a private conversation. When we wanted to talk we went for a stroll round the huge camp, and he showed me the place where the smugglers were shot and confessed to the fear besetting all the refugees – that they were at the mercy of the Thai soldiers every night when the UN officials left the camp.

Khao-i-Dang was both a city and a prison. The Thai authorities were at pains to make it not so attractive as to lure yet more illegal immigrants (as the refugees were classed). The learning of English, for instance, was officially disallowed because that would give the impression that every one of these illegal immigrants to Thailand was bound for the United States. The informal markets were regularly closed down. The aid officials and the US embassy were operating with extreme tact and caution. On the say-so of the Thais all the refugees could be forced back into Cambodia against the guns of the occupying Vietnamese. This was no mere threat. Many Cambodians had already lost their lives in this way. The Thais and

14

the Vietnamese are the traditional enemies of the Cambodians, so nobody in the camp could feel in the slightest bit secure. They were desperate to get out as soon as possible.

Someth and his family were accepted by the States, but between acceptance and actual departure there was a long delay, and the incredible tedium of camp life. I remember pointing out that several of the refugees had planted small vegetable gardens by their huts, and suggested that this might prove a distraction. Someth replied tactfully but firmly that having spent the last few years slaving in the fields the last thing he wanted to do was grow vegetables. So I suggested he should begin his memoirs.

It is likely that in many of the families who escaped from Cambodia someone has had a go at writing an account of his experiences. But, although there have been several books about the Khmer Rouge written by Westerners, very little of the story has been told by the Cambodians themselves. Someth believes that the best Cambodian writers must have been killed. There are other reasons. Autobiography itself, a long-established tradition in the West, is not a particularly familiar art in Cambodia. For Someth, it is sometimes surprising to be asked to give details of daily life that to a Westerner will appear irresistibly exotic, although for the author they are nothing more than normal.

And there is another reason why satisfactory accounts of the period are thin on the ground – the traumatic nature of the experience itself. To describe the nature of life under the Khmer Rouge in the kind of detail that might begin to satisfy the wonder and horror of our curiosities, somebody must be prepared actually to *relive* that experience in his imagination. Someth began this task in Khao-i-Dang, and continued while working as a janitor on the *Washington Post*. For the last few years he has been studying in England. Watching him plough through successive drafts, I have sometimes wondered whether the pain of this effort has not been too great. It has involved a lot of sleeplessness and misery.

We could have taken short cuts – a tape-recorder and a ghost-writer – as one might with a busy politician or a film star. But to do real justice to the experience, it was necessary for Someth to learn both English and the art of writing simultaneously. On the intermediate drafts, he was helped with points of grammar and expression by Nicola Richards, and it has only been at the final stage that I have been directly involved in reshaping the already rich material. It has been a happy as well as harrowing experience, and I am convinced that only this method could have secured the unique quality of what follows.

JAMES FENTON

January 1986

Preface

I dreamt I was in the middle of nowhere. The men in black uniforms were choosing the healthy teenagers to join their forces. They put us in groups and they pointed at me. I was immediately happy and excited because I knew that I was going to be well fed. A big party, the kind of thing I had not seen for years, was taking place. There was meat, fish and rice, followed by a dessert made from sticky rice, palm sugar and coconut milk. I ate a great deal.

At the meeting they told us what to do. We had to be loyal to our territory and nation. We had to be honest with the High Revolutionary Committee. We had to be ready to die in the defence of our country, and especially in support of the Angkar. I listened to these orders with surprise.

Now we were formed into groups, sections and companies. As we were loaded into trucks and driven away, I assumed we were off to the Recruitment Centre for training. We seemed to drive the whole day through thick jungle, until we came to the sound of fighting. They had sent us straight into the battlefield, untrained! When I jumped off the truck, everyone around me was shot and died immediately. I ran and ran, always pursued by the sound of gunfire. Yet I couldn't see anybody chasing me. I seemed to run for hours and hours.

Then I became aware of a wisp of smoke, seen through a pair of curtains, and a white wall decorated with anatomy charts. Piles of books were lying in disorder on the table. The sound of gunfire continued. I wondered where I was. Gradually I realized that the gunfire was the bath running next door, the smoke was from the house opposite, and I was lying in a comfortable bed. I was in England, in Oxford. I was a student preparing for my A levels. I snuggled under the duvet and relaxed.

I hadn't dreamt like this for a long time. In America, where I spent the first years of my exile, I had very few dreams. But in Cambodia, after long hours of work and starvation, I would lie down yet I rarely felt I had any real sleep at all. I would dream. I would dream I was getting plenty of food, as much as before my misfortunes began. Sometimes I dreamt of all the fun I once had with my family and friends at school. But I seldom had nightmares. The nightmares took place during the day. The good dreams were at night.

In the nightmare I have described, it may seem odd that I was glad to be chosen as a soldier. But I really would have been very fortunate. The soldiers were the only ones who were well fed and, for years of my life, food was the main thing on my mind. If I learnt anything from the Khmer Rouge, it is that food is delicious. Today, even if I am not actually enjoying eating something, I still know how delicious it is. In those days, there were rare occasions when, after ten days of hard labour, there would be one day of rest and eating. And on that day people ate so much they died.

Starvation, hard labour and terror were the normal circumstances of my life. My experiences were no different from those of my family and friends. Any of us could tell the same story. But unlike so many of us I managed to survive. The revolution forced me to become a liar, a thief, a smuggler, a classical dancer, a refugee and finally a stateless person. And now that I have survived I want to tell the story, exactly as it happened.

PART ONE
Back to the Temple of the Black Lady

ONE

In the pagoda

This must be my earliest memory. I am playing with my brother and my two sisters in front of the house. There is a large jacaranda and a small mango tree in the forecourt. The streets are quiet. There are horse-drawn carts, bicycles and *cyclos* – bicycle rickshaws. The *cyclopousses* never use bells or horns – they flick their brakes with a soft, rattling sound in order to draw the attention of possible customers. Every time we hear that noise we glance out at the street to see whether our mother has returned with the shopping. We are keen to help – in a not very helpful way – and when she arrives we rush to greet her and take her bags, dragging them along the ground, dropping things and ignoring her pleas to be careful. Mother pays off the *cyclopousse*, who asks for a glass of water. By the time she comes into the house to fetch it, the shopping is all over the floor.

The thing we are looking for is the detergent, the packet of Tide. One of us rips it open and plunges in, stirring around to find the little plastic toy – a doll, a car, a sword or a gun. If it is the wrong sort of toy, we tease the person who has found it. My brother prefers the swords. My sisters collect the dolls. I'm not particular – I like all the toys. Sometimes a quarrel breaks out among us and my mother has to come and settle the argument. But we are not very quarrelsome children. We never fight.

Some time around the age of four, my home life was suddenly interrupted. I was sent to live in the pagoda, to learn the Cambodian alphabet and to be introduced to the Buddhist religion. In those days, Cambodians believed that it was essential for their sons to start their education with the monks. The daughters stayed at home. Their education, when it began at the age of six, would not be expected to lead to anything like a career. Besides, it was out of the question for girls to come into contact with monks. A *bonze* was not even allowed to touch the hand of a girl. But the parents strongly believed that the pagoda was the best place for the shaping of a son's future. As they handed me over, they used the traditional saying for the occasion: 'Here is Someth. Every part of his body is yours. All we want back in the end is the skin and bones.' Every child who heard this sentence would shake with fear. It meant that he could expect no family protection in this new world. If the monks wanted to beat him, he could no longer run to his father. The monks could do whatever they wanted. They were like gods.

I was the youngest student in the place. The first part of our education involved learning chants in Sanskrit and Pali. No attempt was made to explain to us what these chants meant. We were told simply to listen with attention, to learn and to repeat after the monks. We were taught how to address and behave towards our elders. The monks sat with their legs crossed, but it was considered very rude for a child to cross his legs in front of an older person. When we prayed or had our lessons, we sat in a semi-kneeling position. We were not taught meditation at first. Praying involved lighting incense, bowing three times to the Buddha and muttering one of these incomprehensible chants.

My routine began at six in the morning. I had to go before the stern figure of the head monk and recite what I had learnt the previous day. Then I helped the older students prepare the monks' breakfast of rice soup and dried fish. Only when the monks had finished were we allowed to eat. Mornings and afternoons were spent in front of the blackboard, learning the alphabet and reciting our multiplication tables, chanting them in unison, over and over. We lunched on the remains of the food that the monks had begged from the neighbourhood, but in the evening we cooked for ourselves. The monks were not allowed an evening meal, so the material for our supper was provided by our families. The older boys organized the cooking, and if the food was particularly delicious they would add some extra chilli so that the younger boys would not be able to eat so much.

The first thing the monks wanted was to make us scared of the consequences of our bad behaviour. If the older boys slipped out into the city without permission they were beaten with a length of rattan. When supper and communal prayers were over, and we were left to ourselves for the remainder of the evening, the older boys in their turn would enjoy making us children scared. They would tell traditional stories, with plenty of ghosts and devils and evil spirits – stories such as the following:

There was a boy who had always been very dutiful to his mother, taking care of her like a devoted servant. He would wash her feet before she went to bed, and when she woke up there was always a bowl of water at her side for her to splash her face. The mother had never done anything wrong in her life, and when she died she went to heaven. But the boy went to sleep one night and the devils came and took his spirit away.

There had been a mistake. The devils kept a great leather book in which the evil deeds of all the people were noted down. In this book, someone had written that the boy had been disobedient and negligent towards his mother, so he was taken to hell where he learned what happens to people who do wrong in this world. People who ate their food lying down were turned into crocodiles. People who picked at the monks' meals before the monks had had their fill were turned into crows. Those who told lies had their mouths sewn up, and those who drank alcohol were forced to eat fire. Thieves had their hands cut off, and people involved in cock-fighting would meet their opponents on a hot iron platform over a pit of flames. Adulterers were forced to climb a tree of iron spikes. Anyone who had tampered with a boundary fence would be held down while a couple of demons took a saw to his stomach. Before cutting him up, they would discuss where the incision should be made – up a bit? Down a bit? Here? There?

The punishment for an undutiful son was to be boiled in a huge pan, and this is what the devils were planning for the little boy. As he approached the pan, he meditated on his mother in heaven, and she appeared before him and asked the devils what they were doing. When they replied that the boy had not been dutiful to her, the mother denied this, but the devils argued that what she was saying could not be true: the evidence was plainly written on the thick leather pages of their book. All the mother's arguments were in vain and the boy was thrown into the pan. But the mother used her magic powers, and there appeared, suddenly, like an umbrella, a large lotus blossom that hovered in the air just above the surface of the boiling water. The boy fell into the blossom and was unhurt.

The devils were so angry with the mother that they went off to heaven to lodge a complaint. The king of heaven listened to both sides of the argument, and after a few minutes' reflection gave his judgment: the mother must be telling the truth, otherwise she would not have been able to use these magic powers. And so the boy's spirit was returned to his body, and the boy woke up the next morning in his bed.

About eight thirty one of the monks came to tell us to go to bed; we were to hang up our clothes tidily and before we went to sleep we must go through everything we had learned during the day. The dormitory was partitioned with saffron curtains, like a hospital ward. We each had a wooden bed like a low table, a mat, a mosquito net, a pillow and a blanket. Crawling under the net, I began whispering through my lessons until I was too tired to go on. The dogs began to howl. The older boys had told us that when the dogs howled it meant that they had seen spirits. Nobody talked in the dormitory for fear of the monks.

As a boy from a devout Buddhist family, I tried patiently to learn what I had been told, without understanding what it meant. In my spare time at the pagoda, there was nothing to do but sit on the floor, my legs tucked under me, bowing to the ground with my hands together in prayer, thumbs pressed against my forehead, backwards and forwards, backwards and forwards. At the top of the altar, the great gilded Buddha was gleaming in the candlelight. Rays of light emanated from behind his head, and at his side was depicted the *po*-tree under which he was born. Below him on the shelf were a dozen smaller statues, and in front of them stood the jar in which my incense stick burned for my prayer. I only prayed for one thing – the time to pass quickly so I could get out of the pagoda, back to my family and my toys.

I was allowed out at weekends, and once, when the time came for me to return, I cried a great deal and begged my parents not to take me back. But the matter was not in their control. Before removing me from the monastery, they would have to get permission from the head monk, so they told me I would have to go back for at least a week. They bribed me with sweets and biscuits, and I went back on the assurance that there were more to follow. That week, I became a sweet and biscuit king as my father popped in every day and left them with the monks while I was at school. At the end of the week my parents came to see me and I told them that as long as the sweets and biscuits kept coming I would stay.

My parents were very proud of the education I was receiving. It was considered a privilege. But one day later on, a friend of my father's happened to come to the pagoda to bring food for the monks. I cried and insisted that he take me home, I missed my family so much. The man told me to stop pestering him or he would tell my parents. I wouldn't listen. I cried and cried, and eventually the monks themselves became disturbed. The head monk told the man to take me home. He was very unhappy to do so – he must have thought that it was quite against all tradition. But the head monk insisted, and we arrived home much to my parents' surprise. They shook their heads, gave a forced smile and said nothing.

I realized now that my parents loved me very much for, to a Buddhist, I had done the worst thing possible. My parents believed that a child who ran away from the pagoda would be destroyed by the Buddha. Not only that. He would ruin the fortunes of his family for a generation.

TWO
Home

Out of the pagoda I felt free again. I could get up when I wanted and leave my clothes in a mess. Instead of reciting my lessons every evening, I forgot them in the excitement of being home. Before going to bed, my brothers and sisters and I would sit in the small living-room listening to my parents telling stories about Cambodia.

They told us how the Thais once dreamt of owning the beautiful temple of Angkor Wat, which was then the capital of the empire. They invaded, and after a few years of fighting, captured it at great loss to both sides. The king moved the capital to Lung Vek, and around the new city he planted a bamboo thicket, several metres deep and as tall as a house. Twice the Thais attacked it, but neither spear nor arrow could penetrate the wall of bamboo. On the third attempt, the Thais threw gold and silver coins into the thicket. The Cambodians, being poor, hacked away at the bamboo until much of it was cleared. The Thais got in, took the city, and thus defeated the king with the help of his own subjects.

Then the Vietnamese began to slice up the empire, and they overran the part now known as the Mekong Delta. They were not kind rulers. The Cambodians who had stayed on tried to retain their nationality. They organized themselves into a group called the Khmer Krom, and they called their territory Kampuchea Krom. One year, my parents told us, the governor ordered the people in my father's home town to declare their nationality as Vietnamese. The people refused and there were several days of demonstrations. The governor called the people to discuss the order, and everyone packed into a large barn. Vietnamese soldiers were guarding the only door. Half-way through the meeting all the Vietnamese disappeared and within minutes the barn was ablaze. Those who left by the door, even children, were shot. No one escaped. The governor blamed the incident on the Viet Minh.

And who were the Viet Minh? My father told us they were a group of people who lived in the forest and fought against the Vietnamese soldiers. Had he met them? Yes indeed, they would come to the village most evenings dressed like farmers, asking the people for provisions. And would he give them things? Yes, of course, otherwise they would burn your house down in the next few days. So were they worse than the Vietnamese? They were all Vietnamese, my parents would say, and the Vietnamese are never good. Why not? we would ask, and then they would tell us another story.

On this occasion the Cambodians were asked to dig an irrigation canal to join the river Bassac. The governor explained that it would benefit the farmers in the village. When the canal was nearly finished, and all the Cambodians were at the bottom of it, the Vietnamese upstream let the flood water in, and hundreds of Cambodians were drowned.

This was the kind of story we were told before bed. If I got bored, I would look around the living-room at the photographs of my family. Some of them were shown in monks' habits. Many I had never met. On one wall, above the calendar, there was a small shelf with an altar covered in silver paper. In the middle was a photograph of my grandfather between two silver urns containing some of his ashes. It was customary, in those days, when a senior member of the family died, to cremate the body. Before the ceremony, a beautiful coin (of high melting point) was placed in the dead person's mouth. After the cremation the relatives would gather round the furnace to collect the remains. The one who found the coin, it was thought, would have luck, fame and wealth. Not only that – they believed that the spirit of the dead man would come and protect him from all devils. The relatives would take the remains to the pagoda, where the monks would pray for a peaceful existence for the spirit in the next world. Then it was that the finder of the coin was allowed a small amount of ashes by the monks. He would take them home, and display them, as my father had done here, in front of the dead person's photograph.

My father never told me that it was he who found the coin among my grandfather's ashes, and I think he may not have believed in the tradition. The sorting out of the ashes was a very sad

27

job for the closest relative of the dead person; he or she had to gather together all the charred bones, and I think that the tradition of placing the coin in the mouth was designed to encourage the relatives to help do this as quickly as possible.

In front of my grandfather's photograph there stood a couple of statues of the Buddha, and a porcelain vase half-filled with uncooked rice in which my family used to burn incense sticks. On the floor beneath the shelf stood an ancient black and white television which we were allowed to watch at weekends only. There were only two hours of programmes a day, from six to eight in the evening. Mostly they showed French documentaries.

Both of my parents came from Kampuchea Krom. My father's family had inherited extensive paddyfields, which they rented out to the peasants as was the custom in that area. Thirty per cent of the crop went to the owners, seventy per cent to the workers. Some people had signed leases for life. They worked very hard, often late into the night. They had nothing to pass on to their children but their skills. People like my grandparents, by contrast, received enough income from the land to live comfortably without doing any work. My father told me stories about their big house and the solid barn in which they kept the rice. They had several pairs of bulls and a few bullock carts for transport. They had one boy, my father, and two girls.

Despite the Cambodian proverb which says that fruit never drops far from the foot of the tree, my two aunts were very different characters. One married a Vietnamese officer, and set up a thriving dress shop in Saigon. The other earned her living as a gambler. Once a year she would come to visit us, and most of her time was spent slipping off to illegal gambling dens (which were usually in private houses set up and protected by members of the Royal Family). My aunt was always modestly dressed and she detested make-up. She was generous, and we could always tell at once whether she'd had a good day. She would come back with a *cyclo* full of food and sweets, but we never talked about what she had been up to. She took the bad days well, although sometimes her losses were so great she had to pawn all she had.

May Sokhom, my father, was the second child of the family. He talked very little but thought a lot, and for as long as I can remember his chief concern was for the welfare of his family. He would say, 'I have nothing to leave you when I die, so you must

study hard while I have enough strength to work for your education.'
He was strict with himself: he never drank more than a single glass
of rice spirit before dinner, he ate sparingly, never gambled, hated
long hair. My mother used to pray a couple of times a month, but
my father spent about a quarter of an hour every evening in front of
the altar, praying, perhaps, for his father's spirit in the next world.
He read Buddhist texts and his medical books, but he seldom
picked up a novel. He had a happy disposition. When he had a
problem, he would pace the room until he had sorted it out.

His study was simply furnished and he spent several hours a day
there, working on his hobby which was an investigation into
Cambodian primitive medicine. The drawers of his desk contained
neatly labelled boxes, which held the various roots he purchased
from the medicine men in the market. At the other side of the room,
on a small table, stood a polished wooden box with a pair of
elephant's tusks fixed to its sides. The box held three or four ledger-
sized volumes where my father wrote down the results of his
researches. The idea had been to discover what in primitive remedies would be of use to Western medicine. My father would sit at
his desk carefully tasting the roots and writing his notes. His other
hobby was carpentry, but the results of this were unpredictable. He
would knock together little stools for us to sit on and break.

My mother's parents were very poor and could only afford to
rent a paddyfield one season at a time. They were always getting
into debt over the rent, and their crop produced just enough income
to pay for the education of their two daughters. The older girl, Son
Ba, married a Vietnamese landlord. The younger, Son Tem, my
mother, trained as a midwife and married my father when she had
completed her training.

After the engagement, before the wedding could take place, my
father had to go and stay with my mother's family. This custom
allowed the bride's family to have a good look at the groom. They
scutinized everything he did, the way he walked, sat, worked, ate,
talked or even slept. The groom could be sent away if he did a single
thing to offend the bride's parents, or if they felt that he would not be
able to provide for their daughter. Some crafty families would get a
succession of grooms working for them, free, for several years,
before sending them home. My father was patient and, after a year,
was allowed to marry my mother. Occasionally, I would hear her

tease him when he lost patience with his work. 'You wouldn't have got me if you'd been in this sort of mood in those days,' she would say. Then they would look at each other and laugh.

My mother never forgot what it had been like to be poor, and she always taught us (she was stricter than my father) to think twice before buying anything, and never to waste food. She had known starvation, at the time of the Japanese occupation of Indo-China in the Second World War, and she thought that what had happened once could happen again. She used to terrify us with the thought of going for days without food, and I think it was the fear of poverty that made her always keen, when she was not pregnant, to go out to work. She dressed plainly and wore no make-up. She disliked the behaviour of the Vietnamese women she had known, and used to say that they always imposed their will on their husbands. There was a saying that if a lieutenant married a Vietnamese girl, she would be the captain. My mother's attitude was that a Cambodian wife should obey her husband in all things.

After their marriage, my parents worked in a hospital in Saigon, and at this time they were members of an organization, supported by the Khmer Serei, whose purpose was to put pressure on the Vietnamese over the question of nationality of the Cambodians in Vietnam. This group attracted many supporters and soon alarmed the Vietnamese. They sent secret agents to execute any members they could find, and because of this threat the group dispersed and my parents came to Phnom Penh. From that time on, my father could never return to his homeland, although my mother would go back once a year to collect the rent from his land.

My mother's first interest, on arriving in Cambodia, was to find a job, and she was in tears when the clinic told her that her written Cambodian was not sufficiently good. She was well educated and spoke both French and Vietnamese very competently, but she had never had the opportunity to write good Cambodian. It took her about six months to remedy this defect. By then my father had joined the Royal Army and was working in the Recruitment Centre, and later as a surgical trainee in the Military Hospital. They were poor, and it was a help that my mother found work eventually as a midwife in a private clinic. It was here that I was born, in 1957.

The secret organization continued to work and regroup, and once or twice a year colleagues arrived from Kampuchea Krom to talk to my parents. When they arrived, my sisters, my brother, Sovanna, and I would be told to take our toys and play in another room. My father had made us a wooden cart, which Sovanna or I would sit in, with my two sisters chasing behind. It was a wonderfully noisy game. The chairs and bed tended to get in the way. When the noise became unbearable my father put his head round the door and told us to shut up: they were having a serious discussion.

If we were really impossible they sent us outside into the forecourt that was enclosed with a wooden fence along which grew mangoes and a small red fruit the size of a cherry, called *prakop*. Bored with the cart, Sovanna and I would climb the *prakop* tree and throw down the fruit to my sisters on the ground. Often we ate too much and gave ourselves bad stomach-aches. When my parents noticed a queue for the bathroom they gave us a good telling-off, but that never stopped us eating the fruit.

On hot evenings my parents would sit on the bamboo bench under the mango tree, chatting with the neighbours about their jobs and families and sometimes about politics. We children played hide and seek, and gambled with rubber bands and marbles until we were tired and began to pester the adults for stories. These were usually moral fables based on the teachings of Buddha, stories about what happened to people who told lies or failed to respect their elders. There were also ghost stories. When night fell and the stories ended I felt the house was full of strange shadows.

It was my brother Sovanna who told me that when people died they became ghosts and returned to the house which had once been theirs. He and I shared a room, where we kept a jealous guard over our cart, and where the toys I had found in the soap powder were piled in one corner. There was no furniture in the room except for two low, hard beds with woven mats, pillows and mosquito nets. Our clothes were hung from hooks on the walls – Cambodians prefer not to use wardrobes and chests of drawers, which fill up with spiders and cockroaches. There was a bedside light but the switch was placed out of our reach for fear we should electrocute ourselves. When my parents came to turn the light off, they would check that the mosquito nets were properly tucked under the mat. Then we were left alone and Sovanna began to tell his ghost stories. Sometimes I fell asleep before he had finished.

One night I awoke to find myself alone in the house. I didn't know where the family had gone, but I started to think about people becoming ghosts when they died. An old man next door had died a few days previously, and I could hear the funeral music from his house. When a dog barked in the street I thought it had seen a spirit. I got up and ran out into the moonlight in search of my family. The thin, reedy sound of the pipes next door made my flesh creep. When there was a death such as this, the widow would shave her head and put on white and sit weeping over her husband's corpse. I couldn't bear it any more. I rushed back to bed and began screaming, imagining that I could see and hear ghosts. But all I had seen was a towel hanging from the wall. The light went on and my family returned.

After that I was never left alone again. I insisted on sleeping near my father. He would put me in his bed and in the morning I would wake up in my own. But one night I found myself awake in a strange place. No one was around me and I began to cry. A woman in a white uniform and hat came in and told me to be quiet as I was disturbing the rest of the hospital. I refused to stop, and cried even louder for my father. 'He's visiting his patients,' said the nurse. But finally I made so much noise that she was forced to take me to see him.

It was then that I understood that my father worked in a hospital. After his rounds he took me back to his room and told me to get some sleep, but I was too excited by the strangeness of the place. My father then showed me the hospital and all his instruments. I took the stethoscope and listened to my heart, and from that moment on I always asked for medical toys. I became so involved with them I sometimes forgot my meals. I put the thermometer to great use – I even took the temperature of the cat. When I wanted a day off school, I would claim to be ill and my parents would produce the thermometer. When they left the room I would take it out and stick it against the light bulb. But one day, trying for a spectacularly high temperature, I left it for too long and the thermometer blew up. In those days I was more scared of my teacher than I was of my father.

THREE
School

'Someth,' said my mother one evening, 'you ought to go to bed now. You have to get up early tomorrow and be ready for school.' She had been to the market a few days before and bought all the things that I needed. Now she was packing my new brown leather satchel. She put in a slate, a few pieces of chalk, a notebook and a pencil. On the wall hung my uniform – khaki shorts and a white, short-sleeved shirt which my eldest sister had embroidered with my name and the initials of the school. The name was embroidered above the left pocket, the school initials, PAE standing for Preak Ang Eng, above the right. (Children from rival schools would tease us about these initials, claiming they stood for Eat Your Own Shit.) I still had not worn my uniform and the prospect made me uneasy.

'Will you pack some toys as well?' I asked.

My father told me I was going to study, not play.

'Well, can't I just take them with me?' I begged.

My father was laughing. He knew how to change my mind. 'If you take your toys to school,' he said, 'someone's bound to steal them.'

That settled it. I went to bed with a mixture of feelings, nervous as to how I would get on with the other children, but happy in the knowledge that my brother and sisters were always given a little money before school. It was, I think, one *riel* (about three cents) and that meant a lot to me. One *riel* could purchase two bowls of fried noodles, or a couple of sticky rice cakes wrapped in a banana leaf, or two grilled corncobs with salty-sweet sauce, or a couple of glasses of crushed ice with syrup, or two or three shrimp pancakes, or a dozen marbles from the shop (with a few rubber bands thrown in extra), or coloured chalks, or a packet of boiled sweets, or an ice lolly made of coconut milk and sugar and perhaps a little jak-fruit. The permutations were endless. There were cardboard stencils of

33

animals, telling stories of the rabbit and the snail. There were wax crayons. But the thing we wanted most of all was a black, metal cap pistol, which cost three or four *riel*.

How to achieve it, when money always burned a hole in our pockets? One of the best ways was by gambling with rubber bands. A square was drawn in the dusty playground in front of the school and the contestants stood at an agreed distance. You could be banker if you could show your fellow pupils that you had at least 500 rubber bands, and sometimes there would be quarrels if the banker refused to allow the best throwers to play with him. The square was divided into nine sections, and it was the banker's right to choose the scores for each section. Of the nine sections, one would be negative, one nought, but the rest told you the number of rubber bands you would win if your rubber band landed on that square. If you were good you could win thirty bands with one throw. Selling among friends, you might get one *riel* for 250 bands. There were ten-minute breaks between each hour of lesson, six lessons a day and therefore five breaks. It was just possible, if you were very good at throwing, to earn a cap pistol in one day, rush home with it and make your parents jump out of their skins.

At home we were never punished. The kids next door had their faces slapped or were made to lie on the ground and were caned. We could always hear this going on, and it was enough for my parents to say to us, 'Don't do anything wrong or the same will happen to you.' But at school the teachers were a law unto themselves, and punishment was unnecessarily severe. Our nails were checked every three days and our notebooks were examined every Friday afternoon. If our nails were dirty we were hit on the fingertips once for every dirty nail. Otherwise we might be whipped or caned.

My first teacher was a real monster. When he grew tired of beating us himself, he would delegate the job to his favourite pupil, and if the favourite didn't carry out the task severely enough the teacher would take the cane from him and say, 'This is the way to do it, really hard.' Then he would hit the favourite sharply on the behind. (After 1975, the whole country was disciplined like this. The rulers had their favourites, and the favourites carried out the executions on pain of death.)

One day I spilt a bottle of ink all over my uniform and everywhere under my seat. I was ordered to stand in front of the class and tell them what I had done. Then I was told to kneel by the blackboard for the rest of the lesson, and warned that if I did it again I would be made to kneel on a jak-fruit skin. To kneel in Cambodia means to beg. I suppose I was begging the teacher for forgiveness and I was shamed in front of the class. I went home in tears and told my father what had happened. He was angry and went to see the headmaster the next day, but nothing happened to the teacher. In those days teachers were very powerful and respected figures. The word for a teacher, *lok kru*, could be applied to magicians, medicine men and fortune-tellers as well as school-teachers, and all of these figures were revered in our society. Teachers had almost the same prestige as monks. The word *kru* is the same as *guru*, and that is what they were. (After 1975, all the functions of monks and teachers were abolished. The state became the only teacher.)

I hated my teacher and was very scared of him. I never dared to look in his face and if I got a chance to avoid him I did so. My parents knew about this but there was nothing they could do. My mother always told us that we should stand up to people in authority. 'Do it, you won't get eaten,' she would say. If we didn't understand something we should ask, and if we disagreed we should argue. But my fear of the teacher made me work badly and at the end of the first term my results were poor. In the vacation, my parents sent me to a private school where I loved my teacher so much that I was annoyed when the holidays ended and I had to return to the state school.

One day, during a game with my sister Sisopha, the cover of my notebook was torn. Next Friday came the notebook-checking session. When the teacher reached my book, he glared round the class, held the book up and asked to whom it belonged. I raised my hand and stood up. He flung the book into the corner of the classroom, where it fell into pieces. Then he shouted at me to come to his desk. I did so, keeping my eyes on the floor. I felt like a sheep in front of a hungry tiger. The teacher produced a piece of jak-fruit skin from his drawer, threw it on to the floor and told me to kneel on it.

He chose the jak-fruit skin for its sharp, knobbly texture which made it extremely painful to kneel on. When the knobbles had worn down, or the piece was broken, he brought a new piece and put it in his drawer. On these days we knew what had happened because the smell of the new jak-fruit skin filled the whole class-room – a strong, sweet smell, rather like nail-polish remover. We would sniff the air and wonder how sharp the new piece would be.

The teacher was a connoisseur of instruments of punishment. Sometimes he set us a weekend assignment to find them for him – canes of bamboo or rattan, bits of dry jak-fruit. He would examine our offerings silently, one by one, writing down the marks in his book. Bamboo scored low because it wouldn't last more than a couple of beatings. Rattan, if it was mature, scored high. He would keep the piece in his hand throughout the lesson, hitting his desk with it to underline what he was saying. When the marking was complete, he would give the book to his favourite who then read out our scores.

I knelt on the sharp skin all afternoon, and when the others went out for break I had to remain there, weeping by the blackboard. At the end of the day he told me to get up and collect the pages of the book. I was to copy out all my notes by Monday morning.

My sister Somaly collected me from school, but I did not dare tell her or my parents what had happened. I thought I might be further punished by them. On Saturday morning I tried to copy out all my work. My father thought it strange I was not playing with the others. He came up behind me and asked what I was doing. It was too late to hide the work. He asked what had happened to the old notebook. I began to cry.

'Good children never cry when their parents ask them what they are doing,' said my father, patting me on the head. He promised he wouldn't punish me, even if I had done wrong to a friend at school. So I told him everything and showed him my knees. He was furious with the teacher and told me to stop working. We went out to Wat Phnom, the only children's park in the capital, for a treat.

FOUR
Phnom Penh

I was always very excited before going to the park on Saturdays. We had no car in those days, and there were six of us children, so my parents would hire three *cyclopousses* to get us there. As soon as my mother had dressed me I ran out into the street to spot the empty *cyclos* passing the house. When I saw one in the distance, I shouted to my parents, 'Mummy, Daddy, he's coming.' 'Calm down, Someth,' they would say, 'there'll be plenty more. Get back in the house.'

The *cyclos* were the main form of transport in the city. There was no city bus service as yet, and comparatively few people had cars. There were some old black Citroëns, with their long running-boards, a few Peugeots, and the Volkswagen Beetle had recently arrived. Some people had Vespas or Mobylettes, but for the most part you went by bike or *cyclo*.

The *cyclo* was a three-wheeled vehicle with a hooded seat in front. In rainy weather the hood was put up and a tarpaulin could be fixed to protect the passenger completely. The driver sat perched up behind, exposed to the elements. Even though Phnom Penh, lying on the flood plain, was absolutely flat, the driver had to have strong leg muscles to cope with the kind of loads he was expected to carry. Some drivers could manage four or five people, sitting on each other's knees, and often they carried large loads of shopping or merchandise.

Usually the *cyclopousse* was a peasant who came up from the country when the harvest was done. He didn't own his vehicle. He hired it on a daily basis. At night-time he would ask the owner for permission to sleep in it. The *cyclo* became his home. He had very few possessions. For his work he wore shorts, a shirt and a palm-leaf hat. All his money was in a pocket in his shorts, secured with a safety pin. He kept his trousers under the passenger's seat, neatly

37

folded so that they were always perfectly creased even if they were covered with patches.

Apart from his toothbrush and his comb, for which there was a little compartment, his other most useful possession was a *kramar*, or checkered towel, a typical Cambodian garment. You could wear it round the neck, like a scarf, or on the head, like a turban. When you washed, it was a loincloth, and when you dried yourself it was a towel. At night it became a sheet. Women working in the fields might use it as a sunshade, or it could turn into a hammock for the baby. The *cyclopousse* might have bought some fruit. Then his *kramar* became a shopping bag.

On the streets there were single-horse carts, coming from Ta Khmao bringing vegetables and fruit to the market. A water vendor pulled the shafts of his cart, while his wife or children pushed from behind. The icemen had bicycles and a dripping trailer. They could carry three large blocks at most, and they covered the ice with rice husks to protect it from the sun. Occasionally you would see an elephant, down from the north, with a load of rare barks and woods and roots used in medicine. The howdah on its back was large enough to sleep in.

The pavements were full of life. There were bicycle vendors sitting on stools under the trees, with inner tubes hanging from the branches over their heads and a bowl of water beside them, for finding punctures. They used raw latex from the plantations in Kompong Cham, and for a quick repair they took a burning rag soaked in petrol and blew the flame against the patch. I remember the horrible smell of the latex in the Coke bottles – like rotting excrement. Other street workshops included watchmenders, people who welded plastic covers on to documents or important books – they heated a small iron on a charcoal stove, rubbed it over a lump of soap, covered the plastic with Cellophane and rubbed the iron along the edges – and little stalls for radio repairs.

You could buy satay beef on bamboo skewers. There were carts selling dried squid or beef, which the vendor grilled over charcoal, beat till tender and served with pickled papaya on a lotus leaf. Women sat behind bucket-sized clay stoves with a wok of boiling oil in which they made you a banana fritter. Or they grilled the bananas over charcoal, coating them from time to time with salted water, which they applied with a brush made from a banana-leaf stem, so that the skin was as hard as a roast potato. There were coffee stalls in the morning and soup stalls in the evening. Little boys went round the streets, clicking out a rhythm on two pieces of bamboo to drum up customers for soup. Women came down the streets with kerosene lamps and wide baskets on their heads, calling out in a singsong voice the names of the various sweetmeats they had to sell. My family referred to these as Midnight Treats. At dawn it was the turn of the little boys again to come down the streets with bags of fresh French rolls over their shoulders, singing '*Pain, pain, fresh and crispy!*'

The hill from which Phnom Penh gets its name is a rocky outcrop with a temple on the top, housing many statues of the Buddha. At its foot was the children's park. There were swings, see-saws, roundabouts and an iron slide shaped like an elephant. There was also a pond with a fountain of urinating boys, which I used to imitate for a joke.

On arrival we were impossible to control. While our parents paid off the *cyclopousses*, the four of us ran to our favourite things – Somaly and Sisopha to the swings, Sovanna and I to the slide. Every so often we boys would go to the swings and push our sisters really hard, so that they screamed. My parents ticked us off. They used to sit patiently on the double swing with the twins, who were too small to play.

We never wanted to go home, but still there might be the excitement of shopping. The New Market, in the city centre, was busy from dawn to dusk. Under the high concrete dome the Chinese ran the butchers' stalls and the Vietnamese were the fishmongers. They bought the fish early in the morning from another race, the Chams, who lived in boats on the Tonle Sap, a little north of the city. The Chams looked like Malays, and they dressed in green and white check sarongs and white collarless shirts. They had turbans and long bushy beards. Cambodians are relatively beardless (the men used to pluck their beards with tweezers) and our parents would tell us not to wander far from the house or the bearded men would catch us. Most Buddhists thought that milking animals was wrong, and there were no fresh milk products in our cooking. (We used powdered milk for infants and condensed milk in coffee, but I remember the first time I tasted fresh milk it made me throw up.) The Chams were the only people in the country who kept dairy cattle. Their religion was Islam, and they practised circumcision. I believed as a child that this meant chopping off at least half the penis. We thought that if the bearded men caught us the same thing would happen.

For the most part the Chams kept to their own area to the north of the city, where they had villages and mosques. The Vietnamese lived slightly closer to the centre, on stilted or floating houses. Some of them were Christians. Others followed a different kind of Buddhism from ours. Their monks wore grey robes; they shaved their heads but not their eyebrows. The women wore black trousers and conical hats and were very talkative. They kept their live fish – catfish and *trey ros* – in petrol drums beside their wooden stalls. While they were busy gutting and laying out their wares, their husbands would be meeting the trucks that came from Sihanoukville with the seafood: rainbow-coloured lobsters, horseshoe crabs, squid, prawns and sardines. In the evenings the Vietnamese would cook meals to sell to the *cyclopousses*.

We always thought of the Chinese as the noisiest people in the country. Their butchers' stalls were flanked with hanging sides of beef and pork. The men wore T-shirts and shorts and filthy aprons. They chattered to each other as they worked, chopping with such astonishing speed that I always thought they would cut their fingers off. They sold every part of the animal – stomachs and intestines hung above their heads, and on either side of the tiled stall lay a cleaned pig's head, stuck with a burning incense stick.

I rushed ahead of my family in the excitement of being out of the house. Shopping was women's work and the whole building resounded with the noise of bargaining, the bright cleavers of the butchers severing the meat, the sharpening of blades, the splashing of the fish in the tanks, and the whistles of the policemen trying to maintain order among the vendors. The rubbish was piled in one corner where there were cats and dogs, and in the early morning you would see rats. There were flies everywhere, and the fish had to be sluiced with water regularly to keep it clean and fresh. Nowhere in the market was there a fixed price for anything, so my mother spent a good time beating the prices down. For some reason, I was never afraid of getting lost. One way or another we would meet up again.

Buddhists were forbidden to kill, so most of the Cambodians

worked at the edge of the market selling live chickens or ducks, and great heaps of vegetables and fruit. This is where you came for fresh turmeric, ginger and lemon-grass, bright yellow pumpkin flowers, brinjal, taro, smooth and angled loofahs, wax gourds, bottle gourds, bitter cucumbers and four-angled beans. There were pale pink water-apples, tied in bundles with their leaves, purple mango-steens, vivid red, hairy rambutans, some of them half-peeled to reveal the opalescent flesh, like a lychee.

And there were yellow star-fruit. Magicians were forbidden to eat these: if a magician so much as walked under a star-fruit tree he would forget everything he had known so far. The star-fruit was never grown in the pagoda grounds but it was thought to have special powers in exorcism. When someone was possessed by a devil, his family would send for the *lok kru*, who would use his skills against the evil spirit.

This happened once to a friend of mine, when I was about ten. I dropped in to see if he wanted to come for a walk, and found him on his back on the bed, being held down by his family. He didn't recognize me, and I was told that he had been talking gibberish for a few days. They said a devil had possessed him and he was now enormously strong. The devil spoke from the boy's mouth and announced that he would make him run out in the traffic and 'take him away' because 'he has ruined my house'. The *lok kru* sat at the boy's head, cross-legged and in baggy trousers. In his left hand he held a lighted candle, a bowl of water and a stick of incense. In his right was a bunch of leaves, which he dipped in the water and sprinkled on the boy's head.

The devil spoke with a high-pitched whine. His grammar was very bad. To begin with, he taunted the people who were holding the boy down. 'I go get him first, then I go get all you.' Then he addressed the *lok kru*: 'You not good, you not as strong like me, you never get me.' Then he mumbled for a while before bursting into a screeching laugh. The *lok kru* was whispering a magic formula. His eyes were closed. At one point he stopped for a time. Then the devil said: 'You *see*? You no get me.'

The *lok kru* then spoke to the devil. 'You wait,' he said, 'I haven't used all my powers yet.' He told one of the boys to fetch a branch from the star-fruit tree.

Meanwhile the *lok kru* built a small altar. He took two coconuts, slicing top and base so that they stood up straight by the head of the bed. He had turned his back on the boy, who now began struggling to destroy his efforts. In the middle of each coconut he stuck three unburnt incense sticks and tied them with a red thread. Between the coconuts there was a condensed milk can filled with uncooked rice where he placed several burning incense sticks. Next he placed a row of five candles, which he lit, and in front of the candles he put the bowl of water. From his bag he produced a pure beeswax candle, and, whispering still, he allowed the beeswax to drip into the water. The spirit had fallen silent, but the boy was still struggling. When the star-fruit branch arrived, the *lok kru* ordered that it be placed on top of the bowl of water. For ten minutes he uttered an incantation over the branch. The devil still said nothing. Then the *lok kru* took the branch and turned round to face the boy again. He began tapping him lightly from head to toe. Immediately a great scream arose from the boy. I knew that before a devil left a body it was supposed to scream like that. I fled.

A few days later the boy was well again. I was told that the last stage of the exorcism involved the *lok kru* catching the spirit in a little bottle, sealing it tight, and throwing it down the loo. The boy remembered nothing of this. He told me that he was very tired, and that it seemed as though he had slept for a few days. I never mentioned the incident to him.

While my mother was shopping, my father might take the opportunity to visit the Chinese medicine shops near the market, looking at the rhino horns, tigers' teeth and thinly sliced tubers, and discussing the purpose of the various remedies. On the glass counter stood a small balance for measuring the most expensive commodities, like the rhino horn itself, which was sold in thin shavings. There was a large root-slicer, like a kind of hinged cleaver fixed to a block. There was also a metal cradle, with a groove in which roots were crushed. The shop assistant would have to use the whole weight of his body to crush the hardest substances. He held on to a bar above his head, and between his feet he clutched an iron disc with wooden handles, rolling the disc up and down the groove. I remember the screeching of the spoon as he scraped the powder from the cradle, passed it through a hair sieve and returned the residue for further crushing.

There was a low bed in the shop where people came for cupping. This was the remedy for minor ailments like dizziness, headaches, flu or muscular pains. A lighted rag was placed for a moment in a glass to create a vacuum when the glasses were applied to the skin, four rows of them down the back. Within the glass the skin was sucked up a couple of inches, creating a round red patch like a love bite. The men lay there for a quarter of an hour, chatting about business or discussing further complaints. The rows of glasses on their backs made them look like caterpillars in the dew. And when the cups were finally removed, gently, one by one, they made the kind of sucking noise that the larger catfish make when they take their food at night.

FIVE
My sister's wedding

My mother had a child every other year and between pregnancies she went back to work in the clinic. Then, as was the custom in Cambodia, most of the care of the younger children was left to the oldest girl, Somaly. She liked the work and she was very good at it. She would bath me when I got dirty; she would carry me on her hip and take me for walks. Since the oldest girl was expected to have a family first, she had a great responsibility. I remember, one rainy day, I pestered her to take me to buy some sweets at the local shop. Cambodian children always got excited when it rained: the downpours came and stopped so suddenly; the yellow dust turned to mud and then the raindrops seemed to dance like glass beads. I liked to stand under the end of the gutter, taking a shower; or we would tear a section off a banana tree and float it in the streams that began. We loved playing ball games or pretending to wrestle in the rain. On this occasion, as we return from the shop, I can see Somaly struggling to hold me on her hip while she unwraps a red and white striped sweet for me. I am bouncing around so much that she loses her footing and we both come crashing down into the mud. When we get home, soaked, laughing and covered in mud, it is Somaly who gets the ticking-off for not being careful.

Later on, when I looked through the family album, I realized that Somaly had not been a very good-looking girl during her childhood, but she became slim and pretty as she reached her teens. Throughout her life she was energetic, constantly tidying up after us. She did not find academic work very easy, and she gave up school after taking the first diploma exam three times. Then she married the man who had been her teacher in the third form.

Phan was a good teacher of maths and French. He was adored by his students. He came from Kampuchea Krom, like my parents, and

44

our family had known him for some time. Traditions had changed since the days of my parents' marriage, and my father would not have wanted to subject a prospective son-in-law to a long testing period. Phan proposed to my sister, and she told him to ask for my parents' permission. Normally it would have been his parents who brought the request but they were dead, and so it was his sister and brother-in-law who came one day to talk to my mother and father. At the time I knew nothing of what was going on. My parents agreed to the match, and a few days later all of Phan's family arrived in their best clothes, bringing presents.

I was excited as the cars drew up and the visitors produced their silver trays of gifts. Everything was beautifully wrapped in Cellophane, and I could see that they had brought the greatest, most expensive delicacies – apples and French grapes. There were also local fruits, peanut brittle, crystallized ginger, sesame caramels, French *petits beurres* and other biscuits. For Somaly they had brought clothes, including a wedding costume. Everything was placed on a table in the sitting-room. My mother produced a simple meal and we sat round the table talking about everything except the engagement. Phan and Somaly were abnormally shy and subdued, at opposite ends of the room. I remember how attentive Phan was to the children, opening the fruit and handing it out to us. And I remember how carefully Somaly cleared the table at the end of the meal. But it wasn't till the next day that we were told this had been the engagement party.

The wedding ceremony involved a lot of preparations. Permission had to be sought from the *gouverneur du quartier*. The guests had to be invited, and since there were very few telephones in Phnom Penh at this time, and there was no clear system of postal addresses, this involved Phan going from house to house on his Mobylette, handing out the gold-embossed invitations. At every house he would be offered hospitality, so this took time. He must have taken a couple of weeks off work. It was also his family's duty to pay all the expenses and hire the special wedding caterers.

They came on the eve of the celebrations and put up an awning that stretched from the house right out across the street, which was sealed off from traffic. The kitchen tent had five great charcoal stoves, made out of oil drums. There were ten tables under the awning, each with places for ten guests. At the entrance stood an arch decorated with coconut leaves. My sister and my parents decorated the house with paper streamers and arranged woven mats under the altar in the living-room where the monks were to sit.

The ceremony lasted three days and three nights. Early on the first morning the cooks arrived with a truckload of crockery and food. Fires were lit and a pit was dug for the pig. Popular music blared out from two loudspeakers, and the songs chosen were all appropriate for the occasion. There was a bridegroom's song:

> I cannot get to sleep, get to sleep tonight.
> I'm going to be married in the morning.
> I have a bride, so beautiful a bride.
> I am so happy –
> I shall not clutch my pillow any more
> But my wife instead.
> She is so beautiful – I shall never leave her.
> But when I think about the marriage night
> I am worried and afraid.
> I am worried about her virginity
> And terrified about what I am going to do.
> Well, anyway,
> I shall do my best . . .

And a song for the bride:

> Can you show me a green chilli that is never hot
> Never hot, and if it is not
> I'll never be jealous of you.
> But chilli is always hot, and that is why
> I have to be jealous of you.
> I have to be jealous because I love you.
> I have to be jealous because I am afraid
> That one day you'll be stolen away.
> And I'm jealous of you every day.

There was a song in which the bridegroom said:

> If you marry me you'll be lucky,
> Because I am so strong;

46

I can do everything,
From *cyclopousse* to office job;
If I was a dealer,
I would sell several cars a day;
If I was a soldier,
All my enemies would run away;
If I was a commissionaire,
I would watch the tables and all the chairs,
And they would never run away . . .
I can do anything.

The guests on the first day were close friends and relatives up from the country. The idea was that they should have a chance to get to know the bride and groom – or at least have a look at them. Throughout the day, the visitors came and went informally. My mother spent some time worrying how we were going to put up so many people for the night. Arrangements were made with relatives who lived nearby. It was on occasions like this that Cambodian parents would enjoy match-making on behalf of their children, much to the children's embarrassment.

The caterers were busy boiling up the stock and washing vegetables for the next day, so the guests helped my mother prepare meals for anybody who turned up. From the kitchen came the sound of light-hearted arguments over the cooking. The house was full of children, and we were overexcited, spraying each other with Pepsi and drinking so much we felt sick. The bridesmaids were in my sister's room, fixing their hair and hanging up their clothes. They had mirrors propped on chairs so that they could experiment with make-up, which they didn't normally wear. One of our games was to nip into the girls' room, borrow an eyebrow pencil and give ourselves whiskers, moustaches or spectacles. My brother and I had hidden our favourite cart so that it wouldn't get broken. We played hide and seek. One of the boys knocked over his sister's make-up and was told that if he did so again he would be taken home.

We played all day and late into the night. Around midnight the caterers produced a great pot of wonderful rice soup with chicken and ginger and herbs. I'd missed out on dinner in all the excitement. Phan had gone home by now, taking some of the guests with him. The parents, long since tired of the noise the children were making,

47

finally persuaded us to go to sleep. We slept three to a bed and I woke just before dawn to the smell of cooking. The pig was being roasted over the pit of charcoal. They were frying the stuffing for the ducks – all kinds of nuts, dried fruit and noodles. Soups were boiling away. Someone was chopping meat with a pair of cleavers. In the kitchen, a curry was being prepared for breakfast. Somaly and her bridesmaids were already making up.

At around eight o'clock, Phan and his two best men arrived, accompanied by about twenty relatives. The ceremony of their entry into the house was the moment Cambodian bridegrooms always hated. They had to wait around in the street, dressed in their fine gold robes, under the gaze of children and strangers. Phan and his group parked about ninety metres from the house and waited until my parents sent out a few members of the orchestra and the *achar*, the officiating priest, to bring them in. The *achar* led the procession in his white shirt and baggy trousers. Behind him came the flute-player, the drummer with his small clay drum and the man with the two-stringed violin.

Phan followed, looking like a king in a fairy story. His hired jacket and loincloth were of the finest cloth-of-gold. He had black shoes and stockings up to his knees. One of the best men held an umbrella over his head, and as he edged slowly forward Phan's expression was a mixture of embarrassment and pleasure. He faced straight ahead, avoiding the gaze of the onlookers, but watching the impression he was making out of the corner of his eye. The best men in their best suits and ties were revelling in the occasion. People used to warn the best men on such days not to dress up so fancy as to outshine the groom. The female relatives brought out their finest jewellery, and back-combed their hair, as if wanting to show off their necks. The young girls, unaccustomed to high heels, made a cheerful but uncertain progress along the potholed road. It took, I suppose, about ten minutes for them to reach the house, but this always seemed a lifetime for the groom.

Phan and his best men were shown by my parents into a room specially set apart. Only close male friends were allowed in. It was then that the men would talk to the groom about the duties of a husband and father. Meanwhile the living-room had been prepared for the monks. All the furniture had been moved out and woven mats laid from wall to wall. My father and the *achar* made detailed plans as to who was to sit where, and a long cushion was placed in the middle of the floor. This would be the focus of the ceremony. The bride and groom were to sit on one side, the monks on the other.

Outside, the caterers rushed around, splashing the ground with water to keep down the dust, and indoors the guests were preparing the food for the monks. The orchestra was playing and the close relatives were taking their places in the living-room. When the monks arrived, we were kneeling on the floor, and we bowed three times to them with our hands folded under our chins. They were offered drinks by the menfolk. Then the *achar* called Phan out. He had put a big red rose on his lapel, and by now Phan looked extremely self-conscious. One of the monks kept up a light conversation with him to put him at his ease.

At ten o'clock the music stopped, the *achar* struck a gong three times and the *achar*'s wife led Somaly out of her room. As a boy and a nuisance I had not been allowed anywhere near Somaly all morning, and when she came out I was stunned by the way she looked. She wore a golden dress decorated with sequins, and a sapphire tiara; when she sat down it had to be with great precision and grace. People complimented her on her beauty and told her to smile and not be shy. This was the moment when the groom normally stole his first furtive glance at his wife-to-be in all her finery.

Now the music resumed, and a member of the orchestra rose to perform a dance. He took a sword and wound his way around the couple, singing and telling them that he was sent by the agent of the Buddha to be witness to their marriage. The sword was to drive away the evil spirits, and as the dancer sang in his special religious language, he congratulated the couple and wished them good luck. Then the tune changed and a second musician rose to his feet and began a comic patter. He had a razor and a pair of scissors. He pretended to be late for the wedding, there was so much traffic in heaven, and then he'd gone into the wrong house and had been chased by a dog, or he'd seen something he wasn't supposed to have seen like a woman dressing, and then he'd burst into the toilet by mistake, and then he'd tried to hire a *cyclo* but the guy wouldn't stop because he couldn't see him, and so on.

The first dancer interrupted this chatter and told the second spirit to get on with the ceremony. The relatives were laughing, the monks were giggling behind their paper fans and Phan and Somaly were doing their best to keep a straight face. The comic dancer pretended to notice the couple for the first time. 'Hey, Phan,' he said, 'you've got a beautiful wife, but . . .' and here he examined her closely, 'maybe her eyebrows should be just a little thinner, and, look, your hair is sticking out at the back.' And he danced around pretending to give the last touches to their *coiffures*.

There was a silver bowl on a stand in front of the couple, and white threads had been draped around its rim. The first dancer laid his sword across the bowl and he and his companion resumed their seats. The *achar* led us all in a chant of gratitude to the Buddha, and then the monks began their prayers and gave advice to the bride and groom on how to behave as husband and wife. Now the relatives came forward in pairs, slightly bowed in deference to the seated group, took a thread from the bowl and tied it round the wrists of the couple, adding their advice to that of the monks. At eleven, food was served to the monks, they prayed again and left, and then we ate. Alcohol was brought in and everyone relaxed.

During the afternoon, Phan and Somaly retired to their separate rooms, and my parents also went to lie down. The guests were washing the crockery and putting it away, or sitting round chatting, while the caterers were basting the pig with a dark red sauce and laying the tables under the awning. (It was at such moments, during weddings I visited later in life, that boys and girls got to know each other. A lot of my friends got married after meeting for the first time at a wedding.)

At seven o'clock, Phan and his best men and Somaly and her bridesmaids took their places at the entrance to the awning to welcome all the guests. They were still in their wedding robes. Phan held a silver bowl full of artificial roses, purple, red and white. Each guest was given a rose, which Somaly pinned to his lapel. Seeing this, I queued up as well and demanded the same treatment. My parents laughed. They were sitting at a table to receive the wedding presents. Beside them was a large bowl, into which they put the envelopes of money brought by the guests. My father (if the envelope was unsigned) would make a note of who had given it. In this way, when that family had a wedding of their own, he would know what sort of sum to give. There were also gifts of glasses and crockery but the main present in those days was money, which the couple might use to help them set up house, or, in the case of poor families, it might even go towards the expenses of the ceremony itself.

The formalities were over and everyone was seated at the tables. The orchestra having discharged their duty, were given their own table where they were joined by the photographer and the *achar*. This was the tipsiest of the tables. Somaly took me to sit with her and Phan and the bridesmaids and best men. They were relaxed now, having changed out of their wedding costumes. I remember how, during the meal, the bridesmaids flirted with the best men, and how they gazed into each others' eyes while they ate. Their parents, at the other tables, would notice this but could do nothing about it till the end of the meal. In the middle of the table was a charcoal-heated soup tureen, containing a bubbling mixture of prawn and squid. Then there were plates of steamed duck and roast pork – all the best things were out of my reach, so Somaly and Phan kept putting food on my plate. At the musicians' table they kept calling for more ice to go with their beer and *sak dom* (rice wine). Occasionally the photographer would get unsteadily to his feet and come over to take a few more snaps. We finished the meal with sliced palm nuts served with sugar, coconut milk and ice, and lots of cake.

At around ten, Phan and Somaly went from table to table offering cigarettes to the guests. Phan had the cigarettes on a silver dish. Somaly took the lighter. The guests tried to detain the couple as long as possible at their table. They would blow out the light before Somaly could get to the cigarette, and they said all kinds of things to make the couple blush. 'I wish you a lot of children – one at the beginning, one at the end of the year.' Or: 'Be patient when your husband is angry, and patient when he squashes you.' Then someone would chip in: 'No, don't let him squash you.' Later on, at weddings the advice I used to give was: 'Tread carefully, and you will reach your destination in the end.' There was a way of saying this which would make the couple turn as red as a pepper.

Finally, Phan and Somaly were taken by my parents to the bedroom which had been specially prepared. There were flowers and fruit on the table, and curtains draped around the bed. The pillow-slips had been embroidered with roses by Somaly herself. A purple light bulb gave a moonlight effect. The relatives crowded into the bedroom, craning their necks to watch as my parents took what we called a chicken-egg banana (the sweetest and best variety), peeled it and handed it to Somaly, telling her to give it to Phan to bite. Then Phan's family did the same with him, and at this stage I was told to leave. Soon the other relatives came out, leaving only the parents with the couple. As I understand it, it was then that the parents traditionally told the couple what was expected of them during the night.

There was a live band outside and the guests were dancing the Twist. But I was too tired to watch for long. Sisopha and Sovanna were imitating the adults, wiggling their hips and making each other laugh. The year was 1964, and Sovanna was ten. He had six more years to live.

SIX
My brother's funeral

From the days of his earliest education in the pagoda, Sovanna became deeply interested in Buddhist teachings and literature. He tended to be a solemn, quiet child, and he had the ambition to become a philosopher when he grew up. At home, when he was not working, he rarely played with the boys next door, but would go to the pagoda and chat with the monks, always returning with a lot of stories to tell. My parents were not particularly concerned about the religious education of my sisters because it was assumed that they would follow the religion of their husbands. If, for instance, they married Chinese men, the parents could not prevent their daughters from adopting Chinese religion. It was the sons who were supposed to remain true to Cambodian traditions.

My parents had every confidence that Sovanna would do this. They weren't so sure about me. Sometimes they would advise me in an indirect way, gently suggesting that I should take Sovanna as an example. But I wasn't particularly interested in religion. I told my parents I would do my best. As for my younger brothers, by the time they were due to go to the pagoda the war had undermined the old customs. The pagodas were full of draft dodgers, and it was said that the monks were no longer really monks. They would change into ordinary clothes at night and go out into the town, visiting prostitutes. My younger brothers therefore stayed at home.

Sovanna always got on well at school. At the end of each year, he won awards for good work and this meant that my parents did not have to pay for his schoolbooks or stationery. All these he won, and the textbooks would be passed on to me. Sovanna was passionate about the Cambodian language and he couldn't understand why all our textbooks were in French, or why official letters and documents had to be written in French. My father explained to him that, for instance, Cambodian lacked scientific terms. But Sovanna didn't really believe in science. He disagreed with Galileo. He thought the earth was flat, and that the atmosphere around the moon was very hot and windy. He didn't believe that anybody had been into space, and he thought that anyone who tried to get near the moon would melt and be blown away. He wasn't alone in this belief. Most devout Buddhists agreed with him.

They believed, for instance, that an eclipse of the moon was caused by a monster called Reahou who loved the moon so much that he wanted to swallow it. To stop this happening, people would make as much noise as possible banging buckets and saucepans. My brother believed that when you died, and if you had prayed enough and were without sin, and if you wanted to come back to this world, you would have the right to choose the womb you were to enter. But only a few people had this right. To be born was to enter a world of sorrow. Sovanna believed that was why babies cried at birth. The purpose of religion was to escape from a world of sorrow to a heaven that had neither happiness nor sorrow, neither heat nor cold, neither light nor darkness. In heaven, Sovanna said, you were neither hungry nor over-full; if you wanted something to eat, all you had to do was think of it, and it would be there in your stomach. I used to say, in that case, why do people ever want to return to the world? Sovanna said that sometimes the Buddha threw them out of heaven for doing something wrong, and sometimes it was simply a matter of boredom – people get fed up with doing the same thing all the time. On this point I agreed with him.

He paid close attention to his dreams, which he believed contained warnings about the day ahead. When he woke up he would start describing them to me, but I would roll over and ask him to be quiet so he got into the habit of discussing his dreams at great length with Sisopha. Many Cambodians accepted the predictive nature of dreams. A woman who dreamt of a ring was going to have a baby. If the ring had many jewels and the light shone from it, the baby would be clever and famous. If you dreamt of blood or catching fish, you were going to come into some money. If you dreamt that one of your teeth had broken off, one of your relatives was going to die. If an animal was chasing you, somebody was in love with you. Snakes meant sex. Fire indicated a serious family row. A dream of a corpse meant that some spirit was coming to visit you, to be near you, although whether the spirit's intentions were good or bad you wouldn't know. Some people used their dreams as a guide to the national lottery – they had a way of working out what number ticket to buy that week. For instance, if you dreamt of a fish, *trey* in Cambodian, you might buy ticket number thirteen, *treize* in French; or, if you thought the spirit was making it a bit difficult for you, you might prefer to try number thirty-one; a dream of a cow, *ko*, might have something to do with four, *quatre*; if you dreamt of a ladder, that might mean you should go for a very high number.

If you dreamt of some close relative who had died, this was a serious matter. It might be that the spirit of this person was coming back to live with you and to protect you, but it might be that the spirit was angry. Once a year, during the festival of the spirits, the family would take food to the pagoda to be offered to the dead relatives. The monks would eat the food on behalf of the spirits. Traditionally in the old days, when people were cremated or, on rare occasions, buried, thorns would be piled on the grave to stop the spirits getting out (or, as I believed, to stop animals from digging up the corpse). But during the festival these spirits would struggle through the thorns and visit seven pagodas in search of food. If they found food they would have enough strength to get back through the thorns and into the grave, but if their relatives had not offered them any food the spirits would be too weak to get back to the grave. They would see all the other food offerings and this would make them jealous. Their bodies would be torn by the thorns and this would make them angry. Then they would wander round like tramps, and by now they were dangerous.

I asked my father why the spirits didn't simply take whatever food they found in the pagoda, but he said that all the food was labelled, and they couldn't take it or they would be punished. I said, well, if I was a spirit I would take whatever food I wanted.

The best thing to do, if you dreamt of a dead relative, was to visit the *achar* and tell him your dream. He would then ask for your date of birth, and the birth and death dates of the dead person. Then he would consult his books and produce a chart, and work out from there what you had to do. This happened to our next-door neighbours. They came home and set up a spirit house on a spot chosen by the *achar*. The spirit house was like a bird table in the West, a little shelter at the top of a pole. Inside they placed two small coconuts with a candle, incense sticks and betel leaves. They put in a mound of food every day – rice, meat and fish – and a hand of bananas. Then the *achar* negotiated with the spirit to come and stay in the house and to stop wandering.

It was for reasons like this that dreams were important to my brother, and he would get up in the morning, knock on the door of the girls' room and have his whispered conferences with Sisopha. I used to tease them about it when I found them together, and they would tell me to stop pestering them. My parents didn't really take their dreams seriously – they might, for fun, buy a lottery ticket once a month on the basis of something they had dreamt – but Sovanna and Sisopha were in dead earnest over their dream analysis. It was a world they shared. We were all three deeply fond of each other, and it was only on the question of dreams that I was the odd one out. If I heard them telling a dream, I used to tease them with a scary interpretation. 'This means that you're going to break your ankle in the next five minutes. Don't move. Don't go out of the house. Stay in bed for the next twenty-four hours . . .' And Sisopha would push me out of the room and close the door.

In 1968, when I was eleven and Sovanna was sixteen, we both took important exams. I was due to go from primary school to high school. Sovanna was taking his first baccalaureate. We were both pleased with what we had done, and when my results came I was among fifty students in the capital who were given a special award. My parents said that after Sovanna had heard his results, which they expected to be good, we would have a party. We hadn't had a big family get-together since Somaly's wedding, and the idea was that we would send messages to our relatives in Svay Rieng province, inviting them to come and celebrate for a couple of days. We were going to have a feast.

On the day his results were due, Sovanna went off early to school. I was lying on a bench outside the house, reading a cartoon book and explaining it to the twins. I didn't pay any particular attention to a visitor who arrived on a black Velosolex, one of the staff of Sovanna's school. It was a hot day. The visitor talked to my mother for a few minutes, and drank a glass of iced tea. When he left, my mother called Sisopha from the kitchen and told us that Sovanna had had an accident but we were not to worry. She and

Sisopha were going to fetch my father from his work at the hospital. Her manner was calm, although she seemed impatient to find a *cyclo*. We continued playing as before.

The story I was reading with the twins was about a boy called Bucket who was very big and strong and used to eat half a cow for lunch and a whole pig for his dinner. His stepmother decided that if she went on looking after him the family would never have enough money, so she began to look around for ways of getting rid of him. His parents went out to cut down a tree, which was enormous and valuable and nearly a metre thick. His stepmother told Bucket to stand by the tree and support it so that it wouldn't be damaged as it fell to the ground. The point about Bucket was that he was as stupid as he was strong. He did as he was told. When the tree fell, it knocked him into the ground like a nail. His parents were very relieved that he was dead, but an hour later he returned, carrying the tree on his shoulder.

At five o'clock Phan came home and told us to come indoors. We were still reading the book when my parents returned with Sisopha. They came into the house without a word. My mother sat down. Sisopha withdrew into a corner of the living-room. She looked shattered. My father paced up and down, as if wondering what to say to us. The book lay open on the floor. Then my father said: 'Your brother's dead now.' One by one we burst into tears. Somaly was in the kitchen. She came in to ask what had happened. My father repeated: 'Your brother's dead now.'

I had been lying on my stomach. Now I sat up and asked my father: '*What?*' He didn't reply. He just sat down.

Sovanna had not just passed the exam – he had got the best mark in Phnom Penh. On the way back to tell us, he had driven his Mobylette into a truck. He had died in hospital ten minutes before the arrival of my parents. Later on, Sisopha began to ask herself about Sovanna's behaviour the day before. He had seemed very quiet and restless, and she wondered whether he had foreseen his death.

I hadn't realized till then how much I loved my brother. I thought of how I had always pestered him and made a nuisance of myself. My father said to me, 'Don't cry too much, now. He has found his way through. It's you who are left to suffer in a world of sorrow.'

Nobody could eat that night. My mother tried to comfort the

girls with the thought that my brother had passed on to a better life. Nobody left the sitting-room. We just sat looking at each other, and the more we looked at each other the more we cried.

So the party for our exam results turned into a funeral. The next day my parents went to the hospital. Phan hired a group of musicians who arrived in white, the colour of mourning. There were four of them, and they took up position in the sitting-room playing pipes and violins. In front of the house, Phan set up two long bamboo poles and white flags in the shape of a crocodile. He bought yellow and white flowers and took a portrait photograph of Sovanna from the family album and placed it in the middle of a wreath.

The body arrived by ambulance and was brought into the house. We fled from the sitting-room while my parents, with the help of Phan and some neighbours, dressed Sovanna in his favourite clothes, white shirt and khaki trousers, and replaced him in the coffin alongside his favourite books. The coffin lid was covered with flowers, and the wreath placed in front of it. Then my father called us back into the room, shaved the heads of all us younger children and dressed us all in white.

The musicians continued to play, and the neighbours came in to comfort us. But two people were particularly inconsolable. One was Sisopha, who had to be restrained from looking at the coffin because every time she did so it drove her into a frenzy. The other was Sovanna's girlfriend, who arrived that morning in the company of her parents, her head shaven and dressed in white. She had known Sovanna for the last year, and had often come to the house to go through her homework with him. She was a gentle and kind girl who became very fond of the twins. Sometimes when the homework was finished she would help the older girls in the kitchen – and it was then that I used to tease Sovanna about her. First, he would be quite pleased. When I persisted he became shy. Finally, he had to kick me to get me to stop. He never actually got angry, but I did my best to embarrass him. Once he must have told my mother about his feelings for his girlfriend, because I remember her telling him on no account to break our customs and play around with her. She was welcome in the house and everything she did showed that she would be a good daughter-in-law to my parents.

Now, she came into the sitting-room, and when she saw the

coffin she stood rigid for a couple of seconds before rushing and throwing herself on to it. She was gabbling incomprehensibly through her sobs and pushing the flowers off the lid, trying to open it. The neighbours, who had not known her, reacted in surprise. My mother and her parents came forward and pulled her away, but she begged to be left there. I went to sit under the mango tree. I was overwhelmed with self-reproach. I couldn't understand how I'd allowed myself to tease and pester Sovanna and make myself such a nuisance to him. My father stood in the doorway, watching me from a distance. I think he knew what was going through my mind, and that I wanted to be alone and think things out. It was the first time I had realized the full strength of love. I hadn't had the slightest idea what I was talking about when I teased Sovanna, but now I had seen the violence of my sister's and his girlfriend's grief. I felt that I had always disregarded his love for me. I hadn't shared his thoughts and dreams. I should have returned his affection more.

As I wept, I watched the crocodile flags blowing in the wind on either side of the gate. I could see the *cyclos* stopping in the street outside to set down the visitors. Strangers paused a moment, and old men bowed their heads in prayer. Monks passed by with their umbrellas and begging bowls strapped to their stomachs so that they looked like pregnant women. The neighbours stopped them and gave them food. Some of Sovanna's schoolfriends arrived, and one of them tried to cheer me up. He told me to stop crying since it would not bring him back to life. Sovanna's class had organized a fund to help meet the expenses of the cremation. The neighbours had taken over the kitchen and were preparing lunch for the family. The schoolfriend brought me out a bowl of food. I took a few spoonfuls.

I couldn't bear to go back to my bedroom, so I spent most of the day outside the house. In mid-afternoon, the *achar* arrived to prepare the places for the monks. He was an old man, dressed in white. He came by *cyclo*, accompanied by a little boy who sat on the foot plate. The boy dismounted first. He was carrying a white cloth bag over his shoulder, containing the *achar*'s betel-chewing equipment and his chewing tobacco. Then, with great difficulty, the *achar* stood up. He was leaning on a stick, and the boy tried to help him. My father hurried out of the house, bowed solemnly to the *achar*, and helped him inside. Everyone got up and bowed. He sat on a cushion, and my mother placed a spittoon at his side. The boy took his place beside the *achar* and passed him a plug of tobacco. The *achar* chewed for a while, picked up the spittoon, spat two or three times, and began to say where the monks should sit.

Everyone began to organize the room, moving mats and cushions into place so that the monks would be able to pray within view of the coffin. In due course, at about five o'clock, the monks arrived and the *achar* led us in a prayer in which we introduced ourselves to the Buddha. Then the monks began the long prayer for the dead. It was in Pali, and many of the people in the room did not understand it. When we were obliged to repeat the chant after the monks, the younger visitors especially could not formulate the words. We simply muttered nonsense under our breath. Finally, the *achar* led us again in a chant asking the Buddha to accept our prayers. My parents gave the monks gifts of incense, sugar, coffee, tea and cigarettes. The monks left and the musicians resumed.

They were joined by a girl with a terrifying high voice who chanted a chant of the dead, telling of the cycle of human life — birth, youth, old age, sickness and death, how fortunate it was to escape from the world of sorrow, how everything turns to dust: bones, flesh, veins, everything turns to dust. The *achar* stayed on with his little attendant. When he needed anything he would send the boy for it, and the boy, who was very bored, was happy to go and fetch some more of the chewing tobacco, or the special kind of betel favoured by his master. The *achar* ate apart from the rest of us, accompanied only by the boy who did not dare take food until the old man offered it to him.

The music continued until two in the morning, and even then not all the guests left. There was always somebody keeping vigil by the coffin. Candles and incense burned all the time. The *achar* and the boy slept side by side on the floor. Other neighbours stretched out alongside them.

My family knew the *achar* well. Every half moon and every full moon, in the evening, my father would go to the pagoda to pray and chat with the monks and the *achar* in the communal hall of the pagoda. It was as much a social as a religious occasion, and it gave rise to great discussions on religious problems. Although the official religion of the state was Buddhism, this was mixed up with other traditions as well, some from India and some to do with local spirits. As long as you believed in Buddhism, you could add whatever other beliefs you wanted. The exception was Christianity, because this denied the validity of your basic beliefs. In the country, if you passed an *achar* you had to remove your hat. I remember a story about a boy who forgot to do this, and the *achar* hit him on the head with his walking-stick. In the pagoda, the arguments between the *achar* and the monks used to get quite complicated. An *achar* would speak in our language but the monks, even when talking Cambodian, had special words which only they used. When someone brought a religious problem to be resolved, the monks might say one thing and the *achar* another. In the ensuing debate, the person who had asked the question might be completely confused as a result.

Next morning Phan went to the market to buy food, and ten monks were invited from the pagoda. A table was set in front of the house. The neighbours prepared the food and laid it in large silver dishes that they had brought from their houses. The monks didn't come indoors. They stood in a row a little away from the table, accompanied by a little boy from the pagoda. The boy had a yellow shoulder bag. The monks each had stacking tins with five compartments. An old woman called to the boy and he brought the tins and his bag and laid them on the table. The boy was given fruit for his bag. The monks' tins were filled with various different kinds of meat and fish dishes. Then, those who wanted to took it in turns to place a spoonful of rice in each monk's begging bowl. All this had to be done in time for the monks to get back to the pagoda at eleven o'clock to eat.

The vigil around the coffin continued as before. When the *achar* stretched out for a nap, all the visitors spoke in whispers so as not to disturb him. Somaly and my mother were kept busy sorting out the bowls that the guests had brought. Sisopha stayed in her room, and I kept very much to myself. Phan and my father went to order the hearse. Then my mother began folding small banknotes for the next day's distribution. She placed these in a bowl and mixed them with uncooked rice.

On the morning of the funeral I woke early and made my way past the sleeping guests to go to the bathroom. The candles were still burning by the coffin and the atmosphere was heavy with incense. Nobody moved. I remember the odd sandpapery feeling of my shaved head as I took the scoop, plunged it into the clay water jar and splashed my face. Back in my bedroom, I picked up my *kramar* to dry my head, and I could feel the odd resistance of the stubble to the cloth. Later, as my hair began to grow back, I remember that it used to get caught in the mosquito net as I was getting up in the morning.

By now the bread vendors were out in the streets and the market traffic had begun. The guests awoke and called softly for French rolls. The boys came in with their sacks of small loaves, which they displayed on the table outside the house. The guests chose the best loaves, and the boys cut them open and sprinkled them with brown sugar. I found that I was fairly hungry. I was given half a roll. The *achar*'s boy brought water for his master to wash with.

The hearse arrived and parked by the gate. It was like a carnival float, built of wood over a truck, and all you could see of the driver was his head. The sides were draped with white cloth, and there were yellow flowers and incense sticks at the front. The driver climbed out, wearing white. He placed a set of steps by the float, checked the drapery and went into the house to take a few flowers from the sitting-room and to place the wreath with Sovanna's photograph on the front of the vehicle. Then he had breakfast with the *achar*.

Now Sovanna's teachers and friends came with the money which had been collected from school, and a little later his girlfriend arrived in the company of her parents, less distraught now but still under close supervision. My mother took her to be with Sisopha in her room. The monks came and conducted a few prayers before the coffin was taken to the hearse. The driver was by now back in his seat, waiting rather impatiently as my father, Phan, and Sovanna's schoolfriends brought the coffin out of the house. They didn't hold it shoulder high, as in the West. Everyone stood as the coffin came past and was placed on the hearse. Four chairs were put at the head and foot, and the monks took their seats for the journey. With some difficulty the *achar* made his way up the steps and took his place beside the driver. The musicians lined up in front of the hearse, the family fell in behind. Sisopha and the girlfriend came out of the house to join us wearing veils of white cotton. Behind us were the schoolfriends, and the neighbours followed. The monks began to pray, mumbling with their fans in front of their mouths. The musicians struck up and the cortège moved very slowly off. My mother and Somaly threw rice and money along the street as we went, and children and *cyclopousses* picked up the notes.

It took us about twenty minutes to get to the pagoda. A clay-lined pit had been prepared and filled with logs. In those days we did not have proper furnaces, so when a body was burnt you could smell what was happening. We stood beside the pit, family and friends. Then the lid was removed from the coffin and the shroud drawn back to reveal Sovanna's face for the last time. It had a dark, greenish tinge. I wasn't scared to see it. I was too sad to be scared. The girlfriend's parents were ready at this moment for a scene, but it was Sisopha who began to wail and sob on seeing Sovanna. She kept saying that she wanted to go with him. Phan and my father were restraining her. We were told to go to the hall and leave the attendants to light the fire. On some occasions, I have been told, families would struggle to stop the fire being lit.

In the hall there was a large bowl of iced water, filled with bottles of soft drinks. We all took our places on the tiled floor. For the next few hours the *achar* talked to us and tried to comfort us. Gradually the guests began to go. The head monk offered us food in his residence, but we ate very little. My father discussed where in the pagoda grounds we might build a *stupa* for Sovanna's remains. The head monk invited us to sleep a little until we were called to collect the ashes.

At this point Phan took the twins away and my parents, Somaly, Sisopha and I knelt at the side of the pit and gently fingered through the ashes to find the remains of the bones. Nobody spoke but we wept a great deal. We put the bones in a white cloth and took them to the monks. After a final prayer, we left the bones with the monks and went home.

When we got home, I asked my parents if Sovanna's possessions could be removed from the bedroom. I couldn't bear seeing them any more. We took out the bed and gave it to the neighbours. We moved the clothes hooks to another wall. We put my bed in a new position, and for the next few years I slept alone.

SEVEN
The new estate

Sovanna's death changed my character. I stopped talking so much and I stopped making a nuisance of myself. The responsibilities of the eldest brother had passed to me, and I worked hard since my ambition was to become a doctor. At school I argued with my teachers whenever I disagreed with them, and occasionally I could see that they were embarrassed because they had not done enough preparation for the lesson.

At home I grew closer to Sisopha, who, being the oldest unmarried girl, had her own responsibilities. Nobody lectured us about what we had to do. We reacted automatically to our changed family situation. Somaly had begun having children and we moved to a larger house. Sisopha's job was to look after my younger brothers and sisters, who were still being born. After twin girls, Bopha and Mealea, came another girl, Orphea, and subsequently there were three boys, Soveth, Orpheau and Sambath. My mother had taken Sisopha under her wing, and was training her in the duties of housework.

She didn't take to this very happily at first. Sisopha was the most talkative member of the family as a child, very clever except at school work, but sometimes too inclined to believe what she was told. I once said to her that the shop down the road had a pair of diamond-studded shoes for sale. Sisopha went to my mother to ask for money to buy them. She loved dressing up, and in her teens she used to spend ages with her friends making up before going out, even before shopping.

She was always very brave. I remember once when I was in primary school I had an argument with a friend who threatened to beat me up the next day. (We had been gambling with rubber bands.) I was scared to death and told my parents. Sisopha, who was about nine at the time, jumped from her chair and said, 'I'll take you to school tomorrow. I want to see what he looks like.' She did come the next day, and she told my teacher that if nothing was done to settle the matter, she would go to the headmaster. The teacher was impressed by her courage. It was something that Sisopha had inherited from my mother. Neither of them was afraid to argue fiercely against unhelpful or incompetent bureaucracy. This came from a sense of protectiveness towards the family. But also, I suspect, they enjoyed it as a sport.

Sisopha was full of initiative. At school she made friends with several distant relatives of the Royal Family and they encouraged her interest in dancing. She began secretly to train with the Royal Ballet, who danced in the palace exclusively for the entertainment of Sihanouk and his guests. My parents, who disliked everything to do with the Royal Family, were rather shocked when, after three or four months, Sisopha told them what she had been doing on Saturday mornings when they supposed she had been visiting her friends. At first, they did nothing to stop her, but eventually when the time approached for her to make her début in front of royalty they exercised their authority and told her she must stop dancing. I think they didn't like the idea of where this might lead her. Sisopha accepted their decision with good grace. Among her later enthusiasms was an air-rifle club, which flourished briefly before being closed down by the government. (It had fallen under political suspicion.) She must have been a good shot – she brought home a silver cup.

With three members of the family bringing in money (my father, my mother and Phan), our finances began to improve, and shortly after Sovanna's funeral my father announced that we were to get our first car. It was a Land Rover, second hand and, as Sisopha quickly pointed out, very slightly dented. There was great excitement. Our first trip in the car was to the cinema – but what did we see? A French film, I think, a cowboy film. *Je Vais, Je Tire et Je Reviens?* The point of getting a Land Rover was partly that we were about to move house. My parents had found a larger house in a quiet area of town, near to the primary school. It had a large forecourt with a mango tree, a water-apple, a tamarind, two papayas and a coconut palm. There was a well, which was an advantage. Previously we had had to buy water from the truck or from our neighbours. But before we moved, there was a long discussion between my parents about the position of the well in relation to the house. It was believed that a wrongly located well would gradually destroy the fortunes of the family. This one lay to the north-east, which turned out to be the correct position. Otherwise we would have been obliged to fill it in.

Our fortunes improved in other ways. My father had found the house through the help of the Kampuchea Krom family who lived opposite, and he used to spend a lot of his time chatting with them. One of the young men in the family had been working with the American engineers on the construction of Route Four, the highway to Sihanoukville (later called Kompong Som), and he had heard of a fifty-acre plot of land that was going cheap. My father intended eventually to retire to the country, and he bought the land sight unseen and arranged for a temporary shelter to be erected. One weekend, he, Phan and myself drove out to visit the new property.

My father drove. Phan sat in the middle holding an old French military map, and I leant out of the window trying not to be sick. It was my first long journey by car. It was the first time I had been out of Phnom Penh, and the first time I had seen paddyfields. This may seem strange, but you have to remember that in Cambodia people very rarely went on holiday, unless they were extremely rich or had some connection with the French. I had never seen the country or the jungle or the mountains or the sea. I had read about the cultivation of rice but this was the first time I had seen the farmers working away in the mud. They sang as they worked and there was much laughter in the fields. It seemed a happy life.

At the edge of the paddyfields there were rows of sugar palms, and the roads were lined with peasants carrying flasks of the juice. At Kompong Spoeu we stopped at a roadside stall. Phan let me try a sip of toddy from a bamboo cup. It tasted like vinegar with a kick in it. My father and I had palm juice and a sticky rice cake. Now the road began to work its way up into the mountains through a dry rocky landscape. At first I felt very sick, and often asked to stop. But then the valley became really dramatic. As I leant out of the window I could see the ground to the right of the car falling sheer away. About 450 metres below you could see the roof of the jungle. My father was sorry we had not brought binoculars, otherwise, he said, we could have seen elephants, tigers and wild boar. He told me that a lot of people had been killed during the construction of the road, when their tractors fell off the edge. At night if you came this way, you might see a tiger sitting at the roadside, like a man. Sometimes they sat on the road itself, and then the important thing was to keep your headlights on. If you dipped them, or switched from dipped to main beam, the tiger was very quick. It would smash the windscreen, pull you out and eat you. If the tiger was blocking your way, the best thing to do was stop the car and remain absolutely still. As he was telling me these things, we hit the mist, and a cool fresh smell invaded the car. My father drove very slowly for fear of going over the edge. At the top of the valley, among beautiful pine trees, was a white villa where Prince Sihanouk used to come to relax. I breathed in the fresh air and forgot my car-sickness, playing a game in which I tried to catch the mist with my fingers.

Phan saw that my father was getting tired, and he offered to take the wheel, but my father was too concerned about the dangerousness of the road. We drove down towards Kompong Seila, leaving behind the pine trees and the mist, and entering the thick of the jungle. There was a tangle of creepers as thick as my arm. It looked as if the trees were chained together. There were dead trunks covered with stag's-horn ferns and parasitic growths. Occasionally there were monkeys. For a while none of us spoke. We were tired yet excited. The toddy seemed to have put Phan into a mood of quiet contentment. He put the map away and relaxed back in the seat. The colour of the ground changed from white sand to dark loam. The road led gently down to Kompong Seila. A row of bark-walled, stilted houses, no more than a dozen or so, followed the edge of the lake. On the verandahs the foresters had hung strips of salted meat to dry – venison and wild boar and the occasional fish. From the road to the front door of each house there was a wooden walkway, and outside several of the houses people had set up clay jars on poles and drawn faces in white chalk on the jars to frighten away the spirits. I don't remember seeing any Buddhist shrines or spirit houses of the kind we had in the capital: the foresters were preoccupied with the spirits of the jungle. If a man went out hunting, his wife was not allowed to do anything while he was away. She wasn't allowed to clean the house or even to comb her hair. If she did so, her husband was certain to be attacked by an animal. The hunters used traps and rifles, old French .36 single-shot rifles which must have come from the colonial army. They also used crossbows, which they made themselves.

These crossbows were on sale in the market at the far end of the village, where we stopped to eat and rest. There were no stalls — people had their goods laid out in rattan baskets: dried meat, a few fish and wild bamboo shoots. We bought local bread and had a piece of venison roasted for us. This we ate with bamboo pickle, sitting in the back of the Land Rover, enjoying the view. Small trees with a loose silver bark like blotting-paper grew out of the dark green waters of the transparent lake. Beyond lay thick jungle, above which we could just make out the Cardamom mountains. My father was lacking a few back teeth, and the venison, which had been hammered out after being roasted on a wood fire, was rather chewy. Between mouthfuls, he pointed out the mountains and told me how the bark of the trees was dipped in resin and wrapped in wild betel leaves to make torches. My father looked tired and a little old, chewing the dried meat, but he was happy pointing these things out. Phan, whenever we stopped here, always went and admired the crossbows. One day he was going to buy one. I remember another thing in the market: there were python skins, stretched out on logs and nailed to dry. The skins were about a third of a metre wide and cut into lengths of about a metre. Nobody paid them much attention as the smell of the skins was foul.

Now Phan took the wheel. My father sat between us, and was soon asleep. And when my father fell asleep I realized that Phan was tremendously excited. This was the first time he had driven without my father's instruction, and it was the first time he had been on the open road. It wasn't so winding now, and there was little traffic except for the buses making their way between Phnom Penh and the sea. They were Austin buses, beautifully painted by the rival companies, with wooden signs around the luggage racks indicating their stops. Those coming from the coast had sacks of charcoal, baskets of fish, bundles of sugarcane and fruit while the ones from the capital had furniture, boxes of batteries and spare bicycle parts. The short-distance passengers hung on top of the great mound of luggage. The ticket collectors clung to the sides, and sometimes you could see them helping themselves to the fruit. Then they would chuck the durian peel and it would roll across the road into the ditch. Phan was learning how to overtake. He had told me to keep my eyes skinned for the kilometre stones. We knew that we had to turn off the road after number 156. Every time we passed a stone Phan would ask in a stage whisper, 'What number was that?'

I said, 'I'm not sure. You're driving too fast.'

'Shhh!' said Phan, glancing at my father. Now the ground turned white again.

At Stung Chhay, Phan stopped the car and I woke my father up. We were by a bridge over the rapids. Two men in shorts were making their way across the river, adeptly jumping from rock to rock, carrying a huge turtle, as big as a bathroom mirror, slung across their shoulders. In the distance was a mountain and a waterfall. The village houses were constructed out of old tar drums, beaten flat. There was a single shop, run by Chinese, selling coffee, soup and general provisions. We bought pots and pans and spoons and plates, rice and dried fish. My father took the wheel again. Five kilometres further on we reached kilometre stone 156, after which a small track led off to the left, scarcely visible and overgrown with saplings. We wound the windows up, so as not to be hit in the face, and drove on slowly through the undergrowth. We were looking for a dead tree trunk, which marked the edge of the property.

We made our way very carefully. The branches pressed against the windscreen, and sometimes we had to get out and clear the fallen logs from the track. There was a strange whooping sound. My father told me that the troops of gibbons normally made this noise at about noon. It was now around two. Probably, said my father, the noise came from a couple of males who had been thrown out of the tribe. Then there was a lower-pitched noise.

'Is that a gibbon as well?'

'No, that's a pheasant.'

A cock crowed and I asked my father whether there was a village nearby. No, he said, that was jungle fowl. Phan said we must get one and sell it to a cock-fighter, but my father said they were too fast. We'd never catch one.

It was almost impossible to see the track. Just occasionally you could tell from a newly cut sapling that someone had been along here recently. I was impatient to see the house. Finally, we reached the dead tree, which was full of woodpecker holes. My father pointed to the shelter, whose tar drum roof was just visible above the tall grass. In front of the hut was a termite hill, about two metres high.

I jumped out of the car, and was about to relieve myself against the termite hill when Phan pointed out that there were incense sticks placed in its summit. The people who had built the shelter must have prayed to the spirit that lived in the hill to get permission to build on the plot. I went towards a bush. My father said, 'Don't go too far. Be careful of the creepers.' The way he said 'creepers', I knew that what he meant was snakes. When you were in the jungle itself, you never called a dangerous animal by its real name. You would never say tiger, you would say cat. Instead of elephant, you would say my lord. And for wild boar you would say little piggy. Every animal had a guardian spirit. You wouldn't want the spirit of the tiger to hear you talking about tigers.

The house had no walls. It was set on stilts about two metres above the ground. There was a ladder made of sticks tied with creepers, and the floor was made of bark, the colour of jungle camouflage. Half of the roof was made of tar drums, and the other half was thatched with grass. A bark gutter collected the rain in a tar drum, which turned out to be full of mosquito larvae. Phan had already found the sloughed skin of a snake, which he set aside carefully before helping my father unload the car. We laid out our mats and set up the mosquito nets, using lengths of creeper instead of string. I was told to stay in the house. The others went off to look for creepers. After a while a breeze got up and the whole structure began to sway gently. I was scared and called out. My father shouted back from the undergrowth. They weren't far away. I paced around the creaking bark floor and began singing to myself to keep up my spirits. I couldn't help looking at the snakeskin. It always seemed to be getting in the way.

And by now I was suddenly disappointed with our new estate. I was tired and hungry. I'd thought that the house would be in perfect condition and that I could wander around wherever I wanted. But there was nothing to see: my father had told me I couldn't go down to the river until we had worked out the lie of the land. Phan returned with a coil of creepers over his shoulder and my father brought forked sticks. We finished setting the house in order. Then Phan very carefully spread out the snakeskin and measured its width with a piece of creeper. He formed the creeper into a circle, in order to tell what size the snake had been. 'Oh,' he said, 'it was no thicker than my wrist.'

'Are you sure?' I said.

'Well . . .' said Phan, uncertainly. My father sat back, leaning against the rooftree, laughing to himself.

We went down under the house and lit a fire, fixing the forked sticks over it. My father took his *kramar* and filtered some water through it into the cooking pot. Dusk was falling as the rice began to cook. 'What's that noise?' I asked. 'Oh, it's only owls,' said my father. Phan gave me a mysterious look. We all knew that owls are supposed to come to take the souls of the dying. It was said that if a pregnant woman heard an owl hoot her child would be stillborn. (It was also said that snakes are afraid of anything with four eyes. If a pregnant woman walked over a snake, the snake would be paralysed – but the woman would miscarry.) Phan took a little rice and some dried fish, placed them on a leaf and began talking to the spirits of the place. 'Come on, buddies,' he said, 'come and get it. Don't fight. There's plenty more where that came from. You only have to ask. But I think it's more than you need.' Phan believed in the spirits, but that didn't stop him joking with them. My father watched this performance. I don't think he'd ever seen what a joker Phan became when away from the company of women. As we ate, the two men discussed what they might do to improve the house so that we could bring the whole family. But this line of conversation soon petered out. Neither Phan nor my father was much of a carpenter.

I splashed some water on my face and went to lie down. There were polished split logs for pillows. The next thing I knew I was waking up at dawn. I crept out from under the net, trying not to disturb the others as I trod along the bark floor. The floor creaked. My father asked what I was doing. I wrapped my *kramar* round my shoulders against the chill, stood at the edge of the verandah and peed into the clearing. It was beautiful. The ground sloped away to the foot of the jungle and you could hardly see the undergrowth for mist. Then the sun rose and the mist began to disperse. I noticed there were jak-fruit trees in the undergrowth. The bushes shook as the monkeys went to the river. Phan appeared at the other end of the verandah and followed my example. He was tightly wrapped against the cold. He told me he had dreamt that the spirits whom he had fed last night had come to have a chat with him. I tried to appear unconcerned. 'Oh, really?' I said, 'Can I go down now and have a wash?'

'No, no,' said Phan, 'when it's as cold as this the cats come and shelter under the house!'

'Cats! Why didn't they climb up and get us?'

'Ah, they can't smell. Their nostrils are all bunged up.'

'So how do they breathe?'

'Through their mouths.'

'Phan, stop teasing Someth,' said my father, emerging.

We went down, relit the fire and cooked breakfast. A strange accelerated tapping sound, which echoed around the forest, told us the woodpeckers were at work. I found that I could make my own voice echo back from the jungle. Phan laid out another meal for the spirits. 'There's a lot of ash in the food, Phan,' I grumbled.

'Oh, spirits love a bit of dirt,' he said, as he called them along to eat.

We had rice soup and dried fish. It was black with roasting over the fire. My father took the fish out of the fire and scraped off the black. 'Well,' he said, looking at the result, 'we could have been more hygienic but . . . too late.' A jeep came crashing through the undergrowth, and soon we saw the imposing figure of the forester, with dark glasses, bush jacket and white plastic topee. He joined us at the fire and accepted some breakfast, putting his rifle down beside him. Phan admired the gun.

'So you found everything OK?' said the forester. 'I see you've got a Land Rover.'

'Yes,' said my father, 'but the track is a bit difficult.'

'You're going to get someone to look after the land?'

'I don't know yet. We've all got jobs in the city.'

'You'll have to keep an eye on the place,' said the forester, between mouthfuls of burnt fish, 'there are people who come and steal the timber.'

'But how will we know?' said my father.

'Just keep your ears open. There aren't many people living round here, so if you hear anybody chopping the trees, go and have a look. Mind you,' he said, taking out a silver cigar case and offering my father a smoke, 'you'll have to be careful. Some of those guys are pretty violent.'

'Is that why you've got a gun?' said Phan, eyeing the old French rifle once again.

The forester looked around for a twig and left it in the fire a moment while he stuck the cigar in an ivory holder. Then he lit up. 'I don't actually shoot them,' he said, 'but they respect this thing. And you lot, you're not allowed to cut the big trees without permission. Small ones, yes, but not the big ones.'

We set out on a tour of the estate.

'Phan,' said the forester, 'you carry the gun, but don't touch the trigger – it's loaded.' We set out in single file, the forester leading with his stout carved stick, beating the undergrowth away. I came next, then my father, then Phan.

'How long has the land been untended?' asked my father.

'About five years. The previous guy was a teacher. Found it hard to cope. Now, here is the river. The water's clean and you can drink from it. We cross here.' As we walked across the dead trunk, I saw how clear the water was, despite the number of branches that had fallen in. There were bright fish darting in and out of the branches. On the far bank there were animal tracks, wild boar and deer. 'When you get a lot of rain,' said the forester, 'all this land floods. This is where the last guys used to plant rice. Still, it hasn't rained for some time. There won't be so many leeches.'

Now we entered the thick jungle. The floor of the forest was damp and smelt of fungus. The leeches came looping along to say hello. I let out a yelp. The forester said, 'Don't worry about them. You just pull them off like this.' And he rolled up his trouser leg, found one on his calf and drew it off using the middle joint of the index and middle finger. 'If you try with your fingertips,' he said, finding another leech, 'it won't work. Look.' And he pulled at the leech, which extended and contracted like a rubber band. He seemed to be covered with leeches already and couldn't care less.

'I'll tell you what happened to a friend of mine,' he said. 'We were walking through the forest along by a river, and we stopped for a packed lunch. We'd got some dried venison, stuff like that. This friend of mine had finished eating and he was looking for a toothpick. Now a leech in dry weather will go hard, like a twig. My friend picked this leech, stuck it in his mouth where it revived on his saliva. Then he took the toothpick out and found it was stuck to his lower lip.'

The going became difficult. The forester cut at the undergrowth with a bayonet he was carrying in his belt. Sometimes there was thorny rattan in the way. Then there were fallen trunks to clamber over or under. I looked up. The tall trees, closely packed, pointed upwards like a great raft of organ pipes. They were festooned with stag's-horn ferns. You couldn't see the sun, although now it was about noon. There were monkeys in the treetops. On the lower saplings there were brilliant green caterpillars fifteen centimetres long, and moths the size of my hand. A tiny bird, like a thumb-sized sparrow, went from bush to bush eating fruit like tiny red cherries. The forester showed us how to take the scales off the rattan-fruit and eat the sour, cloudy yellow flesh. My father knew this fruit. He had been on a mission in the forests of Rattanakiri and Mondulkiri up north, looking after wounded soldiers. 'Ah, I see,' said the forester, 'that's why you're much cooler about all this than these two.'

My father smiled. He was already beginning to find the special barks and tubers that he spent his time analysing. We passed bamboo thickets where the wild boar had been digging for the tender shoots. The forester found a tortoise, which he tied up with creeper and held suspended from a loop like a piece of shopping. 'That'll be enough for a meal,' he said. 'There are a lot of these things round here. You should get a hunting dog. Then you'll never be short of food. There are monitor lizards as well. If you chop the neck of a wild betel tree and cut out the centre, that goes very well with lizard.' We found a wild betel tree and did as he said. But we didn't find a lizard.

It took about four hours to walk around the boundaries of the estate. These were marked with felled trees. The previous owner had set up a boar trap, using a tree trunk about a metre thick. When the trap was sprung, the trunk was supposed to pin down the boar. As we made our way around, I became exhausted and hungry. We washed in the river and went home for lunch. My father was delighted with everything he had seen. Phan plucked up courage to ask the forester where he could get such a gun. He was told he would have to have a contact in the army.

We were sitting around the fire, waiting for the rice to boil. 'Phan,' I said pointing to a bloodstain that seemed to be spreading over the inside leg of his trousers, 'what's that?'

He jumped up and said, 'Shit, why didn't I feel that?' He whipped his trousers off to reveal a blood-filled leech the size of your finger. Pulling it off in the correct way, with a long exclamation of disgust, he tried to throw the thing into the fire. But each time he threw it, it stuck to his hand again like chewing-gum. Finally he mastered the technique. The leech hit the burning logs, and a few seconds later exploded, like a bottle of wine dropped from a shopping bag.

EIGHT
A New Year's trip to the country

My father was a little perplexed. He wanted to improve the estate, but he wasn't sure how. There was so much to do, he didn't know where to begin. Fortunately, at this moment Chan and Long, relations of ours from Kampuchea Krom, appeared in Phnom Penh in search of work. My father suggested to them, after they had drawn a blank in the capital, that they might the farm the estate themselves. They would have the benefit of the produce. We would have a place to go at weekends. We drove down a month later taking Chan and Long, their bicycles, some basic supplies and equipment. The two men liked the property immediately, and set to work improving it. For the first year my father supported them with equipment, food and a little money. I remember being sent down with a thousand *riel* in my pocket (about thirty dollars). My mother put the money in my back pocket and secured it with a safety pin, just like the *cyclopousses*. I'd never travelled alone on such a journey before, and had never carried such a sum. On the bus I kept fingering my pocket to check that I hadn't dropped it. The bus was heavily overloaded, and along the road bribes were handed out at above five checkpoints. I watched desperately for the right kilometre stone, got out and made my way along the track, whistling and singing and feeling scared of the animals. Chan and Long had already cleared the undergrowth from the fields, and the first thing I saw was that the house had been transformed. It now had bark walls and a new grass roof. Loofahs and bananas were hanging to ripen under the eaves. A wild honey-comb, squeezed dry, was awaiting conversion into candles. There were bunches of herbs and lemon-grass and marijuana for the cooking. Under the house there were woodshavings everywhere. They had been making a plough. Beside a bundle of creepers lay a half-finished fish trap. The fire was smouldering. Chickens ran

76

around pecking at the insects, which had been attracted to the loofah trellis and its profusion of yellow flowers. There was a kite watching the chickens from a tree nearby, and when it flew to a new perch the chickens ran for shelter under the house.

Here in the shade were two hammocks strung from the stilts. If you looked up at the rafters you could see the flat, round baskets used for husking rice, the various mattocks and rakes and the long-handled axes. The remains of the suspension of a truck had been stored away, to make *parang*s. They were drying hard wood for handles. Little inverted volcanoes were where the wasps lived, and already there were spiders' webs with a few bees as victims. Chan and Long were mechanics by trade, and they had chalked up their calculations on the beams while designing the wooden plough. It had been carved from one tree. The blade was made of the root, the handle from the trunk. There were no joins. Also under the rafters they had stored pieces of thick rattan that they were going to turn into walking sticks, using the curve of the root. I thought: if I'd taken a piece like that to my old teacher he would have been really pleased.

I climbed the new steps to the verandah, calling out for Chan and Long. Nobody answered. A fair breeze made the washing flap on the line, but by now the house no longer shook in the wind, and the floor no longer creaked. There was a noise indoors, though. I went into the newly constructed kitchen and found a catfish flapping around in a bucket of water. That would be supper. In the main room the mosquito nets had been folded tidily back to either wall and a small altar was in place. The only decoration was provided by ancient cinema posters advertising romantic Cambodian films, the sort of films in which girls get pregnant by the wrong guy, but somehow manage to muddle through.

I returned to the verandah and looked down. Beside the termite hill stood a spirit house, with the remains of home-made candles. A Nestlé condensed milk can had been filled with rice and incense sticks. Now there was a clear winding path down to the river, and the ground was dotted with bonfire sites and piles of timber. The jak-fruit trees had been cleared of weeds and had progressed well. At my feet chopped tobacco lay drying on a mat.

I called out. There was a shout from the undergrowth and soon Chan and Long emerged, drenched with sweat.

'Hey, well done, you made it. I knew someone was coming as I heard the bus stop. I didn't realize it was you,' said Chan. 'So you've done it. Good boy.'

Long said: 'Were you afraid on the track?'

'No,' I replied uncertainly.

They put down their *parang*s, unbuttoned their dripping shirts and fanned themselves. We sat on the verandah. 'What have you got in the basket?' There were mung beans, dried fish and sugar. I unpinned my pocket and handed them the money, telling them to make sure it was the full thousand. My mother had cautioned me against helping myself. They were delighted. Long said, 'We must try some of our sugarcane. There's just enough for a chew.' He went to fetch it.

Chan asked me whether I had eaten. I hadn't. I was very hungry. We went into the kitchen, where he hung up the dried fish and got a fire going in the tar drum stove. We sat on the floor waiting for the rice to cook. Long came up the back steps with a bundle of cane. He placed a bowl of salt and crushed chilli between us on the floor, we dipped the cane in and began to chew.

'Where do you get the chilli from?' I asked.

'Oh, there's plenty of it growing by the dead tree. The birds eat it and spread the seed with their droppings. There's tons of it down there.'

I felt very adult sitting with them, having come down all on my own. 'Do you think I could have a cigarette?' I asked.

They laughed. 'Your father would kill us, you know what he's like,' they said. Chan put a salad of green mango and dried fish in front of me. The catfish flapped in the bucket. They said they'd show me the fish trap after we'd eaten.

All along the track to the river there were butterflies. Seeds were spiralling out of the big trees and the wind came in waves over the grass. Chan was carrying a couple of buckets on a yoke. Long had a can of earthworms and a bunch of short fishing rods that he would stick into the river bank. I was carrying the *kramars*. We saw the monkeys leap away, in the forest beyond the river. Chan told me they had tried to trap one as a pet, but the monkeys always managed to break out of the traps. They said that when the monkeys went to the river, one of them was always set to watch in a high tree and give warning of any danger.

At the river we filled the buckets first, then bathed. Long set the lines at regular intervals along the bank. I waded along beside him. The water was clear and the bottom sandy. Further down, a kind of fence had been set across the river, and the fish trap was in the middle. As we approached there was a tremendous agitation in the trap. 'Great,' said Long, 'we've got something.' It was a catfish about a metre long.

'There's something else for supper,' said Chan, lifting the trap out, balancing it on his knee and carefully untying the flap. Long pulled a piece of creeper from the bank, and as Chan brought the fish out he passed the length of creeper through the gills, making it secure. We continued wading along the river, dragging the fish with us. But at the other traps we had less luck. One of them had been destroyed by a turtle.

That evening we had a catfish and loofah stew well laced with marijuana. After that, I flopped into the hammock under the house. The fire had been built up, and Long was squatting at its side, rolling himself a cheroot and keeping his eye on some sweet potatoes roasting in the ashes. Chan sat on a log, working at his plough.

'Do you ever get scared here at nights?' I asked.

No, they said, it was a wonderful place, very peaceful. But they had a special device in a bamboo flask, which made a spectacular noise, and two or three times in the evening they fired this off, to frighten the animals away.

When I got home the next day, with a bundle of sugarcane, I felt very proud of my adventure. By now the estate was well enough established for my father to take the whole family down at weekends, and it became a tradition that we went down there at the New Year.

The lunar New Year falls on 13 or 14 April. It used to be an excuse for three or four days of celebration. On the first we would visit the pagoda to give presents to the monks. Depending on how well we had prospered, we would buy packets of sugar, tea, white candles, incense sticks and saffron robes. Everything was wrapped in red or yellow Cellophane. We went before the altar of the Buddha to burn incense and offer our prayers for the next year. Then we gave our presents to the monks, who prayed and conversed with us before going off for their nap, leaving the lay people chatting together. There followed some friendly but competitive arguments. The menfolk were trying to show how well they understood the scriptures. The women would egg their husbands on, or start teasing them and telling them what fools they were.

Often I slipped away at this point, seeking out the students who lived in the pagoda for a chat, and as I grew up I used to wander from the pagoda to visit the public celebrations around Wat Phnom. The parks and boulevards around it were a favourite spot for the fortune-tellers, and at this time of the year young couples went to seek out these wise men in order to ask what they should do so as to get on with their parents. The fortune-tellers would ask for the relevant dates of birth, burn incense and pray silently. After consultation of their astrological charts they would read out the appropriate text from the tatty old books in front of them.

The crowd around the hill formed into groups of girls and boys, and they enjoyed singing contests in which insults and compliments were passed from group to group. They made up songs, using any tune that came into their heads. The girls would sing, 'Oh, look at him, he's as handsome as a movie star – what a pity his nose is upside down,' whereupon the boys would reply, 'She's as pretty as an angel, but her face is as round as the moon' (a tremendous insult). There were riddles. A girl would challenge, 'Tell me, what is there between your navel and the top of your legs?' As the boy went pink she would answer, 'Your belt.'

Some games were designed to give the boys and girls an opportunity to touch each other, which they would not have (at least in theory) for the rest of the year. There was a game of forfeits which involved throwing large dried seeds. Each side would throw a seed intending to hit the seed placed in front of the opposition. If the girls lost, through having their seed knocked over, the boys were entitled to take one of these seeds and tap the girls on the knee. The trick was to use this opportunity to press your knee against the back of the girl's knee, giving yourself and her a tremendous thrill.

There was also a game played blindfold, in which you were obliged to take three swipes in the direction of a hanging clay jar. If your stick broke the jar, dark red liquid would pour all over your clothes.

On the second day of the New Year, we made our trip to the estate. My mother and sisters prepared the food a couple of days in advance. There was sticky rice mixed with coconut and milk and wrapped in banana leaves. There were several kinds of pork and beef stew, which could be kept for a few days so that we did not have to cook during the celebration.

We set out early to avoid the heat of the day. The men loaded up the car while the women made the final arrangements with the food. Sisopha always added the civilized touches to the trip: it was normally she who bought the batteries for the old Philips tape-recorder and put in the tapes of Cambodian pop music we would listen to on the way. Phan's ideas about hunting had led him to bring home an old American carbine one day. He had bribed someone to issue him with a licence. When my father wasn't looking, Phan slipped the gun under the back seat. The last thing my mother did was check that all the windows and doors of the house were properly locked.

We were always very excited to get out of Phnom Penh. It was our custom to stop at the first bit of countryside, after Pochentong airport, for breakfast at the noodle shop. Here, we were allowed to order what we wanted. There were so many of us that the waiters had to put two tables together. In addition to my parents, there were Phan and Somaly and their baby, Sisopha and myself, the twins Bopha and Mealea, Orphea and two little brothers. Over breakfast, we discussed which route to take. Route Four was the quickest, but our favourite was Route Three, which passed along the coast.

The first point of interest on this route was Prasath Neang Khmao, the Temple of the Black Lady, a beautiful construction dating from the fourteenth century. The Black Lady had been a woman of mysterious powers. She was invisible, appearing only to those to whom she chose to show herself. She had the power of predicting people's thoughts. In those days, two princes – brothers – conspired to overthrow and kill the king, their uncle. After this murder there was civil war for a couple of years between the rival supporters of the two brothers. In the end the younger brother won with the help of the Black Lady, who had fallen in love with him. After his coronation, she would appear to him every night, warning him of plots against the throne. Everyone she accused, even the king's own relatives, would be executed the next day. When the Black Lady died, the king built this temple in her memory, placing her statue inside.

On the outside of the temple were bas-reliefs of battle scenes in which the Cambodians were fighting the Thais or Chams, our traditional enemies. Rows of horsemen faced each other with lowered spears. Inside the dimly lit building, the atmosphere was heavy with candle smoke, incense and the scent of the flowers which the visitors had left as offerings to the ancient statue of the Buddha. The Black Lady herself was little more than a lump of rock – you could only just recognize her features. We said our prayers, left our offerings and wandered around the courtyard where a few monks lived. Under the trees, children from the village were playing forfeits. There were cakes on sale, and you could have fresh coconut. I remember watching the children's game and how, when it came to the girls' turn to have their knees tapped, they ran off into the corners of the temple as if afraid. And I can still see the little boys waving their fly-whisks over the enamel trays of cakes, or washing at the temple well.

In the villages along the road, the farmers and their families had gathered to celebrate the New Year, dressed in their best clothes, the girls in white sashes, with trays of food on their heads, on their way to the pagoda. In some of the fields where the harvest was not yet in, they had their singing contests as they worked. A girl would sing: 'How can anyone be his wife? He doesn't even know how to use a sickle.' And her friends would accompany her, clapping in rhythm.

Then from the group of boys, someone would reply, 'Don't judge me yet, my dear. I have a lot to offer a wife. Marry me and you'll see how good a husband I can be.' And the girls would pick up mud and throw it at the boys, in shrieks of laughter, among the sheaves of rice.

Along the road, we passed bullock carts with their long curving shafts, decorated with bright metal. Children of five or six years old were driving them, giving orders to their animals as they went. This was the time of year when the domestic animals were given a rest from hard labour. Most of the oxen and water buffalo were kept in the cattle-pens. Their fodder came from the less fertile areas of the paddyfields. Bonfires were kept going day and night by the pens to discourage insects. Another of the boys' jobs was to take the cattle to the ponds and wash them. This was a marvellous thing for a child to do. They loved their animals and they loved playing in mud. They loved riding on the necks of the strongest bullocks or water buffaloes, to impress the other cattleherds. Every animal had a name and the best of them had a bell round their necks. Different herds made different sounds so the children could keep track of the cattle. There was great rivalry between them.

Near Takeo we would stop to buy presents for Chan and Long. There was a kind of clay jar filled with palm sugar. To get at the sugar you had to break the jar. We bought a string of coconuts, which were cheap here, and anything good. At Ang Ta Som the satay chicken was said to be the best in Cambodia. Here, too, we might load up with Pepsi and beer. At Kampot, where the salt flats stretched out to the coast, we bought a few kilos of rough, dirty, granulated salt. From then on, the road was quite near to the sea and if we turned off we could go down to the beach. We sat by the car eating chicken. After a quarter of an hour we were always bored with the sea. My family had no great desire to swim or paddle in salt water. Even at Kep, where the beaches were beautiful and covered with French tourists, we would laugh at the idea that anyone should want to get a suntan.

Now we turn off the main road. We are at the other end of the forest track, heading for our estate. It is 1969, and none of us knows that this is the last New Year we will spend here. It's noon. The gibbons are in full throat. There are parrots and brightly coloured woodpeckers. The monkeys flee from our advance. The track is clear and we can make a decent speed. When we see the clumps of sugarcane we know that we are on our land. We turn by the dead tree, and there are two houses in the clearing.

Chan and Long rush down from the verandah, laughing and waving. They take my little brothers from the car and hold them high above their heads. Everyone is talking at once. We open up the larger house, which Chan and Long have built for us. It is beautifully made. It can accommodate a dozen people easily. We squabble about who will sleep on the verandah. My father lays down the law – girls indoors, boys out. Phan smuggles the gun upstairs rolled in his mat. The menfolk gather for a beer.

Somaly, Pepsi in hand, loves to imagine herself in charge of the estate. She questions Chan and Long about the crops. For someone who knows nothing about farming she has a good line in questions: what has been planted since our last visit, have there been any pests, what sort of fertilizers have been used, has there been trouble from the wild boars? The two men are amused by her performance and play her along, answering in great detail. Of the fifty acres, about two-thirds has been put under cultivation, using the slash-and-burn method. The remainder is still thick jungle. In addition to the sugarcane there are pineapples, mangoes, cashews, jak-fruit, rambutans, bananas, papayas, sweet potatoes, peppers and lemon-grass. They are just beginning to plant durian.

My mother joins us, from Chan's and Long's kitchen, and she says what she always says at this moment: how beautiful their kitchen is, how nicely everything is arranged, how you can immediately find everything you need. Then she laughs and says: 'If you two were girls, and a man came along and saw your kitchen, he'd immediately want to marry you.' I have a mouthful of Pepsi. The bubbles come surging up my nose.

We walk round the estate. They show us where the wild boars have dug up the sweet potatoes, they point to a large pawmark and say, darkly, 'Cat.' They show us the damage the elephants have done to the bananas, and they tell the children to avoid the traps. Now the women set off to the river to wash. The rest of us pull down *parangs* from the beams and go out for a little weed-clearing session. Then it is our turn for the river. We shoulder our buckets, go down to check the fish traps and bathe.

Dusk falls and I slip away from the rest to sit by the great dead tree among the chilli bushes. Several birds are nesting in the trunk: woodpeckers, parrots, cockatoos and grey-winged blackbirds. Best of all I like watching the spotted owls coming back from hunting in the wood with mice, lizards and sometimes little green snakes in their beaks. The blackbirds bring grasshoppers for their young. The sun disappears. The big-eared bats are hunting mosquitoes just above my head. I can hear the beating of their wings. The noise of the crickets is ear-splitting. There are mysterious whirring sounds from the undergrowth. There are shining fungi, and flashing beetles.

My father calls me in to eat. Afterwards we sit around the fire, chewing sugarcane. Now the animals begin to move in on the crops. We shout at the elephants to scare them off the bananas, and the wild boars to get them off the sweet potatoes. Phan takes his carbine and fires it into the air. A second after the shot, you can hear the sound of saplings snapping as the elephants and wild boars make off into the hills.

We all laugh at Phan. He thinks of himself as a great hunter. Every time we come down here, he says that this time we will have a wild boar or a deer for our supper. But he has never succeeded in killing anything. It isn't that he's scared of animals. And he's a good shot – as good as Sisopha. But when it comes to pointing a gun at a living thing, he gets scared. After all, he is a devout Buddhist, and Buddhists are not supposed to kill.

NINE
Sihanouk

Sihanouk was a Buddhist, but that did not stop him having people killed. I saw one of his executions on television. The victim was a mining engineer called Preap In, who had been accused of treachery. I can't remember the details of the case, but I do remember watching the newsreel with my family.

Two army trucks stopped at the state execution ground at Trapeang Kraloeung. The man was taken out, tied to a pole and blindfolded. A group of monks said prayers on his behalf. The military commander ordered his soldiers to line up in two ranks of ten, facing the man. The soldiers in the front row knelt. All guns were loaded. They fired. Preap In sank to his knees. The officer walked up to him, drew his pistol and fired another shot at his temple. My sisters hid their faces, but my father said, 'He was a good man.'

The film of the execution played in all the cinemas of Phnom Penh, alongside the normal footage of Sihanouk's visits to the countryside. As Head of State he was very popular among the farmers. On his travels he always threw pieces of cloth along the road – cheap cotton, two square yards of it, printed with the slogans 'Long life to the Sangkum Party' (Sihanouk's Popular Socialist Community Party) and 'Long Live Samdech Preah Oppayouvereach' (a name he had given himself, which meant that he had come to the throne very young). People fought with each other for this cloth. They thought it had magic properties and that you could cure a fever by placing it over your head. Once one of these favours dropped from the prince's helicopter into our court-yard. I picked it up and saw that it was the cheapest white cotton. We used it as a duster, and, when we washed it, it shrank by a third.

When important visitors came to Cambodia, the students of every school in the capital from the ninth grade upwards were issued with flags and taught the pronunciation of the visitor's name. This was sometimes difficult: Ja-wa-har-lal Neh-ru, or Jo-sip Broz Tito. Written out in Cambodian these names sounded very odd, and might easily get changed to something more like Joseph Prostitito. We had to buy a special uniform and badges made of plasticated cardboard. (You could get embroidered versions if you wanted to impress your friends.) We had to wear shoes and socks (instead of our normal flipflops) and black ties. We had epaulettes bearing the symbol of Sihanouk's party, and what with all the badges and the tie I always felt uncomfortably hot and constricted. But other students looked forward to these occasions because the schools gave us money afterwards. So we lined the road from the airport, waving our flags and shouting, 'Long life to Jacqueline Kennedy', or whoever it was, as the motorcade swept past, with Sihanouk waving and throwing his printed cloths in the road. One student was so keen to pick up a cloth that he was knocked down by the outriders.

Sihanouk's portrait was everywhere around town: in uniform with a sword, in a suit, in monk's robes, dressed in white with a shaved head like an *achar*; on posters, on notebooks; framed in every classroom above the teacher's head; in the shops and offices. In the magazine that he edited himself we saw him helping a farmer dig an irrigation canal, reviewing the troops, shooting a film (for he was also a film-maker), addressing the National Assembly, giving presents to the monks, opening the annual regatta with his wife, Monique. On the radio we heard his speeches, and one year when he had a craze for singing you could hear his songs more than ten times a day. 'In the Night' and 'The Rose of Luang Prabang' were his own compositions. There was a portrait of Sihanouk as a soccer player, inscribed 'Long life to the sport-loving father', and a medal commemorating the dispute with the Thais over the ownership of the temple of Preah Vihear.

My father always warned us not to get involved in politics. 'Look what happened to me,' he would say, 'I was thrown out of my homeland.' He and his friends from Kampuchea Krom disliked Sihanouk intensely, admiring instead a politician called Son Ngoc Thanh, whom Sihanouk considered his mortal enemy. Still, my father never missed the annual conference of the assembly, which was broadcast on radio and which Sihanouk addressed at length. He would send the children out of the room, and afterwards he had long serious conversations about it with his friend from across the road.

Another man who became an enemy of Sihanouk was Khieu Samphan, who taught me maths for a short period in a private school I attended at weekends. He was always punctual and there were no jokes in his lessons, but he was a good teacher who won our respect. He would insist on our homework being done on time, and we obeyed him even though he never punished us. At the end of the lesson he was in the habit of talking for five minutes about the state of the nation. He was concerned about the corruption everywhere. He used to say: 'I can't understand why the trees are planted in the countryside, but they fruit in the capital.' By which he meant that the hard work of the farmers turned into wealth for the city people. He would ask, 'Why is it that the government always paints the opposition red? Ask yourselves why.' He talked about the government's lack of concern for the peasants, and he told us that he believed the peasants would eventually take over the whole of the country.

One day to our surprise, Khieu Samphan was late. We waited a few minutes and were told that he was ill. The next day he had not recovered, and finally we were told that he had disappeared. Nobody knew what had happened to him. If I asked my father he would say, 'Don't worry about that. Just keep on working hard.' The new maths teacher never talked about politics.

I hadn't known at the time that Khieu Samphan was a leader of the opposition. He didn't look like a politician. His clothes were simple and he drove a rusty old sky-blue Mobylette. We used to laugh about the noise it made, like a tubercular cough. My image of a politician in those days was of a fat man in a black Mercedes with mercury windows and a police escort. Khieu Samphan was thin with short grey hair and he never wore sunglasses. He dressed like a peasant, with sandals instead of shoes. His house was simple and small. In all these things he was setting an example. Above all, he disliked the corruption of the capital.

You met corruption at every stage of life. You had to bribe the *chef du quartier* for a birth certificate. When I wanted to take my exams a year early we had to pay to have my date of birth changed. When Chan and Long wanted to stay in Cambodia, we had to pay for their residence permit. You could bribe your teachers for an advance copy of exam papers. If you were stopped by the police you would '*bonjour*' them with a few notes. You had to pay to transfer from a lean job, like teaching, to a fat one, like the customs. If you needed to see someone urgently in an office, you had to bribe his secretary. You could bribe your way through the courts – you could bribe your way through anything. The only people you didn't bribe were the monks: you just gave them money instead.

One of the main centres of corruption was the casino that Sihanouk opened in the last years of his reign. It stood on the Phnom Penh waterfront, not far from the royal palace, and looked rather like a motel. When my father and I walked past it during its construction, my father told me that it was going to be a state hotel for tourists. But then it was inaugurated as a state casino, open twenty-four hours a day. My father warned us not to visit it – gambling just ruined a family's fortunes.

And, indeed, before long it seemed that robbery was on the increase. The row of houses opposite the casino was converted into pawnshops. Outside there were motorbikes chained up. Inside, jewellery was on display. If you walked past the casino at any time of the day or night you could see men and women coming out of the casino and nipping into the pawnshop, then returning to the tables as fast as they could. At the street stalls nearby you could see the gamblers eating noodle soup, and it was easy to tell from their expressions how their fortunes had gone. There was a park where, after dark, you could see prostitutes carrying baskets of oranges and bananas. They walked under the street lamps, and their customers would come up and buy a single orange or a banana. Then they went with the girls to sit by the bushes in the dark. For the price of a piece of fruit, you were allowed a little fondle as you ate. If you wanted to go further you had to pay more. There were also transvestites who lured men into the bushes to rob them. Men on motorbikes amused themselves by riding through the park with headlights on, to get a good look at what was happening. The prostitutes sometimes took their clients into the nearby pagoda, for privacy. When the police whistles blew, the girls quickly hid their baskets of fruit and walked towards the casino with their customers, hand in hand. The police went round with their torches, put the fruit in the van and ate it.

During the day the *cyclopousses* gambled on the pavements outside until they had enough money to go to the casino. Their vehicles were often stolen. There were usually young boys trying to get a view of the tables, but the doormen wouldn't let them in. If they climbed over the fence they were beaten. However, I noticed that newspaper vendors were allowed in free, so I went home and asked my father to show me a newspaper office where I could get some papers to sell. He told me the address of a paper called *Sochiveator*, which means something like etiquette. This was an evening paper that gave advice on manners alongside the news and ran a sexy serial.

At five o'clock I picked up fifty copies, for which I left a deposit on sale-or-return. I cycled down to the casino and approached the doorman. As I was a new face to him, I had to agree to give him all my profits. He counted the copies and let me past. Inside the big building it was smoky and there was a stench of sweat. There were electric fans above each table. The gamblers crowded around playing roulette and blackjack and *vingt-et-un*. These were the small-time punters. If they accused the croupier of cheating, bouncers came up to them and told them that if they thought they were being cheated they could get out. The big-time games were being played in the smaller buildings where the atmosphere was calmer. I could see through the windows that people were drinking beer. There were ten or so people per house. You could see that they were really grand and rich. But the small-time punters in the big building were desperate for the next throw. Young women sat by the richer players offering themselves. And while I was there I heard that a girl had hanged herself in the bathroom. Family quarrels broke out about property. The bouncers moved in. I left.

TEN
The war craze

The new gambling fever undermined the business of the fortune-tellers around Wat Phnom. They sat there almost unnoticed, with their little slates and their charts, lighting incense sticks and cooling themselves with their fans. And they watched, with some regret, the activities of the street gamblers. There was a game in which you bet money on six drawings printed on a large sheet of cardboard – a tiger, a rabbit, a fish, a lobster, a wax gourd and an orange. The dealer had three dice, similarly marked, which he shook between a bowl and a plate – there were often quarrels when he didn't shake the dice for long enough. If it looked as if someone was going to win a large sum, the dealer had accomplices in the crowd who would push the player against the board. Then the game would be cancelled and begun again. When fights broke out, men from the river navy moved in.

Until recently I had not seen many soldiers around town, but in late 1969 they appeared everywhere. They were not armed, and they behaved as if all was normal. Nevertheless, they were an unusual sight. I asked my father about it. He said the soldiers were in town to keep order among the refugees from the countryside, the peasants who had fled from the Vietcong. So why were the Vietcong in our country? My father said they had been pushed across the border by the Americans in South Vietnam.

'So you mean there is fighting in the countryside now?'

'Yes,' said my father, 'that's why there are so many peasants camped out on the pavements.'

'Why don't we push the Vietcong back into South Vietnam?'

Here my father paused and smiled. 'Fighting is not as easy as pushing a matchbox across a line. You have to plan, with troops, ammunition, and so on. Before you make your push you have to be sure that you are stronger than the other side. Otherwise you'll just get destroyed. So far we aren't strong enough to push the Vietcong back. And anyway, Sihanouk has allowed them to stay in our territory.'

'Why don't the other politicians argue with Sihanouk?' I asked.

'That's just what they are doing,' said my father. 'And that's why the soldiers are in town, to eliminate any Vietcong agents among the refugees. You know how keen the Vietnamese are to wipe us all out. Something's going to happen very soon. But don't think about all this. Just get back to your school work.'

It was around this time that we lost contact with Chan and Long. It was no longer safe to travel on Routes Three and Four. According to the newspapers the roads were infested with bandits and guerrillas, who attacked people in their cars, or took them off buses and made them join their forces. It was said that the guerrilla bases were not far from our estate.

Instead of going to the country at weekends we now went to parties with our friends in the capital, or for picnics on the Isle of Sand a short journey away, or fruit picking at Ta Khmao, a few kilometres to the south. Even then, we were warned by our parents to be back before dark. My father and mother spent an increasing amount of time at the pagoda, which became the centre of their social life.

There were headlines in the papers about clashes between the army and the Vietcong along the eastern and southern border, and cartoons of men in black pyjamas and conical hats, slaughtering peasants, raping farmers' wives, and destroying the crops in the fields. The number of refugees increased dramatically until eventually the casino was closed down and turned into a camp. When the buildings overflowed, they set up shacks in the grounds. The gamblers disappeared. The pawnshops closed down. Only the prostitutes continued to work at night in the park.

In January 1970, we learnt that everyone in the high school had to devote Friday afternoon to learn *la technique du combat*. I remember the first lesson in parade ground drill, and how the officer told us to keep our backs straight and stick our chests out. This was fun for the boys, but it was embarrassing for the larger-chested girls. In early February we were learning how to clean a US carbine and take it to pieces. This was a popular part of the curriculum.

Sihanouk was abroad on his travels when a big headline in the newspaper accused him of selling out the country to the North Vietnamese to be used as a military base against the Americans. A cartoon was published of him standing on the Cambodian map, sawing off the eastern territory with one hand and, with the other, receiving a bundle of money from Phan Van Dong.

One day I went into school to find the teachers absent for the first two lessons. At nine o'clock we were called down to the schoolyard and told we were going on a march to the Independence Monument. We were given banners telling the Vietcong to get out of the country, and as we made our way along the streets the students found places to hang these banners from the balconies or across the road. We shouted anti-Vietcong slogans as we went. We were all excited. It was the first such event in our lives. The leader of the students' association climbed up on the monument and delivered a speech through a megaphone, ending by attacking Sihanouk for allowing the Vietnamese to remain in our country. Afterwards, we hung the banners around the school railings and drew caricatures of Sihanouk on the walls, crossing his face out with an X, and calling him a traitor.

That evening I discovered that all the schoolchildren in our family had been at the same demonstration – every school in the capital had gone, and we'd all had great fun. My father said we should have slipped away and come home, as we might have come up against the soldiers. But there had been no military around. My father said, 'Maybe the time has come.'

On the second day Sihanouk's portrait was removed from every classroom. There were no lessons. The teachers were helping decorate the basketball pitch with banners, which by now were attacking Sihanouk strongly. I went from room to room, watching the students scrawling political jokes on the blackboard. My mother told me that evening not to do anything ahead of the crowd, as you never knew which students were your friends and which not. There might be agents in the school.

Nothing had been said on the radio – there was simply martial music being played. When a report of the student demonstration came up on the television Sisopha and I tried hard to see ourselves in the crowd.

After a third day of demonstrations, the National Assembly

reached its decision: Sihanouk was demoted. He was accused of turning Cambodia communist and allowing Vietcong bases along the border. There was to be a general election and a republic. My father and our neighbours from Kampuchea Krom sat around the radio and cheered the news. It was the moment they had been waiting for. They toasted the announcement with Chinese wine.

The papers were full of stories against Sihanouk, and the one that most appalled me was an item that reported that Khieu Samphan, my old maths teacher, had been thrown into a bath of acid for having opposed the corruption of the Royal Family. Khieu Samphan was portrayed as a hero, as the single honest man who had had the courage to stand up for the poor.

I joined the students' association at my school, and we were trained as 'commandos'. I remember one weekend we were taken to Kambol in three jeeps to learn how to use an M-30 machine gun. We had a military escort and sirens. As we left the school we waved at the bystanders. We were proud of our army uniforms, which you could suddenly buy in the market. We behaved as if we were soldiers going to the front line, although we were not sure what a front line was.

We passed a convoy of a dozen Pepsi trucks, loaded with the first recruits. Little kids, no taller than the guns they carried, climbed on to the trucks with the help of older soldiers. Men in blue jeans and baggy military shirts sat on the roofs of the trucks, waving. They cheered the new republic. These were the real soldiers. They were sent to the front line without any training.

The machine gun was very exciting. We fired wildly at the targets and spent something like ten cases of ammunition. We asked for the brass casings as souvenirs.

Over dinner, my father was dismayed at what I described. 'Guns are dangerous,' he said, 'and the more you play with them, the more you turn yourself into a murderer. Believe me and stop all this, will you?'

I looked to my mother for support, but there was none there. 'But I think it's fun,' I replied. 'You allowed Phan to have a gun.'

My mother smiled. 'He's much older than you,' she said. 'He has a family and he knows what he's doing.' Then she saw my face fall. 'Sorry, Someth, I don't mean you're still a child. Fifteen is a man's age, but men at that age can easily get carried away by exciting events. Especially something like weapon training.'

They'd spoilt all the excitement of the day. Seeing I was upset, my father patted me on the back. 'Your mother is right,' he said. 'You are a man, and we're all very proud of you. I remember that trip you made all that time ago, to see Chan and Long, going through the jungle on your own with all that money in your pocket. A child couldn't have done that.' Then he changed the subject.

But the war craze affected us all. My father was caught up in it, because now his hero, Son Ngoc Thanh, came with his troops from South Vietnam to help fight the Vietcong. Phan, too, was caught up in it, and eventually became a soldier. He got a desk job, organizing the distribution of uniforms. He wore a very neat uniform, with shiny boots and a pistol. He was very proud of his stripes, and would bring all kinds of military paraphernalia back from the office for display at home. His uniform was hung very prominently in the main room so that visitors could see it. He put bayonets up on the wall, and refused to drink from anything but standard-issue army beakers. Meanwhile, my father had become a surgeon at the Military Hospital.

People had welcomed the prospect of war if it was going to rid us of the Vietnamese. In the early days of the republic, a large number of the Vietnamese civilians were taken out of the city and massacred, their bodies dumped in the Mekong. Before long there were no Vietnamese left in the capital. They had either fled or been killed.

In the countryside it was quite another matter. The Americans, who had been bombing the Vietcong positions along the border, now invaded Cambodia to force back the North Vietnamese and Vietcong. In the invasion they used South Vietnamese troops who treated the population so badly that they forced the farmers into opposition. The peasants had, anyway, always been loyal to Sihanouk. Now he was head of the resistance, who had previously been his enemies. It was he who had given them the nickname Khmer Rouge. In the early months of the republic, as fighting spread throughout the country, there were American, South Vietnamese, North Vietnamese, Vietcong, Khmer Rouge and republican soldiers, not to mention the forces from Kampuchea Krom. Within a few months, most of the countryside was out of governmental control.

When the American and South Vietnamese forces withdrew, the

situation looked like this: most of the provincial capitals became isolated. They were held by republican forces. We were told that, on the other side, the majority of the soldiers were North Vietnamese, but in fact the North Vietnamese were gradually training the Khmer Rouge to do the fighting themselves. Sihanouk was only nominally in control. He was in Peking. The Khmer Rouge leaders in the country were supposed to be Hu Nim, Hou Yuon and my maths teacher, Khieu Samphan, but Phnom Penh radio told us that this was only a phantom government. All these people had been killed by Sihanouk years before.

As for the republic itself, the most powerful figure was Sihanouk's old prime minister, Lon Nol. He eventually became president, and it was his portrait that replaced Sihanouk's in the schools, offices and shops – everywhere in the city. Lon Nol was a Buddhist, but more than that he believed in magic. The atheists would be destroyed. In his recruiting posters, the Vietcong were shown coming with tanks and bazookas against the throne of the Buddha. But the Queen of the Sea and the Soil produces a magic flood from her hair. All the enemies are engulfed and a crocodile is sent out to finish them off.

The army that Lon Nol commanded also believed in magic with a Buddhist flavour. Every regiment had its *lok kru*, a magician who chanted spells and sprinkled holy water on the soldiers before they went out into the battlefield. The soldiers wore bundles of charms around their necks. They had scarves inscribed with spells, and tattoos that were supposed to protect them from bullets.

What they weren't protected from was the corruption of the officers, who had welcomed the American involvement in Cambodia precisely because they were going to get rich. From the very beginning, everything possible was siphoned off. K-rations appeared on the market along with boots, uniforms and all kinds of equipment. Military petrol supplies found their way down to the level of the little street vendors who sold it in litre bottles at the side of the road. And the officers sold ammunition to the other side. Everyone knew that they were doing it. Inflation was high and salaries were tight: it was easy to tell from the way someone lived just how corrupt and powerful he was. In the early years of the war, a large number of new villas were put up in Phnom Penh with air-conditioning, refrigerators and a Mercedes parked in front. (After you'd bought your first house, there would be a second villa for your mistress, and so on.)

I had a relative – I'll call him Asok – short, stout and with fourteen children. He became a paymaster immediately after the coup, and the villa and all the comforts followed. He had a Japanese colour television – an amazing status symbol – even though there were no colour transmissions to receive. He really did not know what to do with his money. He didn't want to put it in a bank, so he kept it in a safe in his living-room. The safe was the centre of attention. One day, he invited my father, Phan and myself for a meal that he cooked. It was superb. Phan and my father drank White Horse and soda. He opened his fridge and handed me a frozen banana – a novelty. Then he showed me how if anyone tampered with the safe, an alarm sounded. We sat listening to it. I said it would send me to sleep very nicely. He said it was supposed to wake you up.

Asok asked Phan to put his name down as a 'phantom soldier'. He could draw a corporal's salary in Asok's unit, just as long as he presented himself to the commissioners when they came to check. The rest of the time he worked in his regular job. Thirty-five per cent of the salary went to Phan, the rest to Asok and his colleagues. This was the main way in which officers became so rich.

Corruption spread everywhere. People like Asok, who supplied Sisopha and myself with petrol for our scooters, stored gasoline in the houses of their relatives. The whole city was a fire hazard. I remember rushing out early one morning to find a blaze next door. It was the windy season and by the time the fire brigade arrived, several houses had been destroyed. The firemen stood there watching. People were desperately throwing water into the flames. My father approached the firemen and gave them some money. Very quickly, the firemen started hosing our house, which wasn't yet on fire, and ignoring the others. A dozen other houses were destroyed.

There was a slogan people used about how to get a job: 'Money is number one, pussy is number two, influence is number three.'

What with the bombing and the fighting, more and more peasants were fleeing to the capital, leaving large tracts of land uncultivated. Unemployment was high and little was done by the government to help the refugees. Gangs grew up. They stole from everybody, including old people and orphans. At any time of day, you could be robbed. The refugees began to put up shacks along the roadsides. Sometimes the military police came and pulled them down, but the next day they had mushroomed again.

The army was selling weapons to the Khmer Rouge, who were soon in such a strong position that they had cut all the major roads. Rice had to be brought in from abroad. Inflation rocketed – a kilo of beef cost a soldier's weekly wage. The students and teachers began demonstrating against the government.

At one such demonstration, in front of the College of Law, the police opened fire on the students, one of whom was injured. The story was put around that he had actually been killed, and another demonstration was organized. People came from all the schools in Phnom Penh, chanting slogans against the Lon Nol government and carrying banners. When we reached the Independence Monument, I saw two beautiful girls and two boys, all with their heads shaved, sitting around a coffin. They were dressed in mourning and they wept all day long. Funeral music blared from a loudspeaker.

But there wasn't anything in the coffin. I knew this at the time, but I was more interested in demonstrating against Lon Nol. We kept a vigil there for three days and three nights. On the second day, I was in charge of security, with thirty people under my control, looking out for suspicious people who might try to remove us. We found no one. We sent groups of the most beautiful girls from door to door, collecting money for the dead student's funeral. We added drama by saying the dead boy had no family: they had all been killed when his home was bombed. People believed us, and they gave a lot of money.

At the end of the demonstration we held a secret meeting and counted up the proceeds. I had assumed that they would be used to finance another demonstration, but this is not what happened. The organizers simply divided the money among those present. I kept my mouth shut and took the money.

In addition to my school work and activities in the students' association, I took a part-time job at the Groaning Table, where I was able to learn English from the numerous foreign journalists covering the war. It was now late 1973, and the Khmer Rouge were moving closer and closer to the capital. It was well within range of their shells and rockets. People were killed every day. I remember one morning as I was waiting at the tables, several shells landed in a nursery school nearby. The blast broke most of the glasses on the restaurant shelves.

We hit the floor. Journalists and camera crews rushed to the scene, and I followed them. We had to take an indirect route, because the streets were blocked off with barbed wire. When we arrived we found a pool of blood. Eight people were injured, most of them children, and there were pieces of torn limbs everywhere. It took the police and the ambulances a long time to arrive.

Phnom Penh began to look more and more like a battlefield. The soldiers were no longer properly under the control of their commanders, and their pay was always overdue. Many of the officers never showed their faces at the front line – the only action they saw was in the nightclubs of the city. The place was full of deserters, and special teams were set up to arrest them. Sometimes there were fights between these teams and the men they were trying to arrest. Everyone had guns and it was difficult to tell who was who.

Groups of uniformed men came into the restaurants, ordered expensive meals and drinks and, at the end of the meal, called the manager and demanded money. Grenades were thrown at places where the manager refused. Cinemas, theatres and public places were no longer safe but nightclubs, dancing bars and brothels thrived under the protection of army officers.

Finally, in 1975 the Khmer Rouge (led by my old maths master, Khieu Samphan, who had not in fact been killed) blockaded the city. They cut the Mekong, and all supplies had to be airlifted in. But gradually the airport itself was becoming unsafe. Lon Nol eventually left for Honolulu, on the grounds of ill health, but it was too late to rescue the military situation. The place was gradually collapsing.

At the time, my mother was abroad in connection with her work. She had told us that she would be back by 13 April for New Year. My father was very much alone with his thoughts. He had laid in some stocks of dried food, and told Phan to remove all his military junk from the house. The new president, Saukham Koy, ordered a curfew from six in the evening to six in the morning. There was nothing to do but sit at home and listen to the radio.

President Ford announced that there would be no more military aid to Cambodia. And then everything unravelled very fast.

ELEVEN
The city falls

On 12 April, hardly any foreigners arrived for breakfast at the Groaning Table. They were all rushing to the American embassy to be evacuated. The Cambodian journalists ate in a hurry, cleaned their cameras and went off to photograph the Americans leaving. My cousin, seeing we had no customers, said we might as well play at being customers ourselves. We ate an enormous breakfast, Western-style. I had *oeufs sur plat au jambon* with three eggs, toast, iced coffee and orange juice. The others had *Croque Monsieur*. My cousin treated himself to a Bloody Mary. He had allowed the journalists generous credit (although the bills were a kind of fiction) and very few of them had settled up. We were worried about this, but someone said, 'Don't worry, they've not gone far, Bangkok at the furthest. They'll be back one day.'

We weren't particularly worried about the Americans. We fooled around, talking about films and night clubs. Am Rong's officers didn't seem to be in a panic, and the briefing notice reported the military situation as usual: *aucun incident significatif.* When we heard a rocket fall not far away, we did what we normally did – we lay on the ground and began to count. The second rocket fell on the count of fifty – it was nearer. We waited and counted again. The rockets normally fell in threes. Suddenly my ears were blasted and my body seemed to bounce. The glasses fell off the shelf in the kitchen hut. I felt the force of a shock wave, and then I saw the wall of the house next door collapse.

We picked ourselves up and checked for any wounds. We were all fine. The house that had taken a direct hit had been abandoned by its owner, a doctor, some weeks before, since when it had been used by Am Rong's officers as a gambling den. But no one was gambling at that time in the morning. Our breakfast things had been blown off the tables. Am Rong's window had been broken. They had probably been aiming for him.

The Cambodian journalists came back in a good mood. One was pleased with a shot he had got of a rocket falling near some US marines. Another had snapped John Gunther Dean, the ambassador, rushing to the helicopter. They described how the marines had slashed the tyres of American jeeps to block off the evacuation area. Some *cyclopousses* had abandoned their vehicles in the hopes of getting on a chopper. The people living nearby had been stunned by the speed of the operation. It had taken about a quarter of an hour.

People ordered their breakfasts again. It was more like a normal working day. One of the compulsive gamblers was glad he had been sent down to the embassy, otherwise he might have suggested a game in the house next door. Now, some of the photographers began to worry what they were going to do next – all their employers had gone. Drinks were ordered. I finished work and said goodbye to my cousin as normal.

That was my last day at the Groaning Table. My father told us all to stay at home, for fear of the rockets. His friend from Kampuchea Krom came round. He was *chef ilot*, which meant that all the American grain in our section of town was stored in his house. Someone had advised him to take the sign down from his door and disperse the sacks of rice among people he knew. Once people realized there was to be no more food aid, the looting was likely to begin.

We took five sacks and placed them in the rocket shelter, a sandbagged construction we had dug in the courtyard. And now my father began to organize provisions. He sent Phan and me to buy up any food that could be stored – dried fish, tinned foods, Chinese sausages and dried meat.

We took the Land Rover. I'd never seen the street so empty in daytime. All the families were staying at home for the New Year. They sat on the verandahs chatting and playing cards, waiting for the city to fall. The occasional cigarette vendor was out, but most of the *cyclopousses* and the refugees had gone to the pagoda. In the market, two or three Chinese shops were still open, but most of the shops were shuttered. Canvases flapped on the market stalls. Dogs were rooting around among the rubbish.

Phan was quite optimistic about what would happen. He thought that when the Khmer Rouge came, the top men in the army would be changed but everyone else would stay where he was. The army would continue to exist. The civil service would remain roughly unchanged. But at last we would be able to get out into the country. We would be able to revisit our estate. We'll be able to go hunting again, he said. Taking advantage of the empty road, he drove all over the place, accelerating, braking, speeding round corners.

We could see the Olympic Stadium, where helicopters were coming and going. Rockets were falling downtown. You could hear the sirens of the ambulances coming from the front, and the howitzers pumping out their shells from the city. The army had by no means run out of ammunition, but there were no planes coming in.

The shop-owners had left a small gap in the shutters. Inside they were shovelling up rice soup with chopsticks. We had a military bag containing a bundle of notes the size of a brick. My father had told us not to worry about the price – buy up anything we could. Prices had jumped 500 per cent. We took whatever we could afford, mostly eggs and sardines and dried food.

That evening at around seven, the whole city exploded with small-arms fire. It was like popcorn in a hot pan. People were celebrating the New Year, firing off any weapon they had. Phan rushed to his room to get his M-16 and join in, but my father told him not to be so stupid. The electricity failed. The gunfire continued for another twenty minutes. The ammunition expended would have been enough to hold the front line for a day. We lit the petrol lamp and watched the insects darting into the flame.

Early in the morning, a large black car with mercury windows arrived, escorted by a jeep full of soldiers. It was General Dien Del, commander of the 2nd infantry division. He was a friend of my father's, but it was most unusual for him to visit at this time. He told my father he wanted a private word with him. They went into his study and closed the door. When Dien Del came out he looked very grave. He said goodbye to us in a strangely formal manner, got into the jeep and drove off, leaving his car in the courtyard. I asked my father why he had done this. He replied that the general was just going to review his troops at the Olympic Stadium, not far away.

My father seemed restless and worried. I asked him what was wrong. 'It's nothing,' he said, 'I'm just wondering whether I should go on my rounds.'

'You don't have to go to work if you're not feeling well,' I said. 'Your health is more important than your work.'

There was another reason why my father was worried. If there were no more planes coming into the city, how was my mother going to get back? That night he didn't go to work and he didn't get much sleep. He wandered round the room, sighing from time to time. I didn't ask him what it was Dien Del had said.

On the morning of 17 April the radio played martial music instead of the customary Buddhist prayers. The streets were silent and nobody left their houses. Then came the sound of rockets from the south. We had prepared a large amount of rice, hardboiled eggs and Chinese sausages, some of which we ate. Now there was about half an hour of small-arms fire. Sisopha was listening to pop music on the tape-recorder. My father was sitting by the radio. Suddenly, the gunfire stopped and the radio went dead. I walked to the gate. Some soldiers came running past, stripped to their T-shirts and shorts. People handed them civilian clothes. The republic had collapsed.

Down the street from us was the villa of an army officer who had worked in food supplies. He had been gone for about ten days, leaving the house guarded. Now the guards had left, and people broke into the house. They were rolling drums of petrol out into the road and carrying sacks of rice on their backs. Someone else took his car. My neighbours were busy tearing up white material to make flags, which they hoisted on poles in front of their houses.

When the Khmer Rouge arrived about an hour later, many of my neighbours began to cheer them. They were glad the war was over. They were fed up with the inflation, the corruption and the continual rocketing of the city. People shouted and waved their white flags, but the Khmer Rouge did not acknowledge the greeting. They were alert and severe with their guns at the ready, and the first thing that surprised me about them was their youth. At sixteen or seventeen they were younger than me. I had sometimes seen Khmer Rouge prisoners being paraded at Am Rong's office. They were normally in their mid-thirties, in neat new uniforms. The point about those guys, as I learnt later, was that they were fakes, probably recruited from the ranks of the *cyclopousses* for propaganda purposes. The real Khmer Rouge were less neatly turned out. Their *kramar*s were filthy. Their shirts were faded and stained with sweat, and they were not tailored to size. Their trousers were rolled up to below their knees, and they had red flashes on their guns. Their faces were darkly tanned.

As they came along the street they asked if anyone knew the whereabouts of the seven traitors, or of any republican officers. Down the street, from the house which had been looted, they were throwing out framed photographs into the road. I went back indoors.

The radio came to life again. There was a confusion of voices. Then silence. Then someone wished long life to the liberation forces. And now we could hear Lon Non, the brother of Lon Nol, addressing any republican soldiers who might be listening. He asked them to lay down their weapons and shake hands with the other side. There was no point in continuing hostilities. We were all Cambodian and we should join hands and try to reconstruct our mother country. A Buddhist monk repeated this message. Then there was silence again.

Two jeeps came along the street, the first mounted with a machine gun. They were driven by FANK soldiers but contained Khmer Rouge troops. Children were running alongside, laughing and cheering. Someone called through a megaphone telling everyone to bring out their weapons and put them in the second vehicle. Women came out with the guns, smiling. Phan hid his M-16, wrapped in a mat, on the toilet roof.

I stood by the gate again. A new group arrived. They looked as if they feared they might be attacked at any moment. My father called me back into the house, and as I went in some Khmer Rouge followed me, asking for the head of the family. They wanted to know if there were any soldiers in the house. My father seemed to have recovered himself. He was calm and said there were no soldiers here. Phan stood at the back of the family group.

The soldiers' eyes darted round the room. One of them told us we must leave the city at once. The Americans were about to bomb it. We should pack emergency provisions for a few days, but not too much. The evacuation would only be for a short while. Then we would be allowed back. Also, they said, they wanted to find the remaining enemies of the people, the chief traitors.

We dithered for a while. Phan seemed to have lost any sense of danger. He suggested that he and I should stay behind to guard the house. I asked my father. He told me not to be such a fool.

Now a second group of soldiers came by and repeated the orders. They said that if we stayed in the city we would be responsible for our own safety. 'That's it,' said my father, 'we're going.'

TWELVE
The journey out

So it was that, after a five-year break, we once again made our traditional New Year trip to the country. It was as if my father had done all the planning that my mother used to do. He had got together plenty of rice, dried fish, salt, tinned food, plastic water-bottles, spare cans of petrol, blankets, mosquito nets, tarpaulins, pots, pans, plates and spoons. My sisters put our clothes into the Land Rover. Sisopha took the Philips tape-recorder. Phan was still very attached to some of his uniforms, but my father stopped him taking them. I put in my diaries and some of my favourite books: Orwell's *Animal Farm*, Eric Williams's *The Wooden Horse*, Daphne du Maurier's *Rebecca*, a French textbook called Mauger and an English grammar. My father seemed to take nothing. He burnt the ledgers in which he had written all his researches into popular medicine.

This time it was Phan who locked up the house. There were fourteen of us. My father drove. Phan, Somaly, Sisopha and I walked beside the car. Orphea and Mealea were in the front seat. Bopha was perched on the back. My three little brothers and my nephew and two nieces were dotted among the luggage. We set out along the crowded street, carried along by the throng. People were shouting out, trying not to lose their families. Those of us who were walking held on to the car. The Khmer Rouge stood at the roadside, telling us to move along. If anyone tried to turn back, they would jump into the crowd and order him to keep moving in the general direction of the outskirts.

We moved very slowly in the heat of the day. Some people were carrying their possessions on their backs or on bicycles. Others had handcarts which they pushed and pulled. There were overloaded *cyclos* with families balancing on them and parents pushing. Those of us with cars were the lucky ones. Children cried out that they were being squashed in the crowd. Everywhere people were losing their relatives.

After two hours we reached the market place called Phsar Doeum Kor, where there were two piles of bodies in civilian clothes, as if two whole families had been killed, babies and all. Two pieces of hardboard stuck out of the pile, and someone had scrawled in charcoal: For refusing to leave as they were told. From here on, both sides of the road were covered with dead bodies, some soldiers, some not. People were being pushed along in hospital beds. They had come from the Khmero–Soviétique hospital, which had been emptied. Their relatives struggled with the beds, like ants with a beetle. We passed mutilated bodies, some killed by grenades or mortars, others decapitated. There must have been heavy fighting here. There were burnt cars and houses all around.

At the first checkpoint the Khmer Rouge were looking for any military objects – uniforms, weapons and packs. They took some of our medicine, my watch and the Philips tape-recorder, and threw them on a pile of confiscated objects – televisions, cameras and cassettes. They found nothing incriminating in our car, but other groups were less fortunate. They were told to wait beside their possessions. Then, when a group of around ten had been assembled, they were led across the dry paddyfields to beyond the treeline. Then there were gunshots.

By evening we had reached the Clear Water Pagoda, Wat Tuk Thlar. Nobody spoke much. We spread tarpaulins on the ground and ate some food. People came round selling pork at a very high price (they must have found it in abandoned properties) and some people produced blocks of ice and cartons of Fortune cigarettes. There were still families moving on the road, looking for space to camp for the night. Late that night, the Khmer Rouge came and confiscated some motorbikes from nearby. They were still looking for radios and medicine. Nobody mentioned the threat of American bombing any more. I stretched out under the Land Rover and wondered how long we would be away from home, and what had happened to my mother, and what had happened to my school-friends. I wondered if anyone was left in the city. Sisopha had been separated from her fiancé, and was worried about him. Phan said to my father, 'Why don't we go to South Vietnam?' But my father told him that was impossible – he had been thrown out long ago.

Sisopha suggested we might try to go to the estate, but my father was not sure whether we would be allowed to. And besides, we didn't know what had happened to it or Chan and Long during the war. Somaly was comforting her children. Everywhere around, children were crying.

On the second day we reached Pochentong market, and waited with the milling crowd to see what would happen next. The shops had been ransacked. There were torn mattresses everywhere. Some people here seemed light-hearted and were treating the evacuation like an adventure. They were selling loot at around ten times the normal price. People were drinking beer and picknicking in the fields. There was very little movement. It was as if people thought that they would soon be allowed back.

But on the third day we were forced to move further. We got as far as the soup shop where Routes Three and Four divided, the place where we had always stopped for breakfast. The tables were upturned and people were sheltering in it. We camped in the fields a little away from the crowd, and my father told us all to bury our identification cards, for safety's sake. From now on, he said, we were to say that we were peasants from the Pochentong area. There was to be no mention of the military, of doctors or nurses or students.

Here the Khmer Rouge came round asking if anyone was a technician from the information ministry. They needed them to return to the capital to work. But nobody volunteered.

The weather was hot and sticky. We had run out of water, and this was the dry season. If we found a pool, it was always dirty. Sometimes there were corpses in it. I left the family and struck out across the fields in search of water, hoping perhaps to come across someone I knew. Sisopha told me to keep a look-out for her fiancé.

I could see now that Route Four was blocked and that we would not be able to get to our estate that way. In the fields around Route Three there were families camping, and the atmosphere was, in a way, quite cheerful, as if the whole adventure was absurd. People were wandering around, and nobody stopped me as I went in the direction of the nearest village.

Here, there was no sign of life. The huts were open and empty, as if they had been suddenly deserted. There were ragged clothes strewn around. Farm implements lay in disorder. Flasks were still hanging in the sugar palms. There was a fresh smell of manure, but there were no oxen in sight.

At the far end of the village, I came across an old lady sitting in front of her shack beside a large sack of rice. She was feeding her chickens. I asked her if she knew where I could find water. 'Oh,' she replied, 'this year every pool in the village has dried up. The weather's been so hot. I used that pool over there, but it's dried up as well. All these people coming from the capital. They've taken it all.'

'Why's the village so quiet? Where has everyone gone?'

'They left a week ago. They were all told to go to the jungle.'

'The jungle! Then why are you still here?'

She sighed. 'I was told to go, but I said I was so old I didn't care if they killed me.' She spat out some betel. 'I'm sure I'll die very soon, perhaps today, perhaps tomorrow.' And she cried.

'So what did they do when you disobeyed them?'

'They were very angry, but there was a boy about your age who said I was too old to go with them and they'd have difficulty taking care of me. I'd just be a nuisance.'

'I'm sorry to ask you these things, grandmother. Have you cooked anything today?' She hadn't. There was no water and she'd been living on dried rice. So I asked her permission to climb the coconut trees. I left some for her and took the rest back to the camp. Talking to the old woman had made me realize we were never going to be allowed to return to Phnom Penh.

It was dusk when I got back. The family were worried about me. We opened the coconuts and cooked with their milk. Then we tried to rest, but around midnight I heard voices. The Khmer Rouge were ordering people to get back on the road and go to their places of birth. If they came back and saw us still here, we could not blame them if they used force.

Everyone was fast asleep. I woke them up and told them what I had heard. Obviously none of us could go back to our place of birth. We packed up the car and set off again along Route Three, but when we reached the road we ran out of petrol. People were shouting to their families to be off. Those whose motorbikes had been confiscated were asking the owners of vehicles for space to put their things, but our car was loaded up. We began to push, passing along the way groups whose home-made carts had collapsed. There were no longer any of the wounded from the hospitals. What had happened to them I do not know. Every time we stopped for a rest we were forced at gunpoint to move on.

The sun rose and we pushed until noon when we were able to stop and eat some rice and salt. I went off to look for some vegetables. I didn't know what I was going to do. The last time I had seen this area it had been green and rich in crops. Now I could see the destruction that the war had brought about. The palms had been blasted away. There were bomb craters everywhere. The field looked like one of those baking tins for individual Yorkshire puddings. There were bomb cases and mortar fins sticking out of the ground. The stubble was burnt.

I thought back to my family and home, and everything I had done at school. It made me burst into tears. If we were to leave the capital for ever, what was going to happen to my little brothers? They were too young for this hard journey. I kept thinking about my mother and wondering how she would find us if she came back. Would she be allowed to return? I walked round the fields, thinking of all these things and finding nothing. As soon as I got back to the car we were told to move on, on pain of death.

To our delight we reached the Kanthuot river, which still had some water. The bridge had been destroyed, and people camped along the near bank. The further bank was absolutely empty. You could see where the road had been cut with trenches (for this had been the front line during the war). After eating, I went down to the river for my first wash in three days. The water came up to my knees. I lay down in the river fully clothed, and looked up at the cooking fires along the crowded bank. On the far side, something silver shone in the moonlight. It turned out to be a couple of dead fish. Without a thought I put them in my pocket, to give to my sisters for our next meal. In the camp, arguments began to break out over food and belongings. Someone started a fight and was taken off by the Khmer Rouge. Now we began to guard our possessions.

We stayed for two days on the river bank, and some people still thought they would soon be allowed home. I suggested to my father that the time had come to abandon the car, but the problem was how we were going to carry all our supplies. How, for that matter, were we going to get the car across the river? Then Phan bumped into some of our cousins, and my father invited them to join us.

With great difficulty we pushed the car down the steep bank and up the other side. And there we had another stroke of luck: San, Sisopha's fiancé, came along the road looking for his family. He had somehow been separated from his fourteen brothers and sisters. Now there were twenty of us. The luggage was piled high in the car. But after pushing the thing another ninety metres or so along the road, negotiating all the trenches, we decided to give up the effort. There was no point.

About midnight, our camp was surrounded by Khmer Rouge with guns.

'Has anyone here been in the army?'

'No, sir,' said my father quickly.

'Don't call me sir, call me comrade,' said the fierce leader. 'No one is called sir after the revolution. We have been fighting to get rid of these words.' And he went on to ask if there were any soldiers, students, doctors and suchlike among the people camped nearby. We pleaded ignorance, but a man not far away from us confessed to having been a doctor.

'A doctor! In which hospital?'

'The Khmero–Soviétique.'

'So how many soldiers were treated by you? Twenty a day? Forty?'

'No, sir, it was a civilian hospital. If you don't believe me ask anyone around here.'

'You can't fool me, comrade. I know all about hospitals,' said the soldier, and turned to his comrades. 'OK, take him. He's a doctor.' And then turning to the man's family, who had begun to cry, he said, 'There's no point in that. You're lucky we're only taking him.' And they dragged the man away into the dark. Some time later we heard gunshots.

The next morning I went in search of water. The river had by now been so stirred up that it was no good for drinking. Eight hundred metres away I found a small pool, but it was full of bloated corpses, most of them soldiers. I looked closer. The man they had taken away was there, lying on his back, shot in the chest. I suddenly thought that I had wandered too far and must be near the Khmer Rouge base. A voice behind me made me freeze: 'Hold it, hands up!'

I dropped the bucket and turned around. A boy about my age was pointing a gun at me. I thought I was finished.

'What the hell are you doing here, comrade?' he shouted.

'I was looking for water.'

'You look like a soldier. Are you a soldier?'

'No, comrade, I'm a farmer.'

'Then get out of here and don't come back.'

I ran off, still believing he would shoot me in the back. I thought: I'll hear a shot and then I'll be killed. I kept seeing the bodies in the pool. When I got back I told nobody what I'd found out.

We walked on. I had found a yoke in the fields and had tied my bundles at both ends. Already my shoulder was blistered. My father was carrying my youngest brother on his hip and a bag on his shoulders. The children complained bitterly of heat and exhaustion. Food was running low. There had been many fights among the evacuees, and all those who fought were taken away. Old people were dying along the road and had to be abandoned by their relatives.

The road was still very crowded and people were dithering. Many were still looking for their families. We had been walking now for five or six weeks, but we had hardly made any progress. Every hundred metres we would stop, adjust the baggage, mend a yoke, swap the children around. People tried to improvise wooden spokes for their bicycle wheels, and wrap cloth around the outer tubes. We used every excuse for delay. The Khmer Rouge watched us from the roadside. They were smoking Fortune cigarettes and drinking Pepsi. The had transistor radios draped over their new motorbikes. They no longer had their guns at the ready. They could see we were too weak to resist them. They relaxed.

Then there was a novelty – a Honda truck came along the road with a loudspeaker. It was the first functioning vehicle we had seen for weeks. I noticed it was new and had no number-plates. The man in the truck told us to hurry along to the next village before our food ran out. There was a registration centre there. After we had registered we would be fed and cared for.

When we came to the village we suddenly realized where we were. It was Prasath Neang Khmao, the Temple of the Black Lady, the second port of call on our old New Year trips to the estate. And now the monks had gone and the Khmer Rouge had turned the place into their headquarters. Nobody was selling cakes under the trees. The carvings had been ruined by bullets and bombs. A red flag flew from a bamboo pole in front of the entrance.

A large crowd sat in the courtyard, waiting for registration. Our turn came after a couple of hours. We took our belongings and stumbled through the temple entrance. In the small vaulted room, the statues had been stacked around the walls and the shelves of the altar were empty. The Black Lady herself was leaning against the wall, turning her back on the proceedings. Several men in neat black uniforms and with silk *kramar*s stood staring at us mistrustfully. Two sat at a small wooden table, their guns propped against the bench. I didn't yet know that the pens in their shirt pockets indicated seniority. On the table lay two US M-16 bayonets, three notebooks displaying portraits of Sihanouk, a couple of ballpoint pens, some Fortune cigarettes and a silver lighter. It was a Ronson. The officer had stood it to attention, as if he was very proud of it.

We were instructed to place our belongings at one end of the room and to sit on the floor in front of the table. They asked us our names and occupations during the corrupt Lon Nol regime. Without hesitation, my father replied that we were farmers and that none of us had been in military service. But when we were asked our place of birth, my father paused for a moment before replying Phnom Penh.

While our answers were being recorded, the soldiers at the other end of the room were amusing themselves tipping our possessions on to the floor. They went through every single thing, and took all our pens and notebooks away. My bags contained nothing but books. As these fell out, one Khmer Rouge exclaimed. 'What are these books about? Whose are they?'

His face had hardened. One of the soldiers picked up *The Wooden Horse* and went through it, page by page, upside down, pretending to read it. I turned to my father and realized he was stuck for words.

'They belong to me, comrades,' I replied. 'I picked them up along the road because I thought they would be good for rolling cigarettes.'

'Well,' said the soldier reading Eric Williams, 'there are plenty of banana leaves where you're going. You don't need this rubbish.' And he threw *The Wooden Horse* into a corner of the room, on to a huge pile of photographs and money.

PART TWO
Under the Khmer Rouge

THIRTEEN
My father

By dusk the registration of the large crowd was complete. The Khmer Rouge with the pistol came out of the temple and addressed us: 'Friends and comrades, it gives me pleasure to introduce myself as leader of this region. Welcome. As you all know, during the Lon Nol regime the Chinese were parasites on our nation. They cheated the government. They made money out of Cambodian farmers, buying up their produce cheaply and selling it in Phnom Penh at extortionate rates. Because the politicians could never resist money, corruption spread through every ministry. Now the High Revolutionary Committee wants to separate Chinese infiltrators from Cambodians, to watch the kind of tricks they get up to. The population of each village will be divided into a Chinese, a Vietnamese and a Cambodian section. So, if you are not Cambodian, stand up and leave the group. Remember that Chinese and Vietnamese look completely different from Cambodians.'

About ten people stood up and walked to the place reserved for them.

'Are there any more?' shouted a man with an AK–47, looking ferociously through the crowd.

We all looked at each other anxiously. In Cambodia there were many families who had no knowledge of any Chinese ancestry but whose faces looked Chinese. No one stood up. The soldier asked again. Still no one stood up. Then the four guards who had been at the temple were told to go through the crowd. Anyone whose face looked foreign was dragged out. Most of them protested, but they were not believed.

By now it was dark and we were told that it was too late to make the journey to the settlement. We would have to stay in the temple overnight; we were given permission to walk around the grounds to find firewood, but we were not allowed to put up shelters.

People rushed with pots and buckets to the temple well, hoping to get there before it was exhausted. Those who found water began making fires. Others took out their groundsheets and began making their beds. At around nine o'clock, while we were eating, a soldier came to warn us not to wander around during the night. We had to stay where we were, and if we wanted a shit we had to do it as near as possible to the crowd. If we didn't take him at his word we would be 'responsible for our own safety'.

None of the adults could sleep. We were all gazing at the fires, which were kept burning against the mosquitoes. Nobody talked. I could see husbands gazing at the faces of their wives and children. They were tense and depressed. My three little brothers were in a deep sleep, and my father sat next to them with his *kramar* in his hand, fanning the mosquitoes away. From time to time he would look at me, then at my sisters, then at my little brothers and finally, with a sigh, at the ground. Sisopha, on my right, lay sobbing at the pains in her joints. She had never suffered such strain before.

In the small hours my youngest brother woke up and cried. My father tried to lull him back to sleep, but he wept and asked where my mother was and where we were. 'Be good,' said my father gently, patting him on the forehead, 'she'll be with us soon. We'll be home in a short while. Come on. Get back to sleep.' His voice was trembling and there were tears in his eyes. I was crying.

The Cambodian section left the temple the next morning, and that was the last we saw of the Vietnamese and Chinese groups. They sat there watching us go. We set off through the dry paddy-fields and came to the foot of a mountain called Phnom Chi So, named after Sister So, the mother of the Black Lady. At the summit there were two temples built about half a century before Prasath Neang Khmao.

Beside a muddy pool we found several newly built huts, about five metres square, thatched with palm leaves, with no walls and without the usual raised floor. They were like cattle shelters. We sat in a field while a Khmer Rouge soldier called out for the heads of families and showed them to their huts. My father's hut was next door to that of Somaly and my cousin's family. Not far away stood several proper houses, roofed with tiles and occupied by Khmer Rouge families.

After a short rest we began trying to improve our huts, putting up tarpaulins for walls. A boy came round to tell us to fetch our rations from the village commune. When my father returned, he had a small amount of rice and a little salt. We cooked, ate, and went on improving the hut, digging a small ditch around it in case of rain, rearranging the roof and smoothing the ground. By dusk our shelter was in good shape.

At night the new residents had camp fires. Some of them burned their rubber flipflops in order to have light. You could still see the worry and depression. Among the Khmer Rouge families there were petrol lamps glowing. People sat laughing and chatting. The petrol lamps were a novelty for the little boys of the area. The fuel had been taken from abandoned cars. The thin wicks were encased in the metal inner tube of a ballpoint pen. The bottle was glass and the stopper was cork. What attracted the little boys was the brightness of the flame, like a welder's torch, and the smell of the petrol. The Khmer Rouge were delighted with their new lamps. We slept on the bare ground.

We were escorted up the mountain the next day, to cut saplings for beds. There followed a mass meeting in the field beside the camp, in which we were divided into groups of ten with two Khmer Rouge to a group. The camp leader gave a very long speech. He began by saying that money had been abolished under the new regime. He spoke of the hardships the Khmer Rouge had undergone during the past years of war, of the lack of medicine in the jungle, the struggle against bombing and the devotion of the soldiers to the Party. He compared the lives of the poor with those of the rich under the old regime. He outlined the aims of the High Revolutionary Committee: to get rid of class distinctions and to achieve equality for the population of the whole country. Those who went to work would be given rations by the committee. Those who did not would receive nothing.

The meeting was addressed by one comrade after another, each trying to find new ways of saying the same things. There were long pauses. It was not until dusk that the speakers had all had their turn. They were uneducated men – you could tell that they had not spent more than a few months at school. Their speeches were resumed the next day when a new face, that of the village leader, appeared. We were told that we would be planting sweet cassava and sweet potatoes.

A band of teenagers in neat black uniforms came marching up to the meeting. We fell into groups, which were further subdivided into subgroups under the supervision of one of these boys – 'The reason being,' said the village leader, 'the smaller the group, the easier it is to find spies from the old regime. The enemies of the peasants must be crushed to pieces.'

These subgroup leaders went from hut to hut the next morning to collect their members. We gathered in the field and set off in single file, the village leader in front, the camp leader at the back and the others interspersed, carrying large *parang*s on their shoulders. We reached the large, dry, infertile area where we were supposed to work. Our tools were brought by ox cart from the village and we began to dig.

It was hot and I was thirsty. There was no sign of water in the field, only waves of vapour from the June sun. At noon we were told to rest. Those who were clever had brought food with them. They started to eat, while the improvident ones, such as my family, wandered round the field looking for shade. At last my father and I found a place to shelter and we were joined by my sisters, who were too tired for conversation.

Under a large tree, away from the new residents, the leaders were sitting in a circle eating their lunch. They were chatting happily, and some of them took their wristwatches off to admire them. Their food had arrived by ox cart.

I could bear my thirst no longer. I went up to them and asked for water. All activity in the circle came to an abrupt halt on my approach. They slipped their watches into their shirt pockets and assumed grave expressions, looking at each other in surprise as I asked for water.

'Why didn't you bring your own water from the village?' said a fifteen-year-old. 'We don't have enough for you.'

'Comrade, I didn't realize we were going to work here all day, and anyway, I wasn't told to do so.'

'Even though you weren't told,' said the boy severely, his voice rising, 'I think you should have known.'

'Yes, comrade, I know I should have realized, but – I'm sorry.' I turned to leave, knowing that what I was about to say would have put me at risk. I was told to stop. One of them stood up and said:

'Listen, comrade, you'll have to drop the word "sorry". You are not allowed to use it here or anywhere else, as long as the High Revolutionary Committee exists. Here is some water and food for you. Next time don't forget to bring your own. Now take it and eat it before the rest period is over.'

I rushed back to my family. As soon as we had eaten it was time to work again. We went on till six.

When I got back to the hut I found that the few books I had been able to retrieve had been torn to pieces and were piled outside. Most of them were burnt. I asked my little brother what had happened. While we were away the Khmer Rouge had come searching from hut to hut, destroying all books and removing some of our clothes and medicines. They had been in a happy mood. We were lucky that my sisters had taken their jewels to the work-field, concealed in their underwear. But now we started to worry about our background. My father thought that the men might have found something to identify us.

He went off to fetch our rations, and when he had not returned after two hours we became alarmed. But there was nothing to do except pace around the hut. Finally, he came back with a little rice packed in his *kramar*. This time there was no salt. He had been delayed because heads of families were being questioned very closely about their former occupations.

At midnight the camp was quiet. Many people were asleep. Others sat in the darkness discussing the situation. They spoke very quietly and carefully. My father and I were the only ones awake in our hut. He was resting on the ground with his right hand on his forehead, sighing from time to time. I lay next to him. He asked me, 'Someth, what would you do if I was not here or – ?'

I sat up. 'Why are you asking such a terrible question?'

'Why do you think? Do you think we can succeed in hiding our background? Do you think I'll be spared when my occupation is known? You saw with your own eyes what happened to that other doctor. That's why I ask.' I was on the verge of tears. He went on, 'Come on, Someth, I mean it. I must know.'

My tongue wouldn't move.

'Someth, I've been thinking about this a long time. I have to tell you the truth about the day General Dien Del came to our house. He asked me to leave the capital with him, but I refused because I could not leave you all behind . . .'

A slight noise near the hut made him stop. We listened intently, but it was only the wind blowing dead leaves along the ground.

'I know exactly what will happen to the Cambodian people,' said my father, 'and to our family. Now, come on, answer me.'

'Dad, why didn't you tell me before? A few weeks ago I was very happy indeed. I thought that the war had finished and the corruption was over.'

'You are right, Someth, but remember, there is no end to revenge.'

'I understand. Tell me what you want me to do.'

'I want you to take care of all your brothers and sisters. You've done very well so far. You're good at coping with new circumstances. But please remember – take care of them and don't do anything that might put their lives at risk. Don't behave as you did under Lon Nol. Under the new regime, anyone who does wrong could have his relatives wiped out.'

I told my father that I would remember everything he had said. Then I begged him to get some sleep because I was really worried about his health. We stopped talking and I began watching my brothers and sisters. From time to time they would turn over and groan in their sleep. Their bodies ached from work. I wondered if I would be able to carry out my duties. Was I too young for the responsibility? And who were the enemies of the peasants? And how did my father know precisely what was going to happen under this regime?

My mind was full of questions and I could not sleep. I went to check the water in the buckets, and started a fire to cook some food to take with us. While I was doing so Phan joined me from the next hut. 'Couldn't you sleep?' he asked, squatting by the fire to warm his hands.

'No, I had backache. What about you?'

'Not very well. Is Father still asleep? He looked very depressed yesterday.'

'I think he fell asleep a few hours ago.'

'Do you have any water left?' asked Phan. 'I used up all mine yesterday, and I've not even washed my face yet.'

There was very little in the buckets, so we decided to go off together to the pool. It was still dark and nobody was stirring among the huts. The further we went, the more I felt that it wasn't wise to stay quiet. I put both buckets in my right hand and began to clank them together.

'Hey, Someth,' said Phan, 'you'll wake everybody up with that noise.'

'They ought to be awake by now,' I replied, raising my voice, 'to prepare food for today's work.' And I went on to talk about our revolutionary duty. My brother-in-law looked a bit surprised by all this, but while we were filling the buckets we were challenged from the darkness. Two boys were standing behind us at the top of the bank that led down to the pool. They had bright long *parang*s. They asked us what we were up to.

'Comrades,' I said, trying to sound normal, 'we're fetching water to cook our lunch for the day's work. If we don't do it now we'll be late for the meeting.'

'OK, get your water and go back to your hut. But next time don't forget to fill your buckets before you go to sleep.'

We rushed back to the hut in great alarm. The boys must have heard what I was saying, otherwise they would have arrested us for walking around in the dark. Sisopha was annoyed with me. 'Where have you been? We were worried about you.' She lifted the lid off the rice. 'You shouldn't leave a pot on the fire like this. If Daddy hadn't taken it off, all the rice would have been burnt.'

'Someth,' said my father, 'don't do that again, will you?'

I apologized and told him to stop worrying.

One day, great excitement was caused by the announcement that we were not to go to work as usual, but were to take all our belongings with us and attend a mass meeting. There was much speculation as to the reason. Bopha asked my father if this meant that we would be allowed to go home. 'I hope so,' replied my father, sighing. 'We'll find out at the meeting.'

'We'll be with Mother again!' shouted my little brothers, jumping up and down on the bed. My father brushed the tears from his eyes as he watched them.

When the village leader appeared before the expectant meeting, he was greeted with clapping. This was the first time we had applauded him. But the opening of his speech covered the same ground as usual, the struggle to liberate us from American imperialism, the fact that people in the revolution shouldn't need to be reminded to work, we had to work for our own survival, and so on.

Gradually, faces fell among the audience. Then he came to the point.

'We have been fighting so far,' said the village leader, 'to destroy the distinction between rich and poor. This struggle is almost complete, but the last step of the process requires help from you all. So, friends and comrades, will you please present all your belongings to the village committee. We are now as one. Everything in the village will belong to us, the peasants, and not to any particular person any more.

'Remember that we have sacrificed everything to the High Revolutionary Committee. We fought empty-handed, owning nothing more than a pair of shorts. Now we have everything. At the beginning we used axes, crossbows, *parang*s and spears as our weapons. Now we have machine guns, rifles, army trucks and even airplanes. Under the old regime peasants were considered too ignorant to fly planes, but now, as I have been informed by Phnom Penh . . .' And he went on to describe further achievements of the revolution.

At the end of his long speech, a group of teenagers went through the crowd and dragged our belongings in front of the meeting. They went for watches first of all, then tape-recorders, notebooks, pens and pencils, family photographs and some money, which, it was declared, would be worthless under the new regime.

'Every remnant of the old regime,' said the village leader, 'must be destroyed and "new things" created for the new regime. We must help the revolution by spying on each other, because there are enemies among us. The High Revolutionary Committee has a new task for you. Tomorrow we start building a dam, so that in a few months we can plant rice. As we all know, we live on rice, and to get it we must build an irrigation network. If we have irrigation in our grasp, the rice will follow. For farming, we need water; for battle, we need rice.' Then he dismissed us to our huts.

We gathered together the remains of our belongings and returned to the camp, suppressing our anger. Before the meeting we had stripped the tarpaulins off the walls, and now all the huts had to be repaired. That afternoon our subgroup leaders brought us pick-axes, mattocks, spades and baskets for work on the dam. We were told to treat them carefully. They were 'the weapons of the revolution'.

The camp was quiet that night, but I could not sleep for worry at what my father had told me. I wondered what it was that he knew about the aims of the revolution. Were they going to massacre us? As I lay awake, I heard the sound of footsteps approaching the hut. I got up and sat on the edge of the bed. Whoever it was had stopped outside, and stood there quite still for five minutes. Finally a voice said softly, 'Is anyone awake?'

'Yes,' I replied, slipping quietly off the bed, 'what can I do for you?'

'The village committee wants to see you.'

I went out as quietly as I could. It was a Khmer Rouge soldier with a wristwatch and gun. He was about my age. In the shadow of a small tree stood three other men, absolutely still. They escorted me to the other end of the village, where the village leader was waiting in the centre of a circle of seats. This was the first time that I had sat face to face with the Khmer Rouge of the village, and the first time I had looked them in the eye.

'Are you Someth?' asked the village leader, drawing on his cigarette.

'Yes, sir – sorry, comrade,' I replied. 'Do you want something from me?'

'You know the reason why we have called you in the middle of the night. We don't want to interrupt your work during the day. That is the rule we have with interviews of this kind.'

'Yes, comrade, I understand. Now what can I do for you?'

'All we need is the truth. If you tell us anything untrue you'll be in big trouble.'

'I'll tell you whatever I know.'

'Good. I was informed that someone in your family was a soldier. Is this true? Tell me the *truth*.' He shouted the last word.

'No, comrade, no one in my family has been a soldier. Not one of us has even done a day's military service. We are farmers.' My heart was beating fast and my throat was dry.

'Are you sure you're telling us the truth?' asked a man I took to be a senior officer: he was sharp-featured, wore a silk *kramar* and had several ballpoint pens.

'Yes, comrade,' I replied, 'we are farmers.' The village leader seemed to accept this. He told me I could go back to my hut. I thanked him (and was reminded that thanks had been abolished) but asked whether I would get into trouble if I went back on my own and met the patrol team on the way. I was given an escort of three boys. As we were about to reach the camp, I dimly saw two men, their hands bound behind their backs, walking towards the west. They were followed by troops in black uniform. One of the soldiers asked his comrades what was happening. He was told that the men had been officials under Lon Nol. They were going to be killed.

My father was angry, thinking I had left the hut out of mere curiosity, but he calmed down when I told him what had happened. Then he sighed and told me to get some sleep.

At the dam site the next day, all the new residents were shocked to see a group of Buddhist monks being put to work. There were about fifty of them, still in their saffron robes. And when we realized what the plans were for the dam, the whole project seemed nonsensical. In pre-war days, the paddyfields of the area were only planted in the rainy season. There were no streams or rivers nearby, only a few pools. The site for the dam had been chosen for its awkwardness – it was in scrubland a little way up a small hill. The idea was to build a dike five metres high, following the contour of the hill, with a wall at either end to form a wedge shape. Thus the only catchment area for the water was a section of the hill itself. If the water came, it was highly likely that it would sweep the dam away down the slope. As we began to break the hard clay ground, we realized that the work was pointless.

The Khmer Rouge did not work. They stood at a distance from the crowd, chatting and watching over us. While we dug, we discussed the fate of the monks, and wondered whether religion would survive the regime.

During the next month of hard labour, we had little rice and no protein. The new residents became tired and pale, and they lost a lot of weight. In contrast, the Khmer Rouge health improved. They had more food than they needed, and their only job was guarding us.

In August came the anniversary of the recapture of the village from the Lon Nol forces. The Khmer Rouge were issued with new black clothes, a new *kramar*, and Ho Chi Minh sandals. They paraded everywhere in the village, showing off their gear. A palm-leaf pavilion had been erected near the headquarters. Two cows had been slaughtered. A group of teenage girls was involved in cooking the meal, and the smells from the pavilion reached us downwind in the camp. This caused a sensation among us – the mixed aromas of lemon-grass, cinnamon, boiling coconut milk, turmeric and coriander seeds. At noon we were taken to the pavilion in groups and allowed to eat as much as we wanted. There was a large vat of sloppy curry with sweet potatoes, and another vat of rice. The girls served the food with great pride and waited on us attentively. Once each group had had its fill, another came to take its place.

In the afternoon, we were told, we could wander round the village but we were not to go too far. I told my father that I wanted to see the carvings on the temples at Phnom Chi So. There were stone steps up the mountain, with a balustrade on either side. The hill was covered with light scrub and clumps of bamboo. Large unwieldy argus pheasants, with beautiful long tails, flapped from clump to clump, calling out with a low woo-woo sound. There were brown and white pigeons and doves, and little yellow butterflies. The further you went up the hill, the louder the noise of the insects among the flowers.

At the summit, a vague, weatherbeaten statue of a woman (perhaps Sister So herself) lay on its side where it had been toppled from its plinth. The walls of the temples were decorated with Hindu and Buddhist reliefs, battle scenes in which kings were borne into the thick of the fight on the shoulders of their slaves. In the first temple, the head had been knocked off the massive Buddha, and I had to clamber over stones that had fallen from the roof. The smaller statues had mostly been taken. The second building had been shattered by the bombing and its Buddha lay in fragments. Leading down the mountain from this place was a dark stone passage. We had heard from the locals that before the war, no one who ventured into this passage ever came out alive. It was said to be the lair of two 'mortar snakes', huge but short creatures shaped like the wooden mortars used for husking the rice. Worse than this, it was said that if you so much as intended to visit the passage some time in the near future, the mortar snakes would come to your hut and drag you away. I was glad my sisters weren't with me, or they would have been scared, and might have scared me too. Like many people they believed this kind of story.

Coming round the temple, I reached a point where the cliff

dropped sheer beneath me, giving a view of a vast abandoned plain. There were bomb craters, some of them full of water, from the B–52 raids. White egrets were fishing in them. The bushes shimmered in the heat. It was the first time in four months that my stomach had been full, and it was the first time I had been alone.

FOURTEEN
Disappearance and death

I walked along the edge of the cliff, taking in the beauty of the view, until I saw, some distance ahead of me, a Khmer Rouge. He was sitting on a rock, looking lost to the world, his chin in his hand, his elbow on his knee. He was around forty years old, with greying hair, and something about him struck me as very different from any Khmer Rouge I had met so far. From time to time, he looked up at the sky, then down to the ground. My first reaction was that I ought to make my presence known to him before he saw and challenged me. As I walked closer I could hear what he was muttering. He was saying: 'Cockshit, cockshit, fuck, fuck, cockshit.' It was the only time I ever heard a Khmer Rouge swear.

For some reason, when I greeted him, it was in a friendly, relaxed style. 'Hey, brother,' I said, and smiled. He started, and came out of his trance. He smiled as he asked me what I was doing and I immediately lost all fear of him. I told him my name, company and section number, and at his invitation I sat down and asked his name.

'Kong,' he said. 'Have you taken part in the celebration?'

'Yes,' I replied, 'and the food was very good.'

'I'm glad you enjoyed it,' said Kong.

Up the mountain, we seemed to be in quite a different world from the village below. After a short conversation, Kong invited me to see his house, and I accepted because I had always been curious to see the inside of a Khmer Rouge home.

Along the road he asked me what I did. I replied that I was a farmer. 'Don't be afraid,' said Kong, 'I'm not going to investigate your background.' He looked up from the road and straight into my eyes. 'To tell you the truth, I was a teacher in Takeo school.'

'How long have you been here?'

'Three years, I think,' he replied, after a short sigh.

'So now you are teaching the kids in the village?'

'No, it's very difficult to tell you who I am. I'll explain when we get to my house.'

I began to choose my words with care.

Like most of the Khmer Rouge houses in the village, Kong's home was built on stilts about two metres above the ground. Under it were a couple of hen-huts with about ten birds, presumably the property of the commune. Hanging from a beam were a pair of rusty bicycles – they seemed to have been unused for a long time. Kong lived alone at the edge of the village. Inside his house were a few old posters of Sihanouk in various uniforms. In a corner stood three sacks of rice.

He handed me about a pint of palm juice in a coconut shell, sat down next to me and began to tell his story. It was, as far as I remember, in 1971 that fighting broke out around Takeo, and his family had been split between the two sides. On the first day many inhabitants of the town had been evacuated to the countryside and he had come here. People who refused to leave had been killed, others were liquidated a few weeks later when it was found that they had had jobs in government offices, or that they had had relations with foreigners. To avoid being killed he had pretended to be ignorant of everything but farming. After about a year, when there was increased fighting with the Lon Nol forces, he was drafted into an ammunition supply team.

Here Kong paused, and sipped at his sweet palm juice a few minutes before continuing his story: 'At one stage, we began an operation against the Lon Nol forces in Kampot province. For a few days it was a bloodbath, but then we defeated them. We had taken three prisoners, and I was ordered to kill one of them to prove that I really hated Lon Nol's people. Someth, I had never killed before – but I knew that if I did not do as I was told I would be finished. I put on a brave face and killed the man, not with a gun, with a knife. A few days later I was promoted to group leader.

'I was given an AK–47 with a folding stock. I was very proud of it, because it indicated my rank in the forces. I worked for the Khmer Rouge and forgot about my past. I had been told that when the war was over I would be able to go and find my family. Then I would be sent to work in a ministry somewhere in Phnom Penh. But now the war is over and they have gone back on their word. They took away my gun and sent me to work in the fields. Someth, can you imagine how I feel now? I have been cheated and abandoned. Well, that's communism,' he concluded, his voice rising. He was obviously very sorry to have lost his gun.

He got up and refilled my shell with juice. I didn't react. I cradled the shell in my hands and sipped at the palm juice, trying to work out why he had told me the story. If it was true, there was nothing that would break his depression. He had fouled his own nest, or, as we say in Cambodian, he had spat on his chest. But was the story true? I realized that the communists had a lot of dirty tricks which I was too young to understand.

I put the shell on the floor. 'Why did you tell me this? Don't you know that you will be in big trouble if I report this to the village committee?'

'I know, but I'm sure you won't,' said Kong, without a trace of worry.

I tried to frighten him. 'What makes you convinced that I'll keep this secret?'

He replied with a smile. 'I've got this strong feeling about you.'

'Does that rice belong to you?' I asked, changing the subject.

'No,' he replied sharply, 'it belongs to the committee. It's here because the communal barn hasn't been built yet – I was told it would be. Each house was told to keep three sacks of rice, and the head of the Food Centre would collect them bit by bit.'

'So you can use it?' I asked.

'Oh, no, of course not,' he said flatly, 'although, as the saying goes, a hen bred on a rice heap will never resist a few pecks.'

Then he got up, saying that he had to go to a meeting, but if I wanted to stay here alone I would be welcome. However, I thought my family might be getting worried. I said goodbye to him and left. I never knew what to make of him as I never saw him again.

Every evening before the rations were handed out there was a meeting where the same speech was made. By now the village leader, and every group, subgroup and company leader seemed to know it off by heart, and every time they repeated it they put the punctuation marks exactly where they had been the day before. We continued working non-stop on the dam, exhausted and on short rations. Most of the new residents suffered from malnutrition. Some stayed in their huts, not caring that their food would be stopped. The Khmer Rouge families began to suggest secretly that we exchange jewels for supplies. Some of us did this.

Again there was excitement when we were told one day to go to a meeting instead of work and to take our belongings with us. Even at this stage, people still thought that they might be sent back to their homes.

After the usual speech, the village leader said, 'Now, the committee is concerned about the state of your health since you are staying in uncomfortable huts. We have decided to improve them, and while they are being reconstructed each family will be sent to live in one of the comrades' houses. You will return to your huts when the reconstruction is finished.'

Obviously this was the easiest way of spying on us. We were sent to our new billets. My family lodged with a husband and wife and their two daughters. They had been with the revolution since 1970 and were very mean. They didn't like talking to us, and we were afraid of saying anything revealing to them. We lived under continual pressure, at their mercy because they had the right to go through our luggage when we were out at work on the dam. They used to long for night to come, when they would exchange their black uniforms for civilian clothes, and their daughters would wear the make-up and jewels that they had got from the new residents.

My father returned one day from collecting the rations. He looked sad. Without any explanation we had been allotted one-third of the usual amount. Then we found out that someone had been round to the house and removed all our medicine. So, when one of my nieces fell ill with dysentery, we had nothing but a hopeless folk remedy made from a crushed root. There was nobody to look after the girl. Somaly, her mother, was told that she would lose her rations if she stayed behind. In the end she did this, when the girl's condition became critical.

There followed the worst row we had had so far, when Somaly told her subgroup leader what she was planning to do. In the end she was allowed to stay behind on the understanding that her rations were stopped. When we returned that evening from the work-field she rushed out of the house to tell us her daughter had died.

In my anger, I dropped my spade without a word and ran to the commune. There was a long queue for food. I pushed past and went straight up to the man who was doling out.

'Why have my sister's rations been cut off?' I demanded, not realizing I had lost my self-control. 'She only stayed behind to look after a very sick girl. And now my niece is dead. Do you think it would have been right to leave her alone and go to work when she was so ill? I don't understand what you are all doing.'

Everybody in the queue was straining to watch the scene.

'Hey, comrade,' replied the leader of the Food Centre, sarcastically, 'we all have to die some time. What was she going to do for her daughter in her illness? Is she a doctor?' – a remark they used every time anyone wanted to care for a sick relative. If you had said yes, the consequences would have been obvious – 'I don't see the point in her sitting at home and worrying. We've lost far too many lives in battle – why complain about your niece's death? My wife was killed as well, but I never complained about that. Listen, comrade,' and here he raised his voice, pointing a finger at my face, 'you have to talk sense after the revolution. Otherwise you'll be in trouble.'

I began to realize that my anger was about to put me at risk. I shut up and took my rations. As I left, a man who used to be an ambulance driver in my father's hospital came out of the Centre. He had a shifty manner, as if he wanted to avoid me, but it was too late and he had to say hello before hurrying on.

Sem, the ambulance driver, was of peasant origin. He was about thirty and in the hospital he had not had many friends. The nurses used to say, 'Sem could turn white to black.' He was aggressive and had a reputation for badmouthing his colleagues. I do not know when he had arrived in the village, but as I went home I could not help wondering what he had been doing at the Centre. As far as I knew, no new resident would be allowed in the HQ without good reason. If they had been interrogating him, why didn't they do it by night?

I decided not to tell my father about Sem's arrival in the village. I didn't want to worry him, and there was also the problem of talking in front of the Khmer Rouge family. The house consisted of a single large room opening on to the verandah, which formed our living quarters. That evening, we sat around the body of my niece, weeping. Inside the house, we could see life continue as usual. Our hosts had their evening wash, and then dressed up in their best clothes – clothes that we and the other new residents had exchanged for rice and salt. The two teenage girls enjoyed their new position of privilege. They revelled in our humiliation. If Somaly had looked up she would have been able to see them trying on pieces of our family jewellery, making themselves up, and preparing for their usual large meal.

The next morning, when Phan asked if anyone wanted to come to the child's burial, no one could face it. I accompanied him silently, carrying the communal tools while he held his child. The new residents watched us in sympathy. Normally our neighbours would already have been in the house comforting the bereaved, but this was the first death among the new residents, and the customs had been strictly prohibited. Phan thought he would get into trouble if we tried to arrange a cremation. We chose a site on uncultivated ground about fifteen minutes from the village and began to dig. Throughout the whole business, Phan was sobbing. Then, rather delayed, we went to work on the dam.

Time passed, and still nothing had been done to renovate our old huts in the camp. Some of the new residents failed to turn up at the roll calls, but neither the group leaders nor the village leader seemed concerned. I knew something must be wrong. People were disappearing, and none of us knew where.

One evening we saw the regional leader again, for the first time since the Temple of the Black Lady. He told us all that the High Revolutionary Committee in Phnom Penh wanted all former civil servants to go back to their ministries. If there were any in the village, they were to pack up their belongings and be ready the next morning when they would be taken by truck to the capital. 'Please do not be afraid,' he said, 'there is no trick. We absolutely need all civil servants to go back.'

The applause began among the leaders, and spread to the rest of the audience. By the end of the meeting, people thought their dreams had come true. Some chatted excitedly with their families. others sat around trying to work out what was going on. My father gave me a look of warning. Though my sisters were smiling for the first time, I didn't believe a word of what we had been told. As we walked home, my father told us that since we had already declared ourselves to be farmers we would not go.

That night there was talking and laughter till dawn as people packed their belongings and cooked their rations for the journey. In the morning, 300 people were taken off in Chinese trucks. The rest of us went to work as normal, and when we reached the dam construction site we found new faces in our midst – Khmer Rouge boys who were detailed to work with us and listen to anything we said. They kept moving from place to place around the field.

Two days later, fewer than a hundred of the people who had gone off in trucks were sent back to the village. There were no heads of family among them.

The next day at work I met a woman who had gone with the trucks and I asked her what had happened. She looked around carefully before answering. Then she told me that they had been driven from the village as far as the Temple of the Black Lady. There they had waited till midnight before being forced to continue on foot. They walked to a remote village called Phnom Chhuk Sar, White Lily Mountain, where all the heads of family were taken away by the Khmer Rouge. The remainder of them had camped in the village for the night. In the morning they heard shellfire. The Khmer Rouge told them to move back – there was a clash with some remaining Lon Nol troops. They were told to start walking back, and that their husbands would be following them. 'I still haven't seen my husband,' said the woman, 'and I don't know where he is.' As she spoke I saw a soldier coming towards us. I grabbed a basket full of soil and took it off to the dam.

The work-field was much less busy now, with so many heads of family missing and with many more people sick with malnutrition and dysentery. Some of those who were too ill to work were taken by the group leaders to the sick bay. None of us knew where this was supposed to be. Meanwhile, the field where my niece was buried became a gigantic graveyard with a horrific smell. My family became thin and unrecognizable. By contrast, the Khmer Rouge looked healthier each day. Each of them possessed a watch and wore a pen with his uniform.

Our old huts by the pool remained untouched and some of them began to fall to bits. We curled up at night under our stinking sheets, too tired to talk to our families and too afraid to speak out against the regime.

Suspicion had fallen on my family. Every evening, as we sat down to our meagre supper a group of boys we had not seen before would be chatting at the other end of the room. Whenever we rested at the work-field, these boys were always in the shadows nearby, listening to our conversation. And then at midnight one night the Khmer Rouge came and said the village leader wanted to see my father. He left without saying a word.

A night, a day, a week passed without any news of him. I thought: that must be it. They must have found out.

Anxiety, stress and depression combined with hard labour made me ill. Sisopha suffered as well. We missed our work and our rations were stopped. Things got worse as we divided out the smaller share of food, and then my nephew went down with malaria. Phan exchanged everything we'd got with the Khmer Rouge to get medicine. Sisopha and I recovered in the end, but my nephew died about a week later.

On my recovery I decided that I must ask about my father. I put the question to the leader at the Food Centre, while fetching rations. He smiled and replied casually that my father was staying at the Re-education Centre, where he was being well looked after. 'All is well,' he said, 'don't worry about him. Just concentrate on your work.'

While he spoke I noticed Sem, the former ambulance driver. Now he was working at the Food Centre, and wore a neat black uniform. He shot me a strange look when he heard me ask about my father. I didn't ask any more. On my way back home, I wondered how Sem had landed himself with such a job.

We were sent back to our old camp; now, more than half the huts were empty. Between sunset and sunrise, if you were not too tired to notice such things, you could see the Khmer Rouge walking from hut to hut, listening to the conversations inside. Quite often people were asked to leave their homes and go to the open fields nearby. One night a boy came to tell me that the village reconnaissance team wanted a word with me. I went out to the same field where I had been questioned a few months before and was told to sit. There were three Khmer Rouge I had never seen before, and by the light of the half moon I could see that two of them had guns.

'Don't be afraid, comrade. You have done nothing against the High Revolutionary Committee. We just want to ask a few questions if we may.'

'Certainly, comrades, I'll tell you everything I can.'

'Do you think you have told the village the truth – about your not being a student and your family being farmers?'

The boy who asked this question picked up a gun and sat down close to me.

'Yes, of course, we really were.'

'I don't think you were,' said the boy. 'We have been informed you were something else.'

'You must have false information.'

'What do you mean?' snapped another of them, getting up. 'What do you mean by false information?'

'I mean that the information you've got came from somebody who wants to kill my family,' I replied.

'Don't misunderstand me, comrade,' said the man, walking round me as he spoke. 'The village committee doesn't kill people when they discover their real occupations. All we want from people is the truth.' I could tell he was really angry at what I had said.

'I understand very well, comrades,' I went on, 'that the High Revolutionary Committee is only doing what the Cambodian people want. But why do people have to be taken to the Re-education Centre? Could you tell me where it is?'

'It is a place where some people have to go to study the political situation of the country. It's not far from here.'

Then another man butted in angrily, 'We haven't brought you here to answer your questions. Tell me again. What was your father's occupation?'

They became more aggressive now. The other two got up and began pacing around me. I replied, in as normal a voice as I could, that I had told them the truth.

'Well,' said the one sitting opposite me, lowering his voice, 'to be honest with you, the village committee needs students and educated people to be leaders in some of the teams. So tell me if you were a student. The job could be yours.'

'To be a leader would be a very great honour for me,' I replied. 'As a matter of fact I really want to be one. But I know I have no qualifications at all. I am uneducated. My family were farmers.'

'If you're telling the truth, that's fine, but remember, there is no place for liars in the revolution. In the end they will be found out and destroyed.'

'I am very pleased to hear it,' I replied. 'I hate liars. If you find

137

anything I've said to be a lie, you can do what you want with me.'

'You don't have to tell us that, comrade. It'll be all over for you if we find out you've deceived us.'

And so the interrogation continued for another two hours.

One day at the dam site I met a very close friend of mine, named Kuntharo. He was from Takeo province where he had been educated before coming up to the capital to study at my school. He was a clever and hard-working student and we were like brothers, sharing even our depressions. We studied at home together and even went out looking for girls together. At the end of the year we had both done well at school. Kuntharo went home to visit his family. The Khmer Rouge attacked the town and I had not seen him since.

Now Kuntharo was in black uniform, with an M-16 slung over his shoulder. He was part of the team sent to listen to the conversations among the labourers. The first time I saw him I almost dropped my spade and ran towards him, but I realized I might get into trouble. I carried on digging, glancing at him occasionally to see if he recognized me. I picked up a basket of soil and went past him on my way to the dam. He smiled but did not say anything. I emptied my basket, walked past him again and returned the smile. Kuntharo was talking to a colleague. The Khmer Rouge were allowed to work wherever they wanted in the field. Gradually Kuntharo began to move in my direction. We began working together. He dug. I took the soil to the dam.

As we worked, I questioned him about his time with the Khmer Rouge. He said that he had been drafted into their army after his home had been overrun, working in the ammunition supply team, with the additional task of taking wounded soldiers to the infirmary. The rest of his family had been killed during the attack.

I asked him about the Re-education Centre, and he looked around before replying. He told me it was where suspects were held and questioned. Former government officials were interrogated there by several horrible methods: their nails were pulled out, their ears were tied to the wall with wires, they were electrocuted, wrapped in plastic sheets and beaten, stabbed or starved to death, and many other ways. 'You could call that place a prison, if you want,' he said.

'But how did you manage to work with them?'

'Someth,' replied Kuntharo with a long sigh, 'it's a long story.

Let's just say that if you want to get along with the Khmer Rouge you have to work hard and act dumb. They don't like intellectuals at all. They have a theory that, if intellectual people survive, their regime will one day collapse. That's why a lot of people from this village have gone missing.' At this stage he paused for a long while, looking at me in a strange way. There were tears in his eyes. He went on, 'Someth, my dear friend, I ought to tell you your father was killed a few days ago in the most horrible way ... I ...'

Then he stopped and turned his face away. I had dropped the basket and blocked my ears.

'What are you saying?' I raised my voice. 'You must have told them about his job. You bastard!'

'Calm down, Someth,' he replied, refilling the basket with soil. 'You know my loyalty to your family. You know who I am. I swear I wouldn't have done that.'

I knew he had been my best friend at school. 'I'm sorry,' I said, 'I'm sorry.'

Kuntharo was called away by his colleagues. I stopped and stared at them as they left. My family are in trouble now, I thought.

'Comrade Meth,' shouted a group leader behind me, 'come on, work!'

'Comrade,' I replied, turning round, 'I feel a bit unwell.'

But I did as I was told. The more I thought about my father the angrier I felt. I dug harder and harder, without realizing that I was using up more energy than I could afford. I dug and dug until, in the end, I collapsed.

When I opened my eyes, the first thing I saw was my family sitting around me weeping. Then I gradually recognized the blue plastic sheets and the palm-leaf thatch. I was on my bed in the hut. My sisters asked me why I was in such a terrible state. I took my little brother in my arms and began crying again.

'Please, Someth,' said Mealea, 'tell us what it is. You've been crying all the time.'

I waited several minutes. Then I told them the news.

FIFTEEN
Through the ghost city

Now terror became the very theme of my daily life. If I walked past the Khmer Rouge on the way to work, I didn't dare to look them in the eye. In the field I worked on my own, and quite often spent the day without saying a word to anyone except my family. The women worked separately from the men, and the only chance of talking to my sisters was during the lunch break. But the spiteful little boys were always within earshot. Rations were cut down and our working hours increased. Sometimes we were kept in the fields until eight in the evening.

There were now sixteen of us. The Khmer Rouge were killing the heads of families. Malnutrition was destroying the youngest. Phan buried a second child. My cousins lost their only daughter. I was worried at the way my two youngest brothers grew thin. But most of all I was concerned to cover up our background. For, since my father's death, I was the head of the family.

Towards the end of November 1975, at the time when we would normally have been celebrating the festival of the spirits, we were told at a meeting that all the new residents would be moved to Battambang, at the other end of the country. There, said the village leader, we would have more food and less work. We were told to pack everything up and leave the next day. We returned the 'weapons of the revolution' – our spades, mattocks, rakes, et cetera – and gathered our belongings.

That night something strange happened. The Khmer Rouge families paid us a visit, asking us if we wanted to exchange anything for rice, salt or palm sugar. We had nothing left to exchange. Everything had gone on food and medicines. The Khmer Rouge began chatting. They told us how upset they would be to see us go. They said how boring it was working in the paddyfields, and how difficult things would be when we had left. I realized that they must have known beforehand that we were not going to stay here very long. They had used us for all we were worth, sapping our strength and getting their hands on all our belongings. Now they were feeling sorry for themselves.

I didn't sleep. I couldn't help wondering whether we were really going to Battambang or not. Maybe we were going to our deaths like the heads of family. The other adults in the camp were busy preparing the food they had exchanged. At dawn, people pulled down their huts and burnt them in disgust. The Khmer Rouge were angry at this but it was too late to stop it.

People paid a last tearful visit to the graves of their relatives. Among the crowd assembled for departure, some people felt relieved to be off. They felt that if they stayed here any longer it would be their turn next. But others who had relatives in the mysterious infirmary were distressed at the prospect of separation. We sat in the open field, waiting quietly.

A dozen trucks arrived, including one full of soldiers – new faces. They were smartly turned out, and the village and regional leaders treated them with respect. They took off their caps and bowed to them. The village leader made a speech praising our hard work and our devotion to the community. He said they would be sad to lose us. We had never given any cause for complaint. We were exemplary workers, just what society needed. The new faces looked searchingly at us. For exemplary workers we were a sorry sight.

No family was allowed more than four pieces of luggage. The space in the trucks, they said, was for people not possessions. So, as we climbed into the trucks a great pile of bundles was left behind. We were packed tightly – I couldn't turn at all or make my way to the corner where my little brothers had been squeezed in beside my sisters. As we approached the road, revolutionary songs played over the radio. A wave of anger hit me.

Their songs told how the party had delivered the country from slavery, and how happy everybody was. I thought of the village leader's speech and my blood boiled. He had come across like a benevolent father to us all when in fact he was really a killer. If I tried to resist, I knew that I would put my family in danger, as my father had said. All I could do was feign ignorance. This was easy enough, but it was hard to live under the rule of ignorant people. I thought that if I died I might find some peace, but I had to stay alive. I had my responsibilities. And besides, I wanted to see what would happen under the new regime. I wanted to tell our story to my children, and to my grandchildren, like the stories I had learnt as a child.

We passed the Temple of the Black Lady. It was being knocked down and the stones were being piled up in the courtyard. As I watched the soldiers at work, I saw once again the image of my father sitting with his *kramar* in hand, fanning the mosquitoes away from my little brothers, and I began weeping.

And now I saw our journey out in reverse, every place where we had stayed the night. The trenches had been filled in and the bridges patched up with wood. The soldiers along the road looked at us in surprise as we passed. They did not seem to know what was going on. When we passed the place where the doctor had been executed I found myself weeping again. At noon the Khmer Rouge took out their packed lunches, which they consumed with relish to music from the radio. We couldn't get at our food, so we went hungry.

But at the outskirts of Phnom Penh there was excitement among the evacuees. We were longing to see the city again. By Pochentong airport there were piles and piles of cars. All their tyres had been removed to make sandals. On the runway there were damaged planes and the airport buildings were locked up. A red flag flew from the control tower. Then came the textile factory, which was shut down, and the monks' hospital, which was empty. There were soldiers working in the fields, but all the houses were deserted. The Clear Water Pagoda was some kind of military headquarters.

As we came to the university everybody began chattering, straining to get a look at the places where they had lived. I was excited too. We passed the science faculty and the technology institute and the places where I had done my chemistry and biology practicals. And there was the park where I used to walk with my first girlfriend, the lily-pond and the crocodile fountain where we used to sit, talking about what we would do when we had finished our studies. And this was the place where she told me that her mother was forcing her to marry an air force captain. As she told me this, she had been sketching my portrait (she was an art student). Then she gave me the sketch and we agreed not to meet again.

And there was Mao Tse-Tung Avenue, along which I used to

cycle to school. It used to be so full of traffic at this time of day when all the students were going home for lunch. And there was the place where an army convoy knocked into a group of students and killed them. Now the street was empty and littered with torn books. Just for a moment I could see down the length of it with paper blowing everywhere. I wanted to jump off and run home and see what had happened to my house but the lorry turned left down a new track, so we never got back to the city centre.

Very slowly we skirted the edge of the city. The sky turned grey. It was going to rain very soon. We passed Boeung Kak, where there had previously been an area of stilted houses accessible only by boat. This was where we used to come to the lotus farm, to buy the young fruit for eating or the flowers to take to the pagoda. Now there were no houses left and only a few patches of lotus in bloom. Everything had been dismantled. The only inhabited places were the high school and the stadium, which had been turned over to the military.

The Monivong Bridge was still broken. We turned on to Route Five, past the old Cham settlement and the mosque. There were piles of timber where the houses had been, and carts were taking all the villagers away. With all the bumping in the truck I felt nauseous. I made my way with great difficulty to the end, and there I saw that my little brothers looked green. Sambath told me he couldn't breathe. I held him on my shoulder to get some air.

A man shouted out that his mother was suffocating. The soldiers paid no attention. They were listening to the music and chewing sugarcane. As the rain fell we tried to collect it in plastic sheets. The rain fell harder. The man cried out that his mother had died. Nobody could do anything. At dusk the truck stopped and the soldiers took down the dead body and dumped it in a ditch. The man pleaded to be allowed to stay, but the soldiers said he couldn't. There was nobody round here at all. We drove on through the dark. A stench of sweat arose from our drenched clothes.

Just before dawn, I crawled off the truck, stiff in every joint and miserably hungry. We were at a small railway station, where we were told to wait for the train. When we unwrapped our food, prepared so long ago, it had gone bad. The train didn't come, and we spent the next day in a field, wrapped in our tarpaulins against the continual rain, shivering and trying to get some sleep.

I remember collecting water from a ditch full of huge leeches, and how Phan and San and I had to hold the tarpaulin over the camp fire when we cooked our rations. People were so tired they had lost any sense of shame. They were shitting in the next field, perched on the paddy-dike like egrets fishing. They wouldn't go into the water for fear of the leeches.

I woke that night to an extraordinary noise. People were scrambling to pack their belongings and there was chaos in the field. Phan and Somaly had gone, and my cousins were nowhere to be seen. I asked Sisopha what was happening. She didn't know. We shook the water off the tarpaulin and stuffed it into the bag. Now I could see the train had arrived and it was already covered with people. It was a steam train, with a wagon of logs in front. Everyone seemed to think they were going to miss it. They were climbing all over it.

I stood still for a moment. I was half asleep and completely confused. I told my brothers and sisters not to move. People were being knocked down in the muddy field. We were being jostled all the time. You could see children being lifted into the goods wagons, screaming. The people on board were shouting 'Why don't you. take the next train?' But they were ignored.

The Khmer Rouge seemed to have lost control of the crowd. So many people were scrambling on to the train it looked like a scorpion with its babies hanging on to it. Then three shots rang out. I turned and saw the body of a young man lying face down in the mud. People edged away from him. Nobody knew why he had been shot. The crowd parted to let the soldiers through. 'What the hell is going on?' asked the soldier with the AK–47. 'Who told you to get on?' And he pointed to the people on the roof. 'Get off there.' They slid very quickly off the top of the train. The soldiers pointed to a second train and told us to get on to that. The first train moved slowly off.

Phan, Somaly and my cousins must have been on it, for I never saw them again. I found out that the first train had gone to region two, and many months later I learnt that this was the worst of the regions in Battambang. It was here that many of the former soldiers' families were sent. They were working on high ground, under the most terrible conditions. A man who escaped from there told me that he had known Phan and my cousins very well. They had been ill for a long time. Then the soldiers took them off to the infirmary. The infirmary, in fact, was a field about a kilometre from the village. There they were all mortared to death.

SIXTEEN
I thank the revolution

The nine of us who took the second train found ourselves chosen for work in the flooded region on the edge of the Tonle Sap, the Great Lake. First we had a couple of weeks' rest, which would have been welcome if we hadn't been crammed into a small hut built over the water, so that the floods rose through the floor. There was no kind of latrine, which meant that we had to relieve ourselves among the catfish. There were mosquitoes everywhere, and I soon contracted malaria. Surprisingly enough they had quinine, which they administered with a carefully hoarded disposable syringe. I looked at the ancient rusty needle in my arm, and somehow gained strength to recover from the fever. When the Khmer Rouge finally came and told us the rest period was over and alternative accommodation had been found, we applauded so enthusiastically that the bamboo floor collapsed and we all fell into the water.

At Ream Kun village, the organization of the co-operative meant that the family was split up. San and Sisopha went to the married unit, which was in the centre of the village where they were able to look after my three brothers. Bopha, Mealea and Orphea were in the single female unit on the edge of the settlement, and I was in the single male unit at the other end. There were also male and female 'mobile units', which were composed either of widows and widowers or of married people who had been separated from their spouses. The word 'widower' in Cambodian covers someone who has either lost or been separated from his wife.

It was the harvest season and cutting rice was considered the easiest job in the peasant's calendar, but it was not so easy for those of us who were pretending to be peasants. In due course I picked up the skill of using a sickle, but not before I'd given my left hand a nasty gash. At the end of the day, I would walk home alongside the leader of our unit. Not being a soldier, he was friendlier than the average Khmer Rouge, and when I peppered my conversation with fascinating facts about agriculture that I had picked up from books, he was really impressed. He seemed to believe everything he was told.

He was a fat boy, Comrade Mok, seventeen years of age, and given to boasting. Gambling had been his passion before the revolution, and he told us how good he was at memorizing a deck of cards. He had an expert feel for loaded dice, and he reckoned he could tell from the sound of a throw what number was going to come up. He had a large burn scar on his left shoulder-blade that he often showed us, telling how he had survived a B–52 raid.

He had his own portable tape-recorder and a car battery, which he said had been given him when he was in a Khmer Rouge fighting unit. 'So you were a soldier, Comrade Mok?' we would ask, trying to sound impressed. And he would skip with pleasure, laughing and showing his gold-capped teeth. Then he would take the corner of his *kramar* and polish the face of his handsome black Citizen watch. He would look at the sun and say, 'Hmm. Ten o'clock.' I was never quite sure whether he could have told the time without the help of the sun.

He carried the tape-recorder to the fields in a special blue shoulder bag, embroidered in red, and he would play revolutionary songs while watching us work. But he had also acquired some Cambodian pop songs. During the lunch break he and his colleagues sat in a circle facing outwards and turned the volume right down. If they saw anyone coming they would quickly turn round, switch the machine off, and talk about the day's work. When the battery ran down, Mok would send one of his favourites to recharge it by pedal dynamo. This was a good day's work.

Every evening we had to listen to Comrade Mok's speech, which he appeared to have learnt from the co-operative leader, exhorting us to work harder. He himself hardly did a hand's turn in the fields, except when he saw one of his superiors in the distance. The rest of the time he fooled around. His favourite joke was to take and stick and walk like an old man. It was a mistake to laugh at this. Mok would say, 'You just get on with your work. It's not funny to laugh at an old man.' Then he would cane us, hard. That was the point of the joke.

At first, rations in the single male unit were better than before: we had rice and salt, pumpkin and water spinach sometimes, and the occasional issue of fresh fish. But then came the announcement that the cooking arrangements were to be communalized. The cooking team was chosen from Comrade Mok's friends, and we all had to hand over our utensils retaining only our spoons. Lunch was brought out to us in the fields, and in the evening when we returned we found large tin bowls of unpleasant-looking soup waiting for us. Often several flies were already bathing there. We were supposed to eat in groups of ten, squatting on the ground. If we were one person short, the equivalent amount of soup would be taken from the bowl and added to Comrade Mok's rations. Sometimes it was merely tipped on to the ground.

For weeks I had not seen Sisopha or my brothers. When I asked permission from Mok he always refused. However, I often passed Bopha, Mealea and Orphea during work, and one day Mealea managed to tell me that Sisopha was seriously ill. She had been fainting several times during the day, and every time she regained consciousness she called out for our father. I was worried and asked Mok if I could visit her. 'No,' he said, 'you're not a doctor.' I restrained myself from pointing out to Mok that if I had been a doctor he'd have killed me.

As we walked along the paddy-dike a few days later, Bopha told me that Sisopha had recovered. A friend of hers called Comrade Ran, who had a brother working in the infirmary, had given her some good Western medicine. Comrade Ran was the only daughter of a senior Khmer Rouge. Her behaviour was most unusual, and she was to become an important figure in our lives.

'Comrade Ran told me,' said Mealea, as we were cutting paddy together a week later, 'a lot of people are coming to the co-operative tomorrow. Every unit is to be reorganized. She said the work in the widowers' unit is not as hard as ours. The rations aren't that bad either. We think you should join it. All you have to say is you're a widower.'

I had my usual chat with Comrade Mok. Towards the end I began to refer to my wife and to say how much I missed her. He was surprised, and asked me when I had got married. 'About two years ago,' I said, 'when I was sixteen' – managing to lie both about my age and my marital status.

He put a hand on my shoulder. 'Where is she now? What happened to her?' The sickle in his hand was grazing against my cheek like a razor.

I sighed, movingly. 'I don't know. That's just it. We were separated when we were evacuated from our farm.' Mok had his romantic side, and this confession made him sad. One day, he told me, we would all be allowed to go wherever we wanted. And then I would meet her again.

I sighed again and said, 'I'm not even sure she'd recognize me.' And I took a swing with my sickle and sent some seed pods flying.

Now it was Mok's turn to sigh. He shifted the tape-recorder from one shoulder to the other. Then he had a thought, 'Hey, there are a whole new bunch of people arriving tomorrow. Maybe she'll be among them.'

'You think so? 'That's great!' I said, enthused by his idea. 'If only we could get together again!' And we walked on in silence, savouring the possibility.

That evening Mok made his usual speech, at great length. Then he pointed at me and said: 'Comrade Meth, I want to hear your ideas about the Angkar.'

This put me in a difficult position. We had heard a lot of references to the Angkar since we had come to this part of the country, but nobody had told us what it was. In normal language the word meant nothing more than organization or committee. Here it seemed to mean something more. I was nervous – not of talking in front of a crowd, but simply because I couldn't think what I was going to say about the Angkar. I stood up and walked to the front of the meeting. I knew that whatever I said it had to sound stupid.

The crowd applauded me with their usual lack of enthusiasm.

'Friends and comrades,' I began. Then I stopped. My voice was out of control with fear. 'This is a great opportunity for me to express my thoughts about the revolution.' Then my mind went blank. I readjusted my *kramar*. My workmates in the crowd desperately stifled their yawns and tried not to keel over with boredom and exhaustion. 'I would like to offer many thanks,' said my voice, which was so high as to be almost unrecognizable, 'to the forces that liberated us from the old regime. Thanks again,' I said, as it suddenly dawned on me that I was not supposed to use the word thanks. 'This is all I want to say.'

Mok was wildly enthusiastic, and took the trouble to come and congratulate me as I was preparing to retire under my stinking mosquito net. 'That was great, Comrade Meth,' he said, 'great. I'm very proud of you. But I have to say you used the wrong word for revolution. Also, remember that the words "thanks" and "sorry" have been banned, along with other words that show the class distinctions of the old regime.'

'I'll remember, comrade. Good night.'

The next morning I secured Mok's permission to go and look for my wife among the new arrivals. He even offered me some rations to take with me. 'Do you have anything to wrap them in?' he asked. I gave him my *kramar*, which he filled with about a kilo of rice. 'Don't tell anyone where you got it from.'

'I won't,' I said, 'but there's another thing I wanted to ask you about.'

'What's that?'

'It's about being married.'

'What about it? Are you missing all those exciting times?' he said. It was most unusual for a Khmer Rouge to make jokes about sex.

'No, it's not that. It's just – supposing my wife doesn't arrive, do I have any chance of staying in the single male unit?'

'What a stupid question. If you want to stay there's no problem. I'll fix it.'

'I don't mind at all which unit I'm in. What worries me is – I don't want to tell lies to the Angkar.'

'Well, you're right. The Angkar doesn't want liars. I don't want to lose you because you're a good worker but . . . OK, I'll send you to the widowers if she doesn't come.'

I gave him a soulful look and hurried off to the centre of the village. The point was that this gave me the opportunity to visit my brothers. I hadn't seen them since we had been split up. I passed the communal barn where the new arrivals were being registered. There was no one I knew, and I thought it better not to hang around.

It was mid-morning. From the distance I could see the three boys, each with a branch in his hands. They were prodding a small bush. When they saw me, they threw down their sticks and ran towards me.

'What were you looking for in that bush?' I asked them.

'We saw a lizard,' said Orpheau, 'and we wanted to get it.'

'What for?'

'Don't you know?' said Sambath. 'Lots of people round here cook them.'

This was the first I had heard of it. 'Forget about the lizard,' I said. 'Let's go inside. I've got some rice for you.' I picked Sambath up and went indoors. There was nothing in the hut except for a few ragged clothes hanging on the wall, a couple of torn mats on the bed. In the end I found a pot hidden under a rag. I made a fire and started cooking.

The boys bolted their food. They looked skinny. I wondered what would happen to them, and I wondered what I would tell them if they asked where their parents were. My eyes filled with tears.

Sisopha and San came back from work, exhausted. I asked them about rations and work. Sisopha wept, and I knew why. She was reminded of my father, to whom I bear a strong resemblance. I played with Soveth, Orpheau and Sambath until one o'clock, when I had to return to my unit. As I got up to go, Sambath said, 'Someth, will you come and play with us again. I miss you very much. Why are you crying?'

'It's nothing,' I said, 'I've got something in my eye.'

'Let me see.'

'No, I'm all right. I'll see you very soon.'

Then I jumped down the steps and ran back to the unit. Comrade Mok was just about to start the meeting. 'My wife didn't turn up,' I said. He seemed genuinely sad.

SEVENTEEN
Catching fish and monkeys

Comrade Run, my new leader, showed me where I was to stay in the widowers' unit. He was a short, powerful man with a criminal face – bloodshot eyes, thick eyebrows and a ferocious expression. He pointed to some planks of wood leaning against a wall and told me I was to stay the night there. The next day I would be going to the fishing commune at Veal Treng Thnuong. I was not to wander away, as I might be needed at any moment.

I sat on the ground. There were several men lying in a row under dirty blankets, supposedly too sick to work. Some of them indeed looked ill, others not. As soon as Comrade Run had gone, one of them scampered towards me. 'You're lucky to be going to the fishing commune,' he confided. 'How old are you?' I told him.

'Eighteen!' he said. 'That's too young for a widower.'

'It's not that young,' I said. 'Why do you say I'm lucky?'

'You work on fish, you eat fish,' he replied. Then he scampered back to his blanket. Comrade Run was returning. He called me out to see the co-operative leader.

Comrade Huon (the leader) had the register in front of him. He told me to cross out where I had described myself as single and write married instead. When I had done so he closed the book.

'Now,' he said coolly, 'why did you change your mind like that?'

'Well, comrade,' I replied, 'I felt I shouldn't tell lies to the Angkar.'

'It's a reasonable answer,' said Comrade Huon. I breathed again.

We were to take the commune's rations with us. A bullock cart was provided to carry the sacks of rice and salt. There were five able-bodied men and a guide, a Khmer Rouge from the reconnaissance team. The fishing commune was in a remote place: there was no track to it, and we had to clear the undergrowth as we went. During the rainy season, the woods in this area were flooded and became a safe place for the fish to breed. When the waters went down, the pools were full of catfish, carp, snakeheads and walking-fish or climbing perch. This last species used to get excited when it rained, wriggle out of the pond and wander so far from the water that they were in danger of being eaten by egrets. The snakeheads buried themselves in the mud and you could dig for them. One variety of snakehead was known for its habit, when attacked, of eating its young. If they were cornered, they would defend themselves viciously, and because they could reach about twenty kilos or so they were quite dangerous. My mother had never liked buying them whole – she said it would be like cutting a baby, they were so huge. The catfish also would come out of the water, and you could find them flapping across wet grass.

We made our way through the woods. Above our heads we could see the high-water mark, and the fish nests of the past seasons. As we approached the commune, we could smell it half a mile away, and then we heard the buzzing of the flies over the refuse heaps. These were infested with maggots. The commune had run out of salt and been forced to throw away whole catches. Beyond the refuse heaps lay the camp itself, a scattering of tents pitched under the trees. Most of the bivouacs were appalling, miserable constructions of leaves and torn tarpaulins. The commune leader's tent was the exception. Around it stood three large smoking platforms, piled with fish. The fires were smouldering gently, and there were honeycombs hung nearby. In the ashes were the remains of the commune leader's meal.

We stopped by the big tent. A man in his forties, in uniform and with a pronounced limp, got up from his hammock and introduced himself as Comrade Tek. He was pleased to see the rations and the extra able-bodied men he had requested, and while he unyoked the bullocks from the cart he told us to make our bivouacs. Now the commune members struggled exhaustedly back, and piled their buckets of fish and their nets in front of the tent. They made as if to retire for the night, but Tek told them the salt had arrived and they were to gut the catch before nightfall. Finally, when this was done, rations were issued.

They were not bad – rice and the freshest fish I had had in fifteen months. There was no cooking team. People prepared their food on their own or in small groups if they had no utensils. I'd been given a catfish, more than half a kilo in weight. I didn't yet know how to hold it without getting hurt by the spines. So I killed it with a stick, borrowed a *parang* and gutted it, and stuck it over the fire between a split branch. As the skin crackled and the juices sizzled over the flames, the smell drove me crazy. We five new arrivals looked at the different fish we were preparing and wondered which of us had got the best deal. Those who had walking-fish had been given two each. The older residents had obviously had enough of barbecued fish – they were preparing fish soup with lotus roots and water spinach and bitter herbs.

But Comrade Tek was something of a gourmet. His trusted colleagues were preparing for him a kind of fish stew we used to have in the evenings at home. Normally the sauce is made from caramelized palm sugar, soy sauce, garlic and pepper. They had substituted wild honey for the sugar, and the smell of it reached us by our fires. I determined that I would do this myself if ever I found some honey. Comrade Tek directed the preparations from his hammock. He liked eating and he liked smoking. The cigarettes he made were rolled from the pages of old textbooks.

After the meal the widowers all rushed to their mosquito nets. They knew that there would be millions of insects after dark, so everyone made sure they had mended any holes with lengths of creeper. Those who, like myself, didn't have mats to tuck the net under, weighted it down with logs. Even then in the morning I would find mosquitoes so full they couldn't fly. Sometimes I would roll over on to a mosquito in the night, and in the morning find bloodstains on my body.

The social life of the widowers was conducted entirely from within the net, like the bedtime conversations I used to have with my brother. From tent to tent the cigarette ends flared and died like jungle beetles. Then a hand appeared cautiously from under the net and flicked a butt into the dark. And the butts flew like tracer bullets. Then you'd hear an oath as someone had contrived to flick the butt on to his neighbour's net, and a great tussle would ensue. Above the noise of the wind, the insects, the frogs and the feeding fish, the widowers had to shout to make themselves heard. Out of fifty people only three or four had lighters, although everybody smoked, so it was incredibly difficult, without getting out of your tent, to locate a lighter and get it passed in your direction. You threw it from net to net, and you used your own cigarette to signal where your hand was. But the real nicotine addicts, when they ran out of tobacco, had to face the insects.

The widowers were mostly old residents of the area, who trusted each other and spoke with relative freedom. But these shouted conversations had a strange quality, since you could never stop the subject from jumping to and fro around the camp. People wanted to talk about their wives and how they had lost them. But this line of discussion got mixed up with an account of the day's fishing, or a plea not to shit too near the camp. It was odd to hear a man describing how he had lost his family in an American bombing raid, but doing so at the top of his voice, like a street vendor, and the news being greeted with guffaws as another topic crossed with it. People conducted two or three conversations at once, and as these died down and were replaced with snores, the wild dogs began to howl. They had smelt the dead fish. Sometimes they even came to the smoking platforms and pulled the fish away. We were too tired to stop them. And anyway there was enough fish for the dogs.

We rose at six, cooked lunch to take with us and set off for the Tonle Sap. There we worked with throwing-nets, which are quite heavy and require skill. The first time I did it, I managed to send the net backwards and myself into the water. The throwing-nets were for snakeheads, and those we set in long lines were for catfish and walking-fish. It took us three hours to get to the fishing grounds; then we worked for four hours and set off home in time to beat the mosquitoes. I became known as the Young Widower, since I was the youngest in the group.

One day Comrade Tek told us he had invented a new method of getting more fish with less effort. We were to bale a pond. There was a reason for this, but at the time we were outraged. 'Bale a pond!' muttered the widowers to each other. We were given buckets and spades. There weren't enough tools to go round, and when we reached the pond in question, we were astonished by the size of it. In Cambodia it is not unknown for people to bale a pond to get the fish, but the ponds in question are about two metres square, dug at the edge of a field. The fish get stranded there when the flood waters subside and it takes about half an hour to empty them. It's a job for a lunch break.

This pond was about fifty metres square and a metre deep. I

couldn't believe we would be able to empty it in a day. Comrade Tek told us to build a dike around the edge of it. Then we set to work baling it out. At the end of the day it was down by a third, and the next day by another third. But on the next day the clouds looked threatening, and we were told to work through the night, to catch the fish before the rains came.

'We're not going back until we've got all the fish,' said Comrade Tek, who had been sitting watching us all day. 'Dinner will be brought to you.' And so it was. We worked as fast as we could, knowing the mosquitoes were on their way. As darkness fell we had to feel in the mud, and you could hear people shouting when they were stung by a catfish. The angrier they got, the more often they broke the necks of the fish when they caught them. People were working sitting in the mud, and to prevent the small fish running up their trouser legs they tied creepers round their ankles.

At three in the morning the pond was half cleared. Tek relented and we were allowed home. As I reached my tent the rains began and continued throughout the night. There was much absenteeism the next day. The pond was full again and the dikes had broken. We tried to mend them but the land was waterlogged. The team leader gave up, and took us back to camp, where Comrade Tek had spent the day.

We were all in trouble – those who had stayed behind and those who had failed with Tek's new method. He called a meeting, the first we'd had since I'd been there, and lectured us on our laziness. With people like us, the Khmer Rouge would never have defeated the American imperialists. He, Tek, had spent most of his life in the forest, fighting for freedom. He'd never complained. Not a word. He'd even slept in a thunderstorm. And so on.

The story in the camp was that Tek, lame from birth, had been thrown out of his home by his parents, because of his compulsive gambling and drinking. He had organized a gang. The village council had been after him so he fled to the Khmer Rouge. The problem he now faced was that for some reason all our nets had been commandeered by the army. We never saw them again. The baling method was abandoned for a while and we made traps instead. The production of fish dropped rapidly, and so did our rations. We lived on a pulp of rice and lotus root. Comrade Tek had an old perfume bottle full of snake fat. With this he would fry up some swamp eels, which he liked with lemon-grass, galingale (a kind of ginger), turmeric, a pinch of monosodium glutamate, a little honey, tamarind sauce and a garnish of wild herbs.

He ate like a nobleman, fastidiously trying a little bit here, a little bit there, and making every meal into an occasion. His two companions had to match their pace to his – you could tell that they would have preferred simply to guzzle. The camp was a sordid place – it took you several days to get used to the smell of the decaying fish. But Comrade Tek's imagination turned his tent into a luxury hotel. The luxuries were very few. For instance, he had a US army-issue water-bottle, from which he drank the same muddy water as us. The difference was that we took our rusty enamel plates to the pond, and drank from them after washing up. He had a bucket of water in his tent from which he filled his bottle, which he placed at his side as if it were brandy, taking little nips from the cap. But we all sat on the bare earth, and none of us had seen a bar of soap for months. We cleaned our teeth by slooshing water with our cheeks. Tek had a toothbrush hanging from a blue and yellow ribbon. Every morning he wetted it from the flask and dipped it in the ash of the camp fire for toothpowder. We went barefoot. He had Ho Chi Minh sandals. Every night he washed them and propped them up to dry.

The cooking ingredients which we envied so much were provided by his wife back in the village. She ran the catering for the married group, and she had a vegetable patch behind her well-made hut. Theoretically, this was for communal use, but in fact it was a perk. Whenever we were detailed to take the fish catch back to the village, Comrade Tek would tell us to drop in on his wife. She would provide a cotton bag full of useful items. We never tried to filch any of these goodies, because if we had used them it would have been absolutely obvious where we had got them from. The smell from our cooking pots would have given us away.

One day I had delivered the fish, and took the opportunity to visit my family. By chance they were all together. Everyone thought I had put on a bit of weight. I was going to ask what life was like in the village when I noticed a young woman in her early twenties sitting in the corner of the hut, wearing a neat uniform. My sisters, seeing my confusion, told me this was Comrade Ran, their friend. I was annoyed to see her there. Nevertheless, I took out the fish I had concealed in my *kramar* and gave them to my sisters to prepare.

'Comrade Meth,' said the girl, 'where are you working now?' I was surprised she knew my name.

'In the widowers' unit,' I replied shortly. I was watching my brothers eat and I was more worried about them than about her.

'So you're a widower?'

I hardly bothered to reply. She asked what the unit was doing and where it was working. I wished she wouldn't ask so many questions.

'Ah,' she exclaimed, 'you must be working with my father. His name is Tek. He's the leader of the fishing commune.'

'Yes,' I said, 'I know him. He's a nice man.'

'When are you going back? I want you to take this letter to my father.' And she handed me a piece of paper.

I was still looking at my brothers and wondering what on earth was going to become of them. 'Will I be doing anything against the rules of the Angkar if I take this?' I asked.

'No, not at all,' she said. 'We are Old People. I'm afraid New People aren't allowed to write letters.'

Something in her voice made me turn to her. I saw she was embarrassed. 'Who are these Old People and New People?' I asked her, stifling a yawn.

'The Old People are the ones who joined the revolution before 1975, like my family. The New People are the ones who were evacuated from Phnom Penh and the other cities at the end of the war. Didn't you know that?'

'No. What will happen to me, if I'm New People, taking a letter to your father, if he's Old People?'

'Oh, nothing will happen. Believe me,' she said, with a half-smile that revealed one gold tooth. I agreed to take the letter.

That night I was allowed for some reason to stay with my family, and in the evening Comrade Ran came round with coconuts, sticky rice and palm sugar. She and my sisters were making a kind of porridge. We'd already had our meal. This was a sort of midnight feast. Very unusual for those days. One of the boys from the reconnaissance team came up to the hut and asked what the hell we were doing and where we'd got this stuff from. He hadn't seen Comrade Ran, who came out of the shadows and gave him an earful. She'd given us the food because our little brothers had been very ill. And now she told the boy to clear off and not come back.

He apologized – he actually said the word sorry – and backed out very fast.

'Who *is* she?' I asked Sisopha when Comrade Ran had gone. Sisopha smiled for the first time that evening. She was just a friend of theirs, she said. I didn't believe it. I thought we were being investigated. And I didn't understand why I was being entrusted with a letter.

On the way back I read it furtively. It was quite banal and contained no information of any interest, but it was hopelessly misspelt. Comrade Tek received it with surprise and suspicion.

I couldn't understand what was happening to the rice. The communal barn in the village was full but our rations were further reduced. Then the barn was suddenly empty. Communal feeding was introduced among the widowers, which meant that we lost our remaining advantages. At night, the noisy conversations between the tents became a thing of the past. The Old People among the widowers were as angry as the rest of us. We had hardly enough strength for work, and people wandered round the fields looking for anything to eat.

At night Comrade Tek's eating companions made a torch from a strip of car tyre and went off to the pond in search of frogs. At this time of the year the frogs were very fat. We heard the men digging in the mud, and congratulating themselves on their luck at finding a new specimen. Then the chopping began, and in a few minutes you could smell lemon-grass, turmeric and galingale. They were preparing the marinade. And then the whispers began among the mosquito nets. 'He'll be having fucking satay fucking frog for his fucking lunch.' In those days the widowers smoked more than ever. They stopped talking about the wives they had lost, and started discussing food in loud whispers.

In the submerged forest not far away lived several troops of monkeys. They used to raid the fields for wild paddy. One day we were stuck for work (there were no pools left) and were given a day off. We'd all been thinking about smoking these monkeys, and we rushed off to the wood to make traps. I had a friend whose bivouac was near mine. He knew how to make a cage out of saplings and creepers, with an entrance that worked on the same principle as a fish trap. We baited it with wild paddy and went off into the bushes to hide.

Within about half an hour there were ten monkeys in the trap, but the trouble was that every time we tried to take them out they started to bite. We needed someone who knew how to handle them. I ran back to the camp and on my way met Comrade Tek who was going round the fields trying to find a pond for us to bale. When I told him of our problem he offered to come along. He made a small hole in the cage and very confidently grabbed them by the back of the neck, one by one. He held them to the ground and tied their elbows together behind their backs. As the joints were dislocated there came a loud crack. Comrade Tek was enjoying himself. Before he tied their feet he allowed them to hop around a bit. Then he said, 'This is what I used to do with the parasites of the Angkar.'

My friend gave him a look of disgust. For my part I was suddenly terrified, and when Comrade Tek announced that the monkeys would be given to the cooks to feed the whole commune, I was relieved because I knew I couldn't have killed them after all. But my friend was furious. We'd been cheated of our day's catch.

Back at the camp, some other people had had luck, but we were all obliged to hand our monkeys over. A large bonfire was built and the day's squirming catch was piled up beside it. Comrade Tek made a speech. He reminded us that the camp would not have been so deserted if we had had work to do that morning. Mysteriously, on the one day when we had had no work there had been no sick people. So what was this disease we were suffering from? It was nothing more than the disease of laziness, the disease he and his comrades had been fighting for the last century. He warned us to throw off this disease before it was too late.

Now we could see that he had worked himself up into a rage. He approached the pile of struggling monkeys, and killed them one by one without a word. The meeting froze. Comrade Tek was a new man. He despatched each monkey with a blow to the back of the skull. As he did so, people straightened their backs.

'And now,' he said, 'I'll show you the way I used to kill the Lon Nol soldiers when we caught them, and the way to get the liver out.' He laid the last monkey flat on the ground. In the light of the bonfire I could see its watery eyes. 'If you don't know the right place to cut,' he continued, with emphasis, 'you won't get the whole thing out in·one.'

He made a cut to the stomach. Then he pressed hard on the incision with both hands. The monkey screeched. The liver came out whole. Comrade Tek then slit the animal's throat. He said, 'If it had been a man, I would have put my foot in the cut to get the right pressure – otherwise the liver never comes out properly.' He held the liver in his hand, and for a brief moment we could smell it. What he was saying sounded like no more than an anecdote to him. Every time I think of it, I imagine my father was killed in the same way.

EIGHTEEN
All my brothers

No one dared stay in the camp. The fate of the monkeys stayed with us, and however ill we were we worked hard. Once Comrade Tek's eating companions knew that we were scared, they pursued their advantage. As we worked away baling out a new pond, they stood within earshot saying, 'One day Comrade Tek will show them how he does it with human beings.' The widowers no longer trusted each other. We were all afraid of becoming our leader's next victim.

But then the fishing commune was disbanded and we returned to the village for the rice season. I was allowed two hours with my family, and set off to find them. Many of the huts in the area were empty. Whole families had died since the malnutrition began. Other buildings had been cleared to make way for new vegetable fields, dikes and canals. The village was very quiet. There were no animals and few people to be seen. The catering teams were husking rice for the evening rations.

At first I wondered whether I was at the right hut. My brothers were lying on a filthy mat with hundreds of flies hovering over them. They were skin and bones. Their heads and knees were swollen. Their stomachs were distended. I'd never actually seen such a thing with my own eyes, only in photographs of Biafra. They were too weak to get up but they recognized me, and Sambath asked in a weak voice whether I had any food. I had nothing. I turned away in tears.

A couple in ragged clothes were struggling towards the hut. The woman was bending forward as if about to fall. The man supported her. He had a small container in his hand, like a paint tin. Only when they reached the hut did I recognize them as Sisopha and San. With great difficulty they climbed the short ladder and came in. Sisopha lay on the floor and San sat down beside her. My brothers struggled to open their eyes and look at them. They stared at the container.

I felt very angry. I asked Sisopha why she had not stayed behind to look after our brothers. She burst into tears and said that she had several times tried to ask permission to stay at home, but had been told her rations would be cut off.

Then she wiped her eyes. 'Someth,' she said, 'I have some exciting news for you. Do you want to hear it?'

I exploded. 'What? Look at those three skeletons lying over there. Do you think that this is the time to start telling me exciting news? Stop behaving like a child.'

'Please, Someth, calm down,' she replied, crying again, 'and don't blame me. I have taken care of them as well as I can. You don't understand. None of us can do a thing about it. If I don't go to work they don't get any rations. None of us does. They would have gone already,' she said, 'if I had not been working. You must understand this.'

I looked at her, and then at my brothers, in silence. I was thinking how my niece had died, and how the arguments had been the same. Sisopha was right and I was wrong. I apologized and asked her to tell me the exciting news.

'Comrade Ran told me a few days ago that she wants to marry you. What do you think? Don't forget, her mother is head of the canteen in our unit.'

I couldn't believe my ears. Sisopha got up and crawled towards our little brothers, container in hand. Sambath couldn't sit up. She held him in her arms. Then she gave them her rations. San had closed his eyes. He was keeping out of this.

I wondered how Comrade Ran could think of love at a time like this. Nothing could have been further from my mind. All I could think of was survival. If I refused her, she might make trouble for all of us. If I accepted, there was no doubt that she had good access to food. But I had never heard of a marriage between Old and New People. Saying yes would possibly land me in just as much trouble as a refusal.

I had other immediate problems too. That night we were provided with a plough and a pair of cattle. I was going to have to demonstrate my skills the next day, and I'd never handled a plough. I thought of everything I had seen in films or read in books. I thought of Chan and Long all those years ago. I stayed awake thinking about ploughing.

The main problem turned out to be the tension on the reins. These passed through the noses of the bullocks and you had to co-ordinate it very carefully in order to plough a straight furrow. On the first day I was trying to avoid a tree stump when the team veered off and the plough grazed the hind leg of one of the bullocks. I was terrified that this accident would be noticed and I would be blamed. There was blood on the ground. However, on the return journey I turned over the stained clod. Mud soon covered the hind leg and the bleeding stopped. I began to be more practised.

As we prepared the ground for planting, more and more of the New People were dying off. I was growing weaker. I could feel my face changing. My clothes began to wear out. They were wet all day. At night I hung them up to dry and slept in my *kramar*, but they were still wet the next day.

It was a long time since the New People had experienced anything like sexual desire. Men became impotent – an erection would have been an immense surprise – and women stopped menstruating. But the Old People, who had good food and enough sleep, had some spare time for sex if it had been allowed. One night a meeting was called to announce that the leader of the ox cart team had been sleeping with his daughter, who had become pregnant. They were demoted and no longer to be considered Old People. For a few days they were forced to work extremely hard. Then they disappeared.

Now the fields were ploughed and needed weeding. All units worked together. Comrade Ran was with me in the field. As she pulled up the weeds I saw she was working towards me. Finally she was near enough to talk.

'Comrade Meth, did Sisopha tell you anything about me?' she asked, smiling.

'Well . . . yes.' I was too weak to be embarrassed, and too irritated to be polite.

'And what do you think?'

'Well . . .' I couldn't think what to say.

'I want your answer now,' she said, very much the Khmer Rouge.

'Stop pushing me, will you?' I replied. 'I need time to think about it.' I shook the mud off some weeds and threw them on to the pile behind me. We all had our own piles to show how hard we had been working.

'I think I have been waiting long enough now,' said Comrade Ran, throwing her weeds on to my pile. I was pleased to get a few weeds but I was still annoyed.

'Comrade Ran,' I said, angrily, 'listen to me.' I stood up at this point. 'Do you think it is right to talk like this when we are working?'

She wasn't the slightest bit unnerved. 'I don't think I've done anything wrong. Nothing scares me.'

'Well, I don't want to do anything against the Angkar. Leave me alone. We're working.'

'We haven't done anything wrong,' she said. 'Unit leaders are allowed to talk in the fields.' I had recently learnt that she was now leader of the widows.

'But not while I'm working.'

'Give me your answer now. Just say yes or no.'

I was thinking: do I yet have enough weeds to take to the main pile? I didn't think so. Fortunately at this moment I was called away. I told her to be patient and I'd let her know. She looked thoroughly frustrated.

Now I was back in the single male unit. They were short of men. I worked out that about a third of the teenagers had died of malnutrition. The rest looked indescribable – like my brothers or worse. When they reached a critical condition they were taken to the infirmary by their company leaders. This job should have taken a couple of hours at most, but the leaders made it last all day. It was a good excuse for time off.

As we planted the rice I could see my sisters in the distance. Comrade Ran always worked next to them. They talked all the time and frequently smiled at each other. Still, I thought I could tell that Mealea disliked having Ran around all the time. I wanted to talk to Mealea. I had heard that she was very depressed. But I never got an opportunity. Comrade Ran was always there.

The New People were dying fast. We were hungry, too tired to wash or clean our clothes, and we lost all sense of hygiene. We didn't care what we ate as long as we could put something in our stomachs. We didn't mind where we had a shit, or who saw us. Disease spread through the village – cholera, malaria, dysentery, diarrhoea and skin infections. There was something I had never seen before – a swelling disease in which the tissues of the body filled up with fluid, so that people reached two or three times their natural weight. They could no longer support themselves, they were too heavy. In a matter of a week, the swelling intensified and the skin began to burst. The patients began to have diarrhoea. After a day or a night of this they would die.

The Khmer Rouge began to invent their own medicines, made of crushed roots moulded into pills. We called these rabbit droppings. The Khmer Rouge called them multi-purpose pills. There was also a kind of serum and vitamin C liquid, used for injections and kept in Coke or Pepsi bottles sealed with polythene and a rubber band. The needles were dirty and rusty. If you had an injection you never escaped an abscess. Many people died from this new treatment.

Officially the Khmer Rouge were proud of the medical care they were giving us. They told us at the meetings, 'One day in the near future, our medicines will be used worldwide.' Behind the scenes, however, it was clear that they believed none of this. They thought the serum and the multi-purpose pill as dangerous as we did.

I saw this clearly when one of the Khmer Rouge soldiers fell seriously ill with malaria. A friend of his had some American medicine, but none of the Khmer Rouge could read the instructions. The friend went from hut to hut in the co-operative asking if anybody could translate it for him. No one dared. The consequences would be obvious. Then the friend went round the work-field with the same request. A man who was working near me said, 'Why don't you give him the medicine the Angkar has produced? I think it would be much more effective.'

'You're joking,' said the Khmer Rouge, and he insisted that the soldier was dying. Finally the man relented and read out the instructions. The soldier recovered soon after, but the man who read the label disappeared.

Casualties were high among the children. They died falling off the sugar palm trees, which they climbed in search of palm juice. They drowned while trying to steal fish at night from the traps which the Old People had set up for their private use. They began committing suicide. One day on the way to the work-field we smelt something rotten. Comrade Mok investigated and found a boy of ten hanging from a hut beam, decomposed. He held his nose. Then, 'Come on,' he said, 'there's nothing unusual about a dead body. Let's go.' And he spat several times on his way to the field.

The children of the New People, Soveth and Orpheau among them, were taken off to live together in the orphanage. The Old People's children were put in the co-operative school, where Bopha found a job as a teacher (through Comrade Ran's recommendation). She had to teach them their alphabet in the morning, then take them to weed the vegetables or gather manure from the cattle-pens. She was allowed to live with Sisopha and San. Sambath was also at home, being too weak to go to the orphanage, and Bopha was able to bring him some food. But he was already dying. The last time I saw him he lay gasping on the mat, his eyelids so swollen he couldn't see me. Sisopha had finally got permission to look after him, although on reduced rations. On this occasion it was Sisopha who got angry with me for not visiting him more often. Either way, whether it was me blaming her or her blaming me, we both knew there was nothing more we could have done. We just had to express our anger somehow.

Comrade Ran had found a job for Orphea in a village about twenty-five kilometres away, working with the nurses in the field. 'Nurse' is perhaps a misleading word. Basically, her job was to hand out 'rabbit droppings' whenever the workers requested them. There was also a traditional bruise therapy, where the nurse pinched your body in different patterns. (Comrade Mok loved having this done – he loved being touched by the nurses.) It was a while before I saw Orphea again.

Mealea was also offered a 'fat job', one of the easiest going. And she refused it. The job would have been in the performing group, who rehearsed revolutionary plays and songs to perform in front of the soldiers. The members of the group had to be well fed – they were entertaining the troops, after all. And they had to have good black uniforms. Even the Old People longed to be chosen for this kind of work. The members of the performing group caused a sensation among the women wherever they went. They were plump and attractive, and they kept out of the sun: they were the nearest thing we had to film stars. The fact that Mealea refused to join them was extraordinary, but anyway I was deeply suspicious about these promotions my sisters were getting.

Once again we were running short of teenagers in my unit, and I heard Comrade Mok saying that the next day the children were returning from the orphanage and there might be some possible recruits among them. The news excited me because I hadn't seen my brothers for several months; that night I carefully tore the left leg of my trousers along the outer seam, all the way from the heel to the hip, went to Comrade Mok and asked for permission to visit my sister so she could mend them. I would go during the lunch break.

When I arrived at the hut there was no one in. I wondered what had happened to Sambath – he at least should have been there. I took the needle from its place in the palm-leaf wall, and unravelled a thread from an old US rice bag. While I was sewing my trousers I could see Comrade Mok going round the other huts gathering up some teenagers from among the newly returned orphans. Half an hour passed, and still there was no sign of my brothers. I went back to the field.

It was Mealea who finally told me, as we met on the way to work. She hung back from the group, in tears. Sambath had died. Sisopha had fallen ill. San had got the swelling disease and died in the infirmary. Soveth and Orpheau had died of dysentery in the orphanage. They had been eating raw paddy-crabs. There were now only five of us left.

As Mealea told me these things I stopped walking. But she had to go on. There wasn't much room on the paddy-dike. Members of my group pushed past me. Comrade Mok slapped me hard on the shoulder. 'What's the matter with you?' he said, jovially. 'It's nothing,' I lied, 'I was just thinking about my wife.'

NINETEEN
Big Brother, Little Brother

All the unit leaders suddenly acquired little servants, chosen from among the orphans. Comrade Mok's servant was about eight years old. His name was Khoy. He had to guard Mok's possessions while we were in the work-field (someone had been stealing them). He also had to keep an eye on those who were off sick, and make reports on what they had been up to. He told the cook every day what his master would like for the next meal, and in the evening he used to prepare a special little late-night snack – a bowl of rice soup or sweet porridge. In those days the nurses at the co-operative infirmary had acquired a supply of monosodium glutamate, which was much prized by comrades like Mok and Tek. Whenever Mok wanted some, he would send Khoy to the nurses with a message that he had toothache, and they would give him a pinch or two wrapped in a twist of paper.

Comrade Khoy was rather like the Black Lady in the legend. His master listened unquestioningly to everything he said. People who were denounced by him would have their rations stopped. We were extremely scared of his power. To distinguish between Mok and Khoy we called them Big Brother and Little Brother. These names were widely used throughout the units. When we got back from work and saw two pots near the fire, we knew that one belonged to Big Brother and the other to Little Brother.

The rice had been planted. We were told by the co-operative leader, Comrade Huon, of some exciting news, a project to build a dam that would be used to irrigate regions two, four and six. And our rations were to be increased. The Angkar was taking good care of us . . .

The work-field for the Ream Kun dam was the biggest so far. The single males, the single females and the widows from the whole region were involved. And the project would indeed have been remarkable if it had worked. The idea was to dam the Maung river and divert the water into a reservoir from where it would be channelled through canals to regions two and six, which consisted of dry high ground. If the water had been prepared to flow uphill, this would have made a great difference to all our lives. It would have been one of the wonders of the world, which is what the Khmer Rouge thought it was going to be.

The length of the dam was five kilometres. At points it was ten metres high and twenty-five metres thick at its base. We slept on the ground, under the kind of shelters normally used for cattle. We ate at the communal canteen, girls first, then boys. The food was prepared in enormous pans that had been cast from melted-down vehicles. They were rusty and encrusted with old food.

Hunger made us selfish. We sat in groups of ten around the soup bowl, with our rice rations served on leaves, waiting to be allowed to eat. And as we waited we would stare into the soup to work out where the few pieces of meat or fish were. The second the order was given, ten spoons plunged in after the meat. If you managed to get it on your spoon, it might still be knocked off by someone else, and the fight would begin again. In ten such meals I reckoned on finding the meat once or twice.

We were woken at five for the roll call, followed by a half-hour speech from the unit leader. At six we set off for work. Lunch break was half an hour at noon. Work again till five, followed perhaps by a meeting criticizing those who had not worked hard enough. In the evening it depended on the moon. If it was bright, dinner might be brought to the work-field, and we would continue digging till eleven. But when it was too dark we ate at the canteen and had meetings afterwards instead. Because our rations had indeed improved, as promised, I found some of my strength returning.

Sisopha, to my surprise, appeared at the canteen, organizing our rations. She had been nursed back to health by Comrade Ran, who had found her this 'fat job' and provided her with a uniform and sandals. She smiled when we met. She seemed quite well.

In the work-field, the men and women were, for some reason, put to work together. But it was hard to talk. Khmer Rouge boys had been placed strategically around the field to listen to our conversations. We didn't know their faces. They covered their heads with a *kramar* and worked on their own. They had guns and they scared us.

I was put to work with Mealea one day. She dug. I took the earth to the dam. After half an hour it seemed safe to talk. I asked her if she had seen Bopha.

'Yes,' she said, 'once since I've been here. Ran took me to see her.'

'How was she?'

'Oh, I think she's well. She seems to enjoy her new work,' said Mealea, sighing. 'Someth, do you think it's right what she's doing?'

'What do you mean?' I grabbed the basket from her and went off to the dam, thinking about Mealea's attitude. Mealea was as religious as my older brother had been.

'Teaching all those bloody black crows' kids,' she said, when I returned. Mealea always referred to the Khmer Rouge in this way. It was her private slang.

'Well,' I said, looking around, 'I object in one way, but not in another. I know what you mean, Mealea. But we all want to survive somehow. We've no choice.'

'By taking easy jobs when others are slaves? Staying alive when everyone else is starving? I can't do that. That's why I refused to join the black crows' performing group.' The basket was full again and I made another trip to the dam.

'Someth,' she continued, 'I don't know how long I will be able to survive this regime. I'm fed up with it now.' She was crying.

'You're not going to do anything terrible, are you? You're not going to commit suicide?'

'No,' she said, pausing from her work, 'I won't do anything like that. Buddha would never forgive me.' The lunch whistle went and we were separated before I could say to her — what my father had said — that any action of hers might affect the rest of the family.

Occasionally Mealea and Comrade Ran used to pass on some food to me, and sometimes Sisopha, who was always trying to slip me something, managed to get a piece of meat to me at the end of the communal meal. We had enough rice to keep our stomachs full. For lunch we had rice and salt. For dinner, salt and rice. But the lack of vitamins in the diet caused many people in the work-field to suffer from night blindness. I was one of them.

During the day I could see perfectly well, but when the sun was about to set I began to have a slight headache. Then a great shadow came over my vision. Everything became blurred and confused. By the time the sun had set, the headache had gone and I was completely blind. At dawn, the effect was reversed. During the blindness I always imagined that my eyes had turned quite white.

Comrade Mok gathered the night-blind teenagers in groups of ten for the evening meal. We sat in circles. He ordered the cooks to place the soup between us. With great difficulty we directed our spoons to the bowl. Then we realized he had given us dirty water or soil. Mok and his colleagues loved this game.

The blindness came and went. If I was lucky enough to find a piece of liver – even a fish's liver – I would be able to see for two or three nights. The rest of the time, they lit bonfires on the work-field, and those of us who were afflicted were made to dig near them. We could see for about two metres. Some people, of course, began faking: they were put on hard labour and short rations. We were always being tested. Mok would make us walk into thorn bushes, into muddy ponds or towards the graveyards. This last happened to a friend of mine, whose whole foot sank into a rotten corpse.

Since the mysterious Khmer Rouge soldiers had been working in the fields with us, several people had gone missing. We knew they had been killed when their clothes appeared in someone else's possession. There were so few clothes around that you would notice even a palm-leaf hat or a scarf if it had a new owner. The unit was divided into companies of thirty, further subdivided into groups of eight or ten. Each of these had a leader. And now a lot of the leaders were disappearing. We were very glad when this happened to our company leader, Comrade Mau, a tough little teenager and a devoted servant of the Angkar. To my amazement Comrade Mok chose me to replace Mau. He told me to stand up in a meeting one day, and then and there he announced my promotion.

Comrade Ran gave me a black uniform to go with my job. She sent for Little Brother and gave him the clothes. He gave them to Big Brother and Big Brother gave them to me. She had almost got us into a position where my family had become Old People, and she was still pestering Sisopha to know my answer to her proposal. Then she sent Mealea with a gift of Ho Chi Minh sandals.

I lost friends through my promotion, and I found it hard to make my speech at the company meeting without alienating the New People further. If I was too soft I would be in trouble with the

Khmer Rouge. But I couldn't adopt the threatening tone of the Old People. I used to say, 'We must all understand that we are living in the land of the revolution and that we have to work very hard in order to reconstruct the country.' My speech never lasted long. I would leave time for the group leaders (there were three of them under me) to do all the threatening.

I was entitled to one day's rest a week, but I never took advantage of this right. I didn't have to. There was no real work for me to do. I spent the day sitting on the dam watching my company labouring and listening to the other leaders discussing methods of improving the work. When anyone made some new suggestion I always said I thought it excellent. Dig a little further away? Good idea. Bring the digging a little closer to the dam? Good idea again. I took care not to have any ideas of my own.

When there were no soldiers around, the discussion turned to the Khmer Rouge girls in the other unit. Most of the leaders were boys at the age of puberty, and they watched the girls like hawks. Normally a girl wore her shirt buttoned down to her cuffs, but if the day was particularly hot and she rolled up her sleeve this was immediately noticed with appreciation. Or if a girl took off her *kramar* for a moment, thereby revealing a little of her neck, the effect was sensational. The leaders were sex starved, and their discussions turned mainly on how plump this or that girl had become. The most daring remark would be to do with the size of a girl's hips.

The nearest the leaders got to sexual contact was the bruise therapy. They might nudge each other and say, 'Come on, let's go to the nurses for a bruise.' The brave ones went alone. The shy ones always went in groups. The nurses too were shy – or pretended to be. They would wrap their *kramar*s round their faces, like Muslims, holding the ends between their teeth. The leaders sat there, shirtless and legs crossed, and they normally took care to put their shirts over their laps. Then the nurses reached forward and pinched them, making a pattern of bruises in rings across their chests. Often this went on for half an hour with nobody saying a word. The pinching had to be very painful to be effective.

The Khmer Rouge girls had a way of flirting with the leaders. They knew when they were being talked about, and they used to speed up work so that they were always passing the leaders carrying a basket of soil to the dam. They had a way of bending over in their black sarongs which showed their behinds to best advantage. Comrade Ran didn't go in for this kind of behaviour, but she got talked about nevertheless. She was, after all, quite plump, and plumpness was everything.

Despite the rest and better rations, I still had trouble with my eyes. Comrade Mok told me I could stay back at the camp to watch the people off sick. I asked him how I was supposed to do this when I couldn't see anything. He said I just had to stay put and act as though I knew what was going on. His little servant would help me. I suspected this was a trick.

Little Brother would come along frequently to say that this person had left his sleeping place or that one was walking around. I called them to ask where they'd been. Invariably they'd been having a shit. I would tell them to let us know before they went. I never bothered to report these incidents to Comrade Mok because I knew he relied on Little Brother.

After a few days I was taken out to the work-field at night. I was not allowed to work, but sat next to the bonfire watching the company digging. At the end of the shift Comrade Mok led me by the arm to return to the camp. Normally this took twenty minutes, but we seemed to go on for longer. I asked what was happening. Mok said it was nothing. He let go of my arm and told me to walk straight ahead.

After a few minutes I again asked where we were. There was no reply. I called out for Comrade Mok. No one answered. I walked on and on. Sometimes I bumped into thorn bushes, but at least I had sandals now. I fell into ponds. I fell over rough ground and twisted my ankle. I sat down and waited, and after a while heard voices. I called out for help. Still no answer. I walked in the direction of the voices. I was going through stubble.

I began to smell smoke. I guessed they must be burning the field. I was terrified of walking into the flames. I stopped. I thought I would see the flames when they came close, and then I would know in which direction to go. Nothing happened. I curled up on the ground and tried to sleep, but it was hard to do so. I was still afraid of the fire.

The sun rose. The morning whistle sounded. The headache came and went. My sight returned. I was about 350 metres away from the unit camp, and the smoke had been coming from the fire with which Comrade Mok warded off mosquitoes. I walked back without a word. Comrade Mok saw how angry I was.

'Comrade Meth,' he said, 'I'm sorry. This is the last time I'll test you.'

'Comrade Mok,' I replied, 'you know very well that the word "sorry" is not allowed in the land of the revolution. By the way, I thought it was a very good test, very good indeed.'

Then I went to collect my company, and we set out for the workfield.

TWENTY
Mealea and the black crows

Mealea was the cleverest of my sisters. Her ambition had been to become a philosopher in the Buddhist tradition. She wanted to write, and this would have been very unusual for a woman in Cambodia. She didn't see herself as a feminist, but she was independent and she had no wish to get married until she had set herself up. She had been young when my older brother died, and she often asked my parents about him – her interests were the same as his had been and she found it frustrating that she was not allowed, as a girl, to go and talk with the monks. She never liked make-up. She believed that you had to dare to be what you were. If there was a blemish on your face, you should dare to show it. If there was something on your mind, you should express it.

Now she was in the infirmary, suffering terrible stomach pains. Her periods had stopped. She was thin and pale and her eyes had become cloudy.

A boy in my company got diarrhoea from eating poisonous leaves. It was serious, and I told Comrade Mok the boy was probably dying and should go to the infirmary. Mok detailed two of his favourites to carry the boy in a hammock, and we set off; we had to stop every five minutes for him to relieve himself.

I'd never been to the infirmary before, although it was not far from the village. The three huts were crowded with patients, and as the beds were all full I was told to leave him on the floor. Then I went over to the registry. Here the nurses were eating mangoes and oranges, laughing and complimenting each other on their looks, and joking about pimples. They had a mirror, the first I had seen in ages. The infirmary had smelt foul. In the registry there was perfume.

When I told them I was the boy's company leader, they looked surprised, and became suddenly friendly. They offered me a

176

bamboo flask of palm juice. I was still recovering from the shock of seeing patients lying in their own excrement. I held the flask in my hand, and asked about Mealea. I learnt that she had been taken from the infirmary by Comrade Ran a few days ago. I was very relieved. Trying not to gag, I knocked back the palm juice and left.

Bopha was with her pupils in the field, gathering baskets of dung. She looked well. She had a new uniform. She told me that Mealea had been nursed by Comrade Ran's mother. She was feeling much better, but looked as if she had something on her mind. I wondered whether I should tell Bopha what Mealea had said to me, but I didn't want to upset her. I've often regretted not having said more.

The dam was finished. Hundreds of lives had been lost on it. Many New People had been accused of working for the CIA or the KGB. When the Khmer Rouge referred to the KGB they actually said KCB, pronouncing the letters in the French style. It took me a few days to work out what they were on about. Later, the New People used to mutter to each other that the KCB must be Khmer Communistes de Battambang. Some of the Old People had also lost their lives: they were accused of illicit sex and thrown into an open pit.

To celebrate the completion of the dam, the performing group came to entertain us. They sang of our love for the Angkar – it was as wide as the sea, it had no boundary. We were masters of our work. There was no more exploitation. We could do whatever we wanted. The canals were the veins of the Angkar. We were no longer reliant upon rain. We could produce as much rice as we wanted. I rolled myself a cheroot, and as usual, after the first puff, I was tapped on the shoulder. The cheroot wandered off around the crowd. The singers looked very sleek. They'd plucked their eyebrows. Mealea could have been among them if she'd wanted.

Now we were harvesting the paddy. Several New People had escaped from regions two and six, and instead of sending them back Comrade Huon accepted them. He needed all the people he could get. Two of them joined my company, and seemed at first extremely scared of me. But when they learnt I was not one of the Old People, their attitude changed. I asked why they had fled, and they told me that their conditions had been even worse than ours. People had had their throats cut with sharp leaves, or their livers removed. The sick had been taken out and shelled to death, and it was now that I learnt that this had been the fate of Phan and Somaly. They hadn't been able to work so they had been killed.

Now Bopha told me that Mealea had got into trouble. It was only much later that I pieced together a full version.

A part of Bopha's job was to keep the children's notebooks in her house. Once a week they were checked by the co-operative leader, Comrade Huon. He was a thin, sharp-faced man with a strawberry mark and a habit of making sucking noises as he spoke. The last time Bopha had taken the books to him, he had stopped at a page written in an adult hand. It was like a journal entry, dated at the top, and Bopha's recollection is that it read as follows:

When I think of my happy life with my family under the republican regime, it seems to me now that we are living in hell. I have never slaved like this before. I have never been fed like this before. At the very least I would have had an hour of rest after a day's work, plenty of rice and dried fish, and clear water. Even the *cyclopousses* and street vendors had something to put in their stomachs.

Now I really hate this regime. It turns men into animals. It has nothing but bloodlust. The people who rule this country now are worse than anything I've ever seen. The death of my father, the death of my lovely brothers and relatives, and the death of my people are the real proof of this. I wish I had been born in another country. That doesn't mean that I hate being Cambodian. I love my country. I love my people very much. But this is what this regime has made me wish.

I don't know what has made me write this. I know it will be considered serious. But I can't stop. It's the only way I can get rid of my depression. I know very well that if this is found I will be killed. Maybe even the rest of my family. But please, brothers and sisters, forgive me. I know I have done wrong but I just couldn't stop it.

'Who wrote this?' said Comrade Huon.
'Wrote what, Uncle?' asked Bopha.
'Read it,' said Comrade Huon, handing her the book. .
Bopha read it. 'I don't know, Uncle,' she said.
'It must have been an intellectual. It can't have been one of your pupils, Comrade Bopha.'

She didn't reply. She told me later that she had felt like a dead body, for she had recognized the handwriting immediately as that of her twin sister. Comrade Huon turned to his little aide-de-camp and ordered him to fetch the register, which contained examples of the handwriting of all the New People. Nobody spoke. Bopha tried to think of a way out. She knew that Mealea had signed the register and that she would be found out. She was left-handed. The only thing Bopha could do was tell the truth before the boy returned in the faint hope that she might limit the damage to our family. But she couldn't betray Mealea.

The boy returned with a stack of notebooks and placed them on the table in front of Comrade Huon. Then Bopha broke down. 'It's Mealea's writing, Uncle.'

Mealea was taken to see Comrade Huon the next day. She confessed she had written the note, and promised she would never do it again. Nothing more was said and she was allowed to go back to her unit.

The harvest was in and we were back on a new reservoir. I couldn't see how it was going to work. There was no river or stream feeding it. It was just a marked out square in the middle of nowhere, to be surrounded with high dikes. We dug outside the square where the water collected and we used it for cooking and washing. Inside the square there was no water at all. It became a convenient place to shit. We were draining the land rather than flooding it.

My company was joined by a couple of demobbed Khmer Rouge, who lived and worked as we did. Their job was to listen in on our conversations. One of them was called Comrade Khann. He acted friendly, worked hard but was often joking. When he arrived he used to call me brother-in-law, by which he intended a compliment to Bopha. Comrade Khann's first victim was a boy of fifteen called Meng.

He began, 'If somebody gave you a bowl of chicken soup, with lots of herbs and spices and a kilo of cooked rice, would you be able to finish it?'

'Of course,' replied Meng, stopping digging, 'I could eat twice that.'

'I bet you couldn't,' said Comrade Khann, still digging, 'your stomach would burst.' And he laughed.

'Maybe in the old regime, but not now,' said Meng. 'I haven't had anything like that for a long time.'

'Keep digging,' said Comrade Khann, 'we can talk at the same time.' And he continued to question Meng about his taste in food. And Meng talked and talked about all the things he would like to eat. The conversation was making me hungry too.

Then Khann said, 'Comrade Meng, all that food was very good, but it was expensive. Only rich people could afford it – government officials who swindled the peasants.'

'Comrade,' Meng replied, wiping the sweat from his brow, 'everything was expensive because of the collapse of the *riel* against the dollar. You didn't know that, did you?' I wondered where Meng had picked up this expression, of which he seemed a bit proud. It certainly had an effect on Khann.

'No, I didn't know that,' he said. 'Oh dear, I think I have a headache. I think I'll just go and get something from the nurses.'

He came up to me and asked my permission. I told him to get back to work as soon as possible. A few minutes later, one of the nurses came up to tell me that Comrade Khann was unwell and had been taken to the infirmary. Actually, it should have been my job to take him. I reported the matter to Comrade Mok, who seemed unconcerned.

That night the general meeting was cancelled in favour of a special meeting of company and unit leaders. Comrade Huon was there, which indicated the matter was serious. We were sitting in the dark a long way from the camp. After the report on work progress, we were told that Comrade Khann had very good news for us. He certainly looked very important.

'My respects to the meeting,' he began, 'my respects to all the comrades. My news is that I have found an enemy in this co-operative. Don't be surprised if anyone from your unit goes missing. That will be the one.'

Comrade Ran stood up. She asked which company this enemy was in. She was very curious.

I thought: oh no, it's Mealea.

'I'm afraid I can't tell you,' said Comrade Khann, with a satisfied smile. 'It is a secret of the Angkar. But you'll learn after the person has gone.'

Two days later I was told to go and talk to Comrade Huon who was sitting on the dam. I stuck my spade into the ground and approached him in terror, still thinking it was something about Mealea.

'You're looking pale, Comrade Meth, is there anything wrong with you?'

'Nothing at all, Uncle,' I replied, 'it's just the weather.' I sat down beside him and pulled out my tobacco. It was dry and crumbling. Comrade Huon offered me some of his.

I unzipped the pouch. In addition to his tobacco, Comrade Huon had a wodge of lined paper, the remains of a school notebook. I squeezed the tobacco tight, so there would be something left over, took a piece of notebook and rolled the cigarette between the palms of my hands. I licked it well and rolled it again, nipped off the loose strands and pocketed them.

Comrade Huon was very relaxed, and his tobacco was excellent. 'Well, comrade,' he said, 'a member of your unit will be taken away in a few minutes – the one we talked about the other night. By the way, how is your company? All doing well?'

'Yes, they're doing terribly well. No one's in the camp. They're all here.'

'Good, Comrade Meth, keep it up. You're a fine leader. You can go back to your work now, and pay no attention if anything happens.' And he slurped characteristically.

I went back to my place. After half an hour, four unarmed soldiers arrived. They were talking to Comrade Huon and cracking jokes. I could hear their laughter as I bent over my spade. One of the soldiers sang a revolutionary song. Comrade Khann moved up to dig by Meng. They were chatting and laughing as well. Then Meng put down his mattock and approached me.

'Comrade Meth,' he said, breathlessly, 'Comrade Khann wants me to show him my new rat trap. I set it just on the other side of the dam. He wants to see it now. Can I go for a few minutes? I won't be long.'

I went up to Comrade Khann. 'Can't you wait till lunch break?' I said.

He put his spade down, winked at me and said he wanted to see it now.

I let them go. They rushed hand in hand over the dam, like two children. The four soldiers followed them.

Within a few days we all knew that Meng had been killed. It was Khann who told Mok. He claimed that Meng had been tortured first for two or three days, then given a huge meal of chicken soup and rice. Then he had been killed. After that, there was a member of my unit who, whenever soldiers appeared on the dike, would shake uncontrollably.

Comrade Khann had earned the respect of Comrade Mok. He gave up working and they sat together on the dam. I knew that Mok was a fool and just as trusting as Meng. But I didn't guess the speed with which Comrade Khann worked. Another special meeting was called, in which Comrade Huon told us that we had to take care of our own companies, because Comrade Mok was going on a mission to the co-operative for a few days. Comrade Khann sat beside his leader, in that same self-important mood. Comrade Mok looked worried. At the end of the meeting, only Huon and Khann and Mok stayed behind.

This is what I think happened. Mok and Khann were sitting together on the dam, and Khann led the conversation on to sex. Mok's penchant for boasting made it impossible for him to resist telling a story. They were both teenagers who had spent some time with the Old People and it was highly unlikely that either of them had slept with a girl. Mok said he *had* done so, and Khann expressed surprise that a girl in the single female unit would have agreed. She would have been too scared of the consequences. At this point Mok thought that the manly thing to say was that he'd raped her. Khann was fascinated and asked for the details. Mok told him proudly, in just the same way as he had boasted to us about his gambling and being wounded by the B−52. In just the same way as he'd said he'd been a soldier − which none of us believed.

But did Khann believe that Mok really had raped a girl? It doesn't make any difference. If he had believed him, it would have been another reason to be jealous of Mok who was superior to him. Mok was a unit leader, Khann was just a fink. If he didn't believe him he still had a perfect chance.

Huon and Khann probably killed Mok that night. There were no soldiers around the camp, and the Re-education Centre was half a day's walk away. Nobody saw Mok go. The next morning he had been due to wake us with his whistle as usual. But it was Comrade

Khann who woke us with Mok's old police whistle. And when he did that we all knew he was on the way up.

In the days that followed, Comrade Khann gradually assumed all of Mok's duties, and he began to sleep in Mok's hammock. He liked the hammock and even started bringing it with him to the work-field, for his lunch break snooze. The reason he took these ostentatious snoozes was that Mok's old favourites, who had always lunched with him, were afraid of Khann. He had no one of his class to talk to. He lunched alone, took to his hammock, placed Mok's radio on his stomach and tuned in very quietly to Phnom Penh.

And now we saw he had Mok's sandals. On the rare occasions when he did any digging he removed them first, because he liked the sandals very much, and the edge of the home-made spade was rather sharp. He liked Mok's sandals better than the soles of his feet. He washed them at night, just like Comrade Tek. Then he began to comb his hair, which was more than poor old Mok had ever done. On his right wrist he wore Mok's watch, but he always pocketed it if he used a mattock. He liked to go and check the time with the nurses. The black-faced Citizen watch would be sure to impress the girls.

We'd seen so many of Mok's effects we knew he must be dead. The clinching detail was when Comrade Khann appeared in Mok's uniform, which was rather too baggy for him and short in the leg. He asked Comrade Huon to ask Comrade Ran's mother to ask Comrade Ran to marry him. She told Sisopha she wasn't interested. Sisopha, who had almost given up with me by then, told me the whole story. I thought they'd make a good match. Comrade Khann was at last officially announced to be unit leader. Within a few days he'd got his teeth capped with gold. The soldiers had people who did this. I couldn't help wondering whether the gold had come from Comrade Mok's mouth.

New company leaders were chosen and unexpectedly I lost all my privileges. Then Sisopha was taken from the cooking team back to the village. When Bopha came to work on the dam I realized all three of us had fallen out of favour. I spoke to her very briefly and she told me Mealea had been taken away.

I didn't learn the details till much later. Another note had been found by the reconnaissance team, although it was not clear that it was in Mealea's writing. Mealea had been back in the infirmary, and again had been rescued by Comrade Ran's mother. They were eating together, and Bopha was with them, when a boy came in and told them that a new consignment of medicine had arrived at the infirmary, and Mealea should go along before it had all gone.

'Can I finish my meal first, comrade?' said Mealea.

'Finish it later,' said the boy. 'It won't run away.'

Mealea put her spoon down and followed the boy. Bopha's pupils told her what happened next. Three of the reconnaissance team jumped out from behind some bushes and grabbed her hands. She was tied up and dragged away to the Re-education Centre.

But at least she had spoken her mind. She had been true to her philosophy.

TWENTY-ONE
The come-and-go disease

Rations were cut, even though the harvest was in, and the working day was prolonged. We were starving again. I worked very hard after my demotion until I went down with cholera and was too weak to walk from my sleeping place to get a drink. I lay there for several days on reduced rations. Comrade Khann paid no attention to me until it looked as if I was going to die. Then he took me to the infirmary.

I was put on the floor next to a patient with diarrhoea. A nurse came and gave me an injection from a Pepsi bottle, followed by a bowl of rice soup and some water. That night I couldn't sleep because of the awful smell. On the second night my neighbour called weakly for the nurses. No one came and she finally died.

Then Comrade Ran appeared with tears in her eyes. She negotiated with the registry and had me taken on a stretcher to her house. Her mother, the wife of Comrade Tek, was clearly embarrassed to have me around, but she nursed me and fed me with fresh fish from the fishing commune, and lettuces from her own garden plot. At night, she showed me where to find everything I needed, and went off to sleep with her colleagues at the canteen. She didn't want to be accused of anything. Footsteps came past the house. I got up and lit the petrol lamp, so the reconnaissance team, if they wanted to, could see that I was alone.

Ran's brother came the next day with Western medicines. I began to recover. Sometimes I sat on the steps and watched the starving people being taken to the infirmary. Carts passed, loaded with rice, on their way to the mountains. A consignment of roots went to the registry – ingredients for the multi-purpose pill. Occasionally a soldier arrived on horseback, some kind of messenger, and once there was a sensation in the village at the sight of a Honda. The children crowded round it, sniffing the petrol fumes with delight. There seemed to be a lot of messages being passed.

Four days later, Comrade Khann appeared, took one look at me and decided I was to return to the work-field with him. He said nothing along the road, but when we reached the camp he laughed and said, 'Comrade Brother-in-law, the Angkar has decided to withdraw your uniform and sandals.' And he flashed his new gold teeth. I replied that if he took my uniform I would have to go to work naked. He thought about this, and decided I could keep the uniform but not the sandals.

Amusement spread around the work-field and people started pointing at Comrade Ran. She had gone to Comrade Huon and asked for permission to marry me. But there could be no marriage between Old and New People. Huon refused and she was demoted from her leadership of the widows. She was very embarrassed. A week later her father took her to work at the fishing commune.

I think it was late 1977. The reservoir was about one-third finished. It looked like an L-shaped road in the middle of nowhere. The demarcated area was dotted with piles of shit and rat traps. The rats ate the shit. We ate the rats. I think it was rat's liver which helped to cure my night blindness.

But now Comrade Huon told us we were to stop work on the dam, and start planting rice. This was odd because it was the wrong season. And when we got to Wat Chass, our new workplace, it looked quite the least fertile of the areas we had dug. All the co-operatives of region four had arrived. There was chaos and no food. Comrade Khann slipped away to the pagoda, leaving us to fix our accommodation. After his dinner, he returned and roused us for another meeting.

The speech of the work-field leader had all the old elements (the miseries of the Khmer Rouge in the jungle, their victory over imperialism) and one new one. We were to have two rice harvests a year. Even three in the near future. Every square centimetre of Cambodia would be turned over to rice. And when that happened we would be more than self-sufficient.

The leader spent a long time congratulating the Angkar on this new achievement. Two harvests would have been possible, with the right seed, with enough water and sufficient fertility. Three harvests were impossible. There were two kinds of seed available – three-month and six-month. The first kind, known as light paddy, took three months between germination and harvest, but the preparation of the soil and harvesting itself took at least two months. For light paddy the ground needed ploughing really well.

Water was also needed: the seedlings had to be under six to eight centimetres of it – but this was raised ground and there was no water to be seen, and no irrigation system envisaged. It was the rainy season: if you planted now the seed would rot under the water; it would germinate but fail to produce seed. So we were on another doomed task.

It was here that I first heard the name of Pol Pot, and that the country he led was called Democratic Kampuchea. We had had no national news of any kind. Now there were loudspeakers on the Wat Chass pagoda, where the food was stored and the reconnaissance team lived. They relayed Phnom Penh radio, which was mostly propaganda about rice. About the world outside we knew nothing at all. We knew practically nothing about what was happening in the next village. Not that we would have been really curious if we *had* known. We were too tired and sick.

The leader of the work-field told us he had some wonderful news. Enemies of the people in region six had been on strike for more food. They had been crushed. 'We gain nothing by keeping them, we lose nothing by disposing of them,' he said, working himself up into a rage. Three prisoners from that region had been found by the reconnaissance team, he said, trying to foment revolution in our work-field. Here they were. 'The wheel of our revolution is spinning forward,' he said. 'No one can stop it. If anyone tries to, he will be run over.'

We craned our necks to see the prisoners. They were in their teens, dressed in rags and obviously suffering from malnutrition. Nobody had seen them before. They could hardly stand up. The reconnaissance team picked them up by the cords that bound their elbows behind their backs, and they stumbled away into the dark. The meeting continued. Behind the leader was a single neon tube, which was as much as the only generator could handle. After half an hour the reconnaissance team returned and passed through the small circle of light, disappearing again without a word. In their hands they were carrying entrails.

Dengue fever was known as the come-and-go disease. Between attacks you could just move around, but it always returned punctually. When I caught it, I suffered between mid-morning and mid-afternoon. It began with a tremendous headache that concentrated on the forehead and the base of the skull. Then a heat spread all over my face, and it was too painful to move my eyes. Then it moved to my spine, and my skin felt as if pricked with a thousand needles. In the next stage my muscles contracted and I began to shiver. When the shivering stopped I would crave something sour tasting – a tamarind, a lime, anything. Whatever I thought of I could immediately taste in the corner of my mouth. Then I'd have visions of the food in question, and I could feel its texture.

Comrade Khann took me to the infirmary. It was worse than the last one. 'Lie still,' said the nurse. 'We are going to burn your spinal cord with these pieces of kapok. It's something we've discovered. It has worked very well on dengue fever.' They grabbed me by the legs and wrists and pressed me to the floor.

I yelled, 'What are you trying to do?'

'We're only trying to cure your dengue fever!'

One of the nurses lit a spill and held over it a piece of kapok the size of my middle fingertip. When it was glowing red, she pressed it hard on my spine with a green leaf. She repeated the process twice on the same spot. A few days later, when I had a terrible stomach-ache, they took me again to the infirmary and gave me five burn spots in different places on my stomach.

I was determined to get out of the infirmary and never return. If the choice was between work and torture, work was much better. Fortunately, just before I was due to leave, Orphea arrived with a consignment of Pepsi-bottle serum for her co-operative, some of whose members were working on the field. She wept to see me in my changed state, and I was astonished at how plump she was. Hidden in a plastic bag she had some Western medicines, including vitamin tablets. I learnt later that she was in the habit of carrying them around in case she met anyone she knew. Orphea was the only one of us who had not been demoted, because being in a different village she was not affected by Mealea's disgrace. I took whatever I thought would do me good, and when I got back to the camp I hid the rest under the hut roof for fear of discovery by Comrade Khann.

The leader of our region, region four, was Ta Vong – 'Grandfather' Vong. We'd never set eyes on him, or been told anything about him, until one day we learnt from the work-field that Ta Vong had been taken to the Re-education Centre. The Angkar had discovered that he had been hoarding rice and selling it to counter-revolutionary forces along the Thai border. This was the first we had heard about such forces.

Next, the work-field leader told us that corpses were being dug up from the infirmary graveyard, and their flesh eaten. He said, 'If you're hungry, work hard.'

I never knew whether people had been eating corpses. He himself disappeared a few days later.

New Khmer Rouge were in control. Meetings were reduced. Work continued much the same. But 'special rations' were introduced. One day in ten we were allowed to eat as much rice as we could manage. The day came. We could smell it on the wind as we came back from the field. Everyone rushed to the barrels, took off their hats and filled them with mounds of rice. The rule was that you had to finish the amount you had taken from the barrel.

We sat down in groups of ten, waiting for the order to eat. Then we gobbled. The sight of real rice, as opposed to the pulp or soup we had been eating, drove us crazy. We ate without chewing. I ate till I felt sick. That night people were vomiting and relieving themselves all around the hut. They farted and groaned and heaved. They tried to walk. They couldn't. They tried to lie down. They couldn't. They were in agony. We had to step through the detritus in the morning for the roll call. Five people from my unit were missing. Little Brother was sent to look for them. He came back holding his nose, picking his way through the sour, fermenting, undigested food. They were dead.

The special rations system was abolished after a month.

TWENTY-TWO
Here is your pen!

This was the way with the Khmer Rouge: we would work for months on one project, like this paddyfield where I guess that two out of ten of us died or were killed in the course of three months. Then one evening, well before the ploughing was finished, the new field leader appeared at the commune meeting and told us we were to go back to our co-operative. What that meant, quite simply, was that all our work had been pointless. There was nobody else in this isolated region to continue it, and anyway, the land we had been preparing was so dry and infertile that it would never have been much use. Now we were told that the rice growing on our co-operatives was in urgent need of protection from birds. We had to pack our things, return communal property such as ploughs and oxen and bullocks to the work-field headquarters, and go back the next day.

At about five o'clock in the morning our unit leader, Comrade Khann, told us what our duties would be. The next work would not be difficult. We would have to stay in the fields waiting for flocks of birds, and as soon as we saw them we had to shout and make as much noise as possible. We had all our belongings with us at the meeting. Mine were: one torn mosquito net, one broken spoon, one ragged *kramar*, one yoke, one torn tarpaulin.

'And now,' said the unit leader, 'we can leave,' and he got on to his rusty Chinese bicycle and pedalled away ahead of us.

At this moment there was a great movement in the meeting. Everybody who still had relatives back at the co-operative went off in a state of excitement, hungry and exhausted though they were. But I was not excited. None of my family was at Co-operative 102, and I envied those who had parents or relatives waiting for them. They would be fed in secret when they arrived. But when I arrived, who was going to give me any food? Who would welcome me? I thought of Comrade Ran's mother, who was the only person I knew there. But would she recognize me? I was skin and bone. I had no idea what my face looked like.

I was near the end of the group walking along the track. From time to time, Comrade Khann cycled back to order the stragglers to hurry. His bicycle – that is, the communal bicycle, the unit's only bicycle – was black and very old and without brakes. Digging his feet into the dust track, he would bring the bike to a halt and tell us to get a move on. He was in a childish good humour and to look at him you might think he had nothing to do with the revolution. But I knew it was dangerous even to joke with Comrade Khann. What-ever you said he might distort and relay to the Angkar. And there was another thing: without my wishing it I had been his rival in love. Comrade Ran had rejected him.

Along with his other possessions, Comrade Khann had inherited Comrade Mok's batman, Little Brother. He was walking along with us, with a shoulder-bag on both shoulders. His own bag probably did not contain much more than mine, except that he would also have had two sets of clothes – two neat black uniforms in good condition. His master's bag would have more in it: tobacco, Western medicines, clothes, US camouflage blankets, mosquito net, pens and paper. You could tell it was the unit leader's bag for several reasons: colour – bright blue or yellow; a red flash sewn on to it; the green nylon American hammock, trussed up with string, like a joint of meat; and, finally, the US-issue spoon of bright, stainless steel that stuck out of the bag, or was slipped into the hammock string (either way so that it could definitely be seen).

We had set out around six o'clock in the morning, with empty stomachs. When I needed water, I took off my palm-leaf hat (which also served as a rice bowl) and scooped a drink from the ditch beside the track. My group consisted entirely of male teenagers. Behind us came the female group, which included Bopha. Although I had seen her working in the field, I hadn't been able to talk to her for the last three months. We walked through the heat of the day, about thirty kilometres, arriving at the co-operative in the mid-afternoon.

The unit leader got off his bike. 'All right,' he said, 'we're going to stay here. You must leave your things here. You can go to see your relatives if you want – but be back within an hour.' Then he went off to visit his mother. I prepared a place to rest on the ground and tried to forget my hunger. But the more I tried, the more hungry I felt. Our unit was near the commune's cassava field. Along the edge of the field was a row of sugar palms, which produced the sugar for the co-operative.

I ought to explain something about the sugar palm. During the harvest season the trees produced flowers, each about the size of a small, floppy rolling pin. Every day, in the early morning and late evening, someone had to climb the palm and cut the end of the flower, which was then squeezed into a bamboo flask tied to its stalk. Twice a day the flasks were replaced, and the juice inside was boiled down to produce the sugar. This job, which took eight to ten hours, was the favourite occupation of the Old People. It was an easy job and there were plenty of opportunities to drink the juice on the side. More than that: the Old People were able to filch some of the thick brown discs of sugar and use them as currency to trade with the New People for clothes, jewellery and especially watches. Sugar and salt were the things that the New People wanted most.

I lay down, resting the back of my right hand against my forehead. One of the Old People, with a knife like a short sword and a set of flasks tied to his waist, was climbing up a palm. As I watched him, an idea occurred to me. If he can climb palm trees, why can't I? Why shouldn't I do the same? If I get the chance, I'll have a go tonight.

But that evening, after a meal consisting of two boiled green bananas, I was chosen as part of a ten-man detail to work in the fields at the back of the village, rebuilding broken dikes. I gathered my belongings again and promised myself that on the next opportunity I would climb one of the sugar palms.

We set off at about ten. When we reached our destination a couple of hours later, it was too late to build a temporary shelter and we had to sleep in the open on the dike. The next three days passed slowly. The nights especially were cold and windy. It drizzled and, worse, our rations had not been sent on. We had to live on apple-snails and paddy-crabs, which were roasted in the fire. On the fourth day, when we were called back to the village, I thought to myself: here is my chance.

That night I waited till everyone was asleep, crept out from my mosquito net, and made my way towards the sugar palms. They were about eighteen metres high. I looked up, wondering whether I had enough energy to reach the top. I was weak from hunger. I had never climbed such a tall tree before, and this was the first time that I had rebelled against the discipline of the Angkar. I was scared but I was also more hungry than scared. What I was doing could cost me my life.

I began, slowly and carefully, to climb the tree. It took me the best part of half an hour to get to the top. Once there, I drank as much of the palm juice as I could. I drank and drank, and then I had to pause, since my stomach was like a balloon. As long as I was at the top of the tree I felt safe. The village ahead of me was quiet and dark. To my left lay the cassava field. To my right, I could see the cattle-pen, where a bonfire was kept burning all night to keep off the mosquitoes. A few of the cows were standing near the fire and I could see them swishing their tails. I felt happy at the heaviness of my stomach. I suppose I waited ten minutes before climbing back down and returning to my sleeping quarters, which were in the open barn. Nobody moved or said anything. I had succeeded.

The next night, and for the next few days, I repeated my routine. I used to look forward to the moment when everyone was asleep, and I became quicker and more practised at climbing the trees. I chose the flasks carefully, first taking a sip to see whether the juice was really sweet, and I never drank to the bottom in case of sediment. I discovered that, despite the Angkar's ban on alcohol, some of the Old People were secretly preparing toddy (or palm wine) in these flasks. One person was in charge of a dozen trees, and of these he might allow himself three flasks for toddy. I always avoided these.

One day at the co-operative meeting, a couple of weeks later, the leader announced that somebody was stealing palm juice from the flasks. The single male unit was near the sugar palms, and the leader suspected one of us. After this I stopped my nightly visits.

It was late 1978 and the rice was due for harvesting. Our job was to scare the birds away from the crop. The day began at five o'clock with the leader's whistle calling us to the roll call, where the able-bodied men received their rations immediately and were sent out to the fields. The healthy got a piece of boiled cassava or half a milk tin of boiled sweetcorn for lunch. The sick received about a third of the rations of the healthy. The cold windy weather continued and as soon as we went out into the fields we looked for anything edible to supplement our diet.

We went out, five or six to the field, and sat on the paddy-dike waiting for birds, which generally arrived at about ten o'clock in the morning and three or four o'clock in the afternoon. There were flocks of pigeons, parrots, robins, sparrows and cuckoos. The worst were the pigeons and sparrows. When anyone saw them coming he would shout to his neighbours, and the message would pass from field to field. As the flock came over us we stood up and yelled; the birds wheeled away to the next field, where you could hear the process repeated. When we were not scaring the birds, we New People were keeping our eyes open for anything to eat. We went for any suitable green vegetation, or for snails, tadpoles about the size of a thumb, baby frogs, grass snakes, mice, paddy-crabs and millipedes. Anything that could be eaten raw, we ate immediately. The rest we concealed by turning over the waistbands of our trousers. After a good day's work it was possible to return to the village with what felt like a cartridge belt of food – a rat, a couple of apple-snails, a few live paddy-crabs – and as we walked home we continued looking for millipedes. We were always longing for rain, because then the birds wouldn't come, and the wild life would crawl out from the centre of the paddyfields towards the dike. But it seldom rained during the day.

At night all the creatures we caught were roasted on sticks over the remains of the cooking fires, but this had to be done in secret (we would say 'with my eyes on my forehead') so that the leader wouldn't know. Within a few weeks, all these animals became scarce, and some New People began eating ants' larvae (raw) and catching red ants from the trees, putting them in water and making a kind of vinegar. They took a bucket of water on a long pole and held it under the ants' nest, shaking it so that the larvae fell to the bottom of the water and the red ants floated on top. These buckets were stolen from the camp kitchen, and hidden out in the fields.

For myself, I confined my eating to baby frogs, paddy rats and crabs. If you want to know what they tasted like, all I can say is that frog is like frog, and rat exactly like rat.

The unit meetings were held once every three days, normally at seven in the evening, after we had eaten. They were punctuated by long pauses, and it was not unusual for members of the audience to

194

keel over asleep; they would be woken up and warned. At the end, the leaders would open the meeting to the people, but nobody dared ask any questions. A year before, one man had asked for the meaning of the word Angkar to be explained – but although he had survived, nobody else had thought of copying him.

Then one day, Comrade Chhith, a boy of about seventeen – a quiet character who seldom chatted to anybody and always sat by himself – suddenly put his hand up and asked whether the unit leader would answer some questions about the revolution and explain a few points which Chhith had not understood so far. His request was granted and he rose to speak.

'Friends and comrades, it is a great opportunity for me,' said Comrade Chhith, 'that the meeting has allowed me to put some questions about the revolution. In every meeting, thousands of them so far, I have been told that the people in the revolutionary territory are equal and that equality has been achieved everywhere. Could you please tell me, comrade' said the boy, looking straight into the eyes of the unit leader, 'what is the meaning of the word "equality"?'

The unit leader, Comrade Khann, stood up to reply.

'Equality,' he said, 'means "the same". In other words it means that the people in the revolution are the same . . .' And he paused as if stumped by the boy's question. 'That is, there is no supervision in the revolution. Everyone is the same.'

The boy stood up again. 'You've just said that everybody is the same and that there is no supervision in the revolution,' he said, and I noticed that his voice was trembling. 'Then why am I always told or ordered to *do this* or *do that*?' And he sat down again.

'Well, that is a very good question indeed,' said the unit leader sarcastically. He was beginning to get annoyed. 'If you are not told what you're supposed to do, none of the work that our Angkar wants will get done.'

Now Comrade Chhith sprang to his feet and came straight back into the argument. 'I see. Now let me return to the word equality. From what you have said, the people in the revolution are equal. But why doesn't equality exist in every unit of the co-operative?' he asked. You could see anger and excitement mounting in him.

'How do you mean – equality does not exist in the units?' asked the unit leader, his tone hardening.

The unit leader was not a Khmer Rouge soldier. He was a peasant who until 1975 had been working under the Khmer Rouge. It was only with the arrival of the New People that he would have been put in charge of a unit. He was not a well educated man. He had the handwriting of a child.

Comrade Chhith, who now returned to his feet, was (I later gathered) the son of an officer in Lon Nol's army. He was obviously well educated, and he had obviously thought out this argument a long time before beginning it. Now he reached the crux.

'Well, let me explain. Take, for instance, our own unit. Why do you all, who call yourselves the Old People, have enough food to eat, when we don't? This is the main question I want you to answer.'

Heads shot up when this question was put, but Comrade Chhith had not finished. He had lost his self-control: 'As far as I can tell, from listening to the songs that were broadcast every evening at Wat Chass work-field, they talked about equality all the time. But I can't see any equality in our unit. We have two meals a day – quite often none. You and your Old People always eat more than three times. Please, comrade, tell me more about the word equality.'

'Comrade,' the unit leader's voice was more menacing, 'you should think very, very carefully before you open your mouth again to ask more questions. We Old People have been fighting very hard over the last few years to achieve equality and freedom for all you here. We've suffered all kinds of miseries while you were in luxury villas in the capital, doing nothing but enjoying yourselves in the decadent culture of the East and West. Do you think that what *you* did was fair to *us*? What right do you have to complain about the food you have eaten? Come on, tell me more about the way we Old People have behaved.'

The boy was really brave but seemed to have recovered his control a little. He stood up again and said, 'The point I want to know from you Old People is – is there any equality in our unit, and, if so, what sort of equality is it?'

The unit leader was calmer in turn, 'I admit that there doesn't seem to be equality in our unit. But if we Old People didn't have enough to eat, we would be starving like you. Leaders have to eat more in order to have enough energy to lead you in the way our Angkar wants. As I told you a few minutes ago, you have to be told, otherwise none of the work would get done. Any more questions?'

'No, I think the answers are very good,' said Comrade Chhith stressing each word. 'Thanks a lot. They are very understandable.'

The meeting broke up at one in the morning. We went off to our sleeping quarters with a lot to think about. I was pleased by the boy's questions, but worried for his safety.

About once a week, the unit and company leaders would have a fourth meal around midnight. On one such night, they sat by the fire watching the rice cook, and the New People watched, as usual, from their sleeping places. As they began to eat, Comrade Chhith got up from his mosquito net and went straight to the fire, sat down and without a word began eating with them. Conversation around the fire stopped immediately, but nobody prevented Chhith from eating. Then one by one the leaders got up and left him alone with his meal. When they had gone, several boys from the unit came over and started to join in. During the whole incident nobody said a word.

Next week, the unit's rations were stopped without explanation. After working a day without food, I could think only of finding some way of filling my stomach. I thought of the cassava field next to the village. If I was careful, I might go there in the night. Most of the people in the unit were asleep by midnight, except for three groups huddled around camp fires, roasting the small creatures that they had caught during the day. The clouds were thick. It would rain very soon, and I thought that this was a good opportunity.

As the rain began, I wandered over to one of the fires and chatted a little with one of the men. When it seemed a good moment, I slipped away in the direction of the cassava field. It took about twenty minutes to cross the open ground, and I stopped and hid for a further ten minutes, listening for voices. Then I tried to pull up a cassava stem, but I was too weak.

I should explain that this form of sweet cassava grows like a small tree, about the height of a sunflower but with a strong woody stem. The part you eat is the tuber, which can grow to the size of your forearm. Most flour used in South-east Asia is made from this kind of cassava, which is also boiled as a vegetable.

Normally I could have pulled up the plant without difficulty, but now I had to dig out the tubers with my hands. I ate as much as I could raw, and then dug up some more to take with me. When I got back to the camp fire everyone had gone to sleep. The rain had just stopped and the fire was nearly out. I put the cassavas among the embers, covering them with wet leaves and blew gently.

I heard a voice calling my name in the camp. The voice came nearer and nearer and I recognized it was Comrade Khann, the unit leader. I called out, 'I'm over here, comrade.'

'Hey, Comrade Meth, what are you doing here?' asked Comrade Khann, joining me at the fireside, squatting and warming his hands.

'I couldn't sleep,' I replied. 'I want to warm myself up. It's too cold over there.'

'Come on, go back to sleep. You have to get up early to work.'

'OK, comrade, I'll go in a minute after I've warmed myself up,' I replied, glancing at the potatoes in the fire to see if they were well covered.

'Come along, now. It's not right to sit out in the middle of the night like this. Come on!' He slapped me on the shoulder, but in a friendly way he was ordering me to leave. I was sorry to lose the cassavas. It was months since I had eaten one properly cooked.

'Comrade,' I said, 'I can't sleep over there. It's too cold.'

'No problem,' said the unit leader, 'I'll lend you my blanket. Come on, let's go now.'

Lend me his blanket! I'd never had that kind of generous offer before. He must be 'chasing a footprint', as we say in Cambodian. I got up and followed him reluctantly to the sleeping quarters, where he gave me his blanket and saw me to my mosquito net.

That night the raw cassava attacked my stomach and I couldn't sleep at all.

The next night I went off to the cassava field again. Nothing happened. By the third night, I'd got into the swing of it. I went off again, and while digging for the cassavas, this time with a piece of dead wood instead of my bare hands – I heard a group of people coming towards me.

As they approached I wondered whether to run or stay still. If I ran, and they happened to have a gun among them, I might get shot. I hesitated. They moved closer. I lay still on the ground and tried to stop breathing. They paused about twenty metres from me, and I could see by the moonlight that there were four men. Each wore black uniform and carried a long *parang*. I knew from this that they were the reconnaissance team, drawn from the most senior of the Old People. We called them *kang chhlob*. When we had first come to this place they patrolled the sleeping quarters at night, and if they heard anyone saying something wrong, that person would be called away by the Angkar the next day and would not reappear. Once they called you, you were never seen again.

'Hey, comrades,' said one of them, 'tonight it's my turn. If we catch somebody here, I'll show you what I can do.'

'OK, comrade,' came the reply, 'stop going on about it. You can do whatever you want but remember, you are not allowed to kill them here.'

I closed my eyes and tried to stop shivering. Hunger disappeared. I could think only of what I would do if I was caught.

They stopped and stood still for about five minutes, watching the field and trying to catch the slightest noise. I held my breath. Eventually they moved on. I thought, I'm alive again! I swore never to come back here at night, however hungry I was.

As soon as they had gone, I got up and tried to work out how to get back to my quarters. I had been lying on a nest of red ants and was bitten all over. I was nervous and did not know which way to go. Very slowly I edged in what I thought was the right direction, but ten minutes later I found myself at the wrong end of the field. I retraced my steps towards the village. As soon as I was out of the field there was a noise behind me.

'You there, stop and put your hands up. You're the one we're looking for.'

I stopped and turned around. It was the four men I had just seen, the members of the reconnaissance team. Although I had seen them often around the village, I never knew their names and I had never even looked into their faces. Whenever they passed, we simply stared at the ground and continued our work.

'What are you doing here?' said another of them. 'We've been watching you all evening and we know what you were up to in the cassava field.'

'No, comrade . . .' I stuttered, 'I'm just going for a walk because I – I couldn't sleep.'

'Going for a walk? Now, come on, move forward very slowly and keep your hands up.'

I did as I was told and as I came closer I noticed their wrist-watches in the moonlight. One of them stepped towards me and grabbed my hands, twisting them behind my back. I looked at the ground.

'Now, you liar, tell us the truth. How many times have you done this before?'

'What have I done, comrade? I don't understand what you're talking about.'

'You've been stealing cassavas from the commune field.'

'No, I'm going for a walk.' By now I was trembling violently and my voice was out of control.

The man in front of me rolled up the sleeve of his right arm and placed his hands on his hips. I noticed a great scar on his forearm.

'Scum, I said tell us the truth before you get hurt.'

I couldn't answer. I could only, with great difficulty, raise my eyes from the ground and look at his face, which I saw for the first time. He had the face and weirdly cruel expression of a man who had spent a long time on the battlefield. His eyes were bloodshot and bulging and the lines in his brow were deep with anger. His hair was greying and his skin was dark.

My mind seemed to drift. I do not know what I was thinking about when I felt a terrible blow to my mouth. His fist had knocked out one of my teeth, and my mouth and tongue started to bleed. My eyes were filled with tears and the pain spread immediately through my skull. The man on my right pulled a piece of parachute cord from his pocket and went behind me. As he tied my arms together at the elbows he kicked me in the back several times.

The man who was tying me up asked his friends, 'Hey, comrades, what are we going to do with him? To the field behind the village?'

'I don't know,' said another, after a short pause, 'I've no idea.'

'If you ask me,' said another, 'we should take him to the field behind the village.'

That phrase 'the field behind the village' meant the killing ground. I'd never been to it but I'd heard about it when I was company leader. There were two main killing grounds for our village. The bigger one was near the Re-education Centre, the former pagoda. When people were taken to the Re-education Centre and later killed, their deaths were reported to the regional Angkar Loeu. But if they wanted to kill one of us for some reason without reporting it, they took the victim to the field behind the village.

The field was about three kilometres away, a patch of open

ground with a small wood at one end. When we went to work, we passed it and we could see from a distance three large open pits from which came the most horrific smell. We could have gone there if we'd wanted to, since they were intended to keep us in terror. But nobody I knew ever went. There was always a flock of crows around.

As I listened to the conversation of my captors, all sense seemed to drain from me. I couldn't understand anything. Blood flowed from my gum where my tooth was broken. I tried to swallow as much of it as I could, thinking that this would conserve my energy. I spat out the broken tooth.

'Listen,' said one of them, 'we've no right to take him to that place unless we get permission from his unit leader. Otherwise we'll be in big trouble.'

'Nobody will know about it, except the four of us, if we keep our mouths shut,' said the guy behind me.

'But we can't fool the Angkar. They're very smart. Sooner or later one of us would tell them.'

'OK, stop arguing. We'll take him to his leader,' said the one who was holding my arms. Then he pushed me forward. 'Come on, you, move.'

They continued hitting me with their fists on the way back to the village. A few people were awake in the sleeping quarters. They were shocked at the state I was in and roused their neighbours, pointing at me and wondering what it was I had done. One of the reconnaissance team went to the unit leader and spoke to him. Then he and his companions left.

It was about two in the morning. I was thrown on the ground with my arms still tied, and Comrade Khann began to ask me what I had done. I told him that I was caught while walking near the cassava field, but he did not believe me and began searching my pockets. He found a small piece of cassava. I was genuinely surprised to see it. He asked me where I had got it from. I told him I had found it during my walk.

'Listen, there's no point in denying what you've done,' said Comrade Khann, 'we've got quite enough evidence. Cassavas have been disappearing every night, and now you've been caught.'

Then he got up from his hammock and kicked me in the ribs. Instinctively I rolled with the blow, but I was too weak to avoid the impact altogether. He came at me again and aimed another kick in the same place. This time I took the full force and fell immediately unconscious.

I was woken by a cold breeze. My mouth and ribs were still hurting, and I tried to move my hands and feet in order to curl up and keep warm. My right foot felt heavy. Opening my eyes with great pain, I discovered that my foot had been chained to a tree.

The sky was clear, showing all the stars and a half moon. From its position I reckoned it was around four in the morning. I was outside the unit camp. I was shivering. My shirt had been removed, I didn't know when. I was wearing only a pair of shorts. I closed my eyes and tried to sleep, but I was too cold. The pain in my mouth and ribs was excruciating. I began to recall the conversation of the four men. Probably they were waiting till daylight to take me to the field behind the village. I tried to resist the pain. I was very scared.

The sky began to glow in the east. I began thinking about my sisters. Did they know what had happened to me? And if I was killed, what would happen to them? Mealea had already been executed for criticizing the revolution. Now that I had been found out, perhaps they would decide to destroy my whole family. And then I thought of Comrade Khann, and how he had been turned down by Comrade Ran, and how she had asked to marry me. Comrade Khann had every reason for taking his revenge. I was at his mercy.

As it started to grow light, Comrade Khann came towards me with three other men. He was armed with a *parang* and another man was carrying a spade. I was going to be killed.

Unlocking the chain from the tree, Comrade Khann threw down my stinking shirt and told me to put it on as it was time to go to work. The chain was still padlocked to my foot; he held the other end. I tried to stand up, but failed. He pulled the chain hard, and repeated the order to go. The second time, I managed to get to my feet and walk. We set out in the direction of the killing ground.

It was not yet light as we went across the fields. At this time of day, everyone would be getting ready for the regular morning roll call, and so we did not meet anyone on our way. I was limping in front, dragging the chain. There was no conversation, just a series of orders barked out in my direction: hurry up, left, right, get a move on. The sun had not yet dispersed the mist, so I could only just make out the small patch of woodland which marked the mass graves.

We walked a couple of kilometres. I knew something of the pleasure that they took in killing people. When we were working on the Ream Kun dam, the men from the reconnaissance team used to come and sit near us, so that we could not help overhearing their conversation. They would boast about how somebody screamed and cried for mercy before he died. They said that after people had had their livers cut out they could do nothing – they couldn't talk, only blink their eyes. They said that fat people had small livers and thin people had big livers. They would sit there laughing together as they exchanged these details. 'You're wrong,' one of them would say, 'I had a fat guy last night and his liver was really big.' And I once heard one of them say that when you put human liver in the frying pan it jumps.

When we were within a kilometre or so of the open pits, they suddenly told me to stop and went a little distance away from me to talk. I couldn't hear their conversation, which lasted about five minutes. When they returned, they told me to start walking again to the right. We were not going to the open pits after all. I had no idea where we were going.

A quarter of an hour later we came to a field. I did not know it. There were several grave mounds, some of them new, some old. Comrade Khann tied my chain to a small tree, took the spade from one of his companions and threw it down in front of me.

'Here is your pen!' he said. 'Go ahead and dig the ground.'

I understood, and I began digging my own grave – began immediately to avoid being hurt. Two of the men left, and Comrade Khann and the fourth man sat on the low dike at the edge of the field, chatting and laughing together just out of earshot. The spade they had given me was made from a piece of beaten oil drum. It didn't work well and anyway I was extremely weak. At around noon, when I had finished digging a grave about half a metre deep, Comrade Khann came up to me and told me to lie in it. He asked me whether I felt comfortable or not. I made no reply. It was slightly small for me. He told me to make it a bit wider. When I had done that, by about three o'clock, I was told to rest. I sat on the edge of the grave, looking into it and thinking I would be inside it in a minute or two. A piece of cooked cassava was given to me. I was not hungry.

'Hey,' said the leader, 'why don't you eat? Is it because you've had too many cassavas in the last few days?' He was smiling and he slapped my back.

'No, comrade . . . I'm very hungry indeed.' I started eating the cassava and continued staring into the grave. I used to like cassavas. This one tasted like rotten wood.

In the distance I saw the two men returning, with three others. They were carrying something which looked like a log, wrapped in a piece of old matting. I thought it must be a corpse. They dropped it on the ground near the grave, and one of them said with a smile, 'You won't be lonely here. We've found a friend for you.'

He unwrapped the matting. There lay the body of Comrade Chhith, the boy who had asked the meaning of the word equality. I closed my eyes.

'Come on,' they said, 'look at your friend.'

They weren't smiling now. They rolled the body into the grave with their feet.

The unit leader walked towards me with his *parang* in his hand and ordered me to fill in the grave. While I did so, I had an intense feeling that something was about to hit the back of my neck and that I would fall into the grave. Dusk was falling as I finished. I was taken back to the unit camp, my right foot still chained. I was tethered to the support of the barn and given a small bowl of rice soup.

That night the unit meeting took place as usual, and after the regular long speech, Comrade Khann came to my case. A boy from the reconnaissance team was sent to fetch me. He unlocked my chain from the pillar and told me to crawl to the meeting. I crawled before the comrades like a dog. Comrade Khann said, 'This person is a thief of the Angkar. He has broken the rules of the commune by stealing cassavas from the field. However, I am very glad to say that the co-operative leader told us not to put him away. However, he will have to work very hard in the next few days.' He paused a moment and then turned to me. 'Now, Comrade Meth, come on and address the meeting and tell us what you want us to do if you are caught again, or if you do anything else to destroy the discipline of the Angkar.'

I stood up and said, 'Friends and comrades, this is a very great opportunity for me to re-educate myself in the way our Angkar requires. If I do anything wrong again, please banish me from the Angkar's territory. Friends and comrades, do not emulate my behaviour.'

At the end of the meeting I was allowed back to the sleeping quarters. As I lay down and closed my eyes, the body of Comrade Chhith reappeared before me with a horrible vividness. He had been beaten to death; the back of his neck was bruised and his skull smashed in. I lay there for about an hour thinking about him. Then suddenly two boys crept in under my mosquito net. 'Comrade Meth, we're very hungry now. Could you take us to the cassava field?'

'Go away from me, will you?' I replied angrily. 'Leave me alone.'

'Come on, nobody will know. You just have to take us there and watch us while we do the digging.'

'No,' I replied, 'I said leave me alone. If you don't, I'll go and tell the leader now.'

'OK, we'll leave you now if you don't want to – but please don't tell the leader what we have said.'

The next day my company leader said to me: 'Oh, Meth, you're lucky you didn't go with those two boys last night. If you had, you wouldn't be here now.'

The immediate effect of my experiences was to make me ashamed in front of my friends and to withdraw from all company. I don't know why I should have felt so ashamed. Before I was exposed as a thief, I used to be held up as an example of hard work and revolutionary potential by my company and unit leaders. Now I worked hard to recover my lost position. Try as they might, the Khmer Rouge could spot no fault in my labour. I worked in continual terror, and as I toiled away I often wondered why I had not been killed. Was it because I had previously been a good worker? Or had Comrade Ran's mother intervened with the co-operative leader on my behalf? And if she had done so, why had she not also intervened to save my sister Mealea's life? These are questions I still ask myself.

Now the harvest season had come, and all the New People were happy at the size of the rice crop. However, as far as I could see it wouldn't last more than a couple of months.

At the co-operative meeting we were told of a new project, another work-field, another dam! The place was called Tram Kang;

it was very near a Re-education Centre, and the water it would hold would be for the use of the inmates. We were advised to be well behaved because the Re-education Centre would be under our noses.

TWENTY-THREE
Re-education – what it meant

Looking back, I can see that the Khmer Rouge were quarrelling among themselves, and their power was now in decline. At the time, none of this was clear. It wasn't just the lack of news. We simply didn't have the energy to think about what was happening, or the opportunity to discuss it. All we were thinking about was how to supplement our diet. When I saw a couple of mice near the new camp we were putting up in the rain and shouted out, everyone dropped their tools and chased after them. I ran too, but my ribs hurt too much and I gave up. In those days I had to use my yoke as a walking stick.

Comrade Khann watched us from his hammock. He was annoyed at this interruption of our work. He called the boy who had caught the mice over to his tent, confiscated them and gave them to Little Brother for his meal. Both Big and Little Brother were now eating with us, and the midnight feasts were much reduced. All the leaders in the work-field were beginning to join in the actual labour. They no longer sat on the dam and watched us. They worked – not hard, but more than they had done. I remember watching Comrade Khann after he had made two or three trips to the dam, leaning on his spade and recovering his breath. We dug until late at night, whatever the phase of the moon. And when we stopped for the evening meeting, Comrade Khann always repeated, 'Friends and comrades, work very hard. The Re-education Centre is under your very armpits.'

Actually, it was about a kilometre and a half from the camp but they took a detour every time we went to work in order to pass it. It was surrounded by ditches stuck with bamboo spikes. The huts for the inmates had no windows. We could hear the groans as we passed, and see the prisoners led out into the fields, chained together. They were forced to pull ploughs, and the Khmer Rouge followed them with whips or thorny canes. If they stumbled in the mud, the soldiers stamped on them and forced them to their feet. We averted our eyes as we passed.

At night as we returned from work we saw two or three prisoners, tied together, being led towards the open grave, which I never saw but often smelt when the wind was in the wrong direction.

The new routine gave us one day's rest in ten. There were meetings all morning. For the first time they began to admit that we were short of food and we were told to work hard because of the shortage rather than because we were people of the revolution. We were working on another of these hopeless reservoirs. The Khmer Rouge were obsessed with rice, and they knew one thing about it – that you needed water. They were obsessed with water, but they hadn't the faintest notion of how to control it. We could have been growing vegetables or sweetcorn. We could have been raising livestock. But they had no notion beyond meeting the needs of the top leadership. We could have been replacing all the fruit trees which had been destroyed in the war. If we'd had nets we could have gone to the Tonle Sap and got some fish. It wasn't like the kind of famine I had read about in Africa, where the weather goes wrong and people starve. The weather was doing exactly what it had always done. The famine was entirely man-made.

Battambang area had been famously fertile before the war. The rice production could feed the entire population of the country. The problem of the peasants in Cambodia had never been creating enough food – it had been a matter of getting a decent price for the food, or questions like ownership of the land. Now all the land belonged to the Angkar, and we were starving.

If the Angkar, which had far more land in the region than it could use, had allowed us one hour a day to dig our own plots and grow our own crops, we could have supplemented our diet to a critical degree. Even with this system of moving from place to place, we could, within three or four months, have been harvesting beans, gourds, sweet potatoes, sweetcorn, cucumbers, loofahs, lettuce, even tomatoes. Those who have never been to a tropical country cannot imagine how quickly seeds germinate and produce fruit.

But if you imagine how quickly mung beans germinate in a centrally heated house, that will give you some idea. If you let the sprouts grow for two months, that kind of green bean will produce edible leaves like spinach, or young pods like French beans. If the pod is allowed to ripen in the third month, you can boil the ripened seed like a mushy pea, or germinate it and begin the cycle again. In Cambodia, every vegetable seed will germinate within a week. You could be eating pumpkin flowers within a month. The only things that took a long time to grow were fruits. But they were an amazing capital investment. I never saw the Khmer Rouge planting fruit.

The weird thing about this peasant revolution was that none of the accumulated wisdom of the peasants went into it. When I was a child I hadn't the slightest idea about cultivation. I learnt from Chan and Long on our estate. And I learnt more without trying than after all this effort by the Khmer Rouge. Even when I was a leader I never heard a discussion about agriculture. It was as if the peasants who ruled us despised the fact that they had been peasants. They were choked with power. They had turned their backs on everything they knew for the sake of politics about which they knew nothing. And because they forced us to pretend that we knew nothing, nobody in the society knew anything. If a skilled engineer looking at what they were doing had laid down his spade and offered to design a wonderfully functioning reservoir, he would have been killed for not being a peasant. The whole society was working at maximum – and brutally enforced – inefficiency.

So it was that on the afternoons of our days off we would go out into the fields to forage. In the most fertile region of one of the most fertile countries in the world, we were looking for any little creature in any little hole. The only thing I found that afternoon was a heap of maggots feeding off the disintegrating corpses of a couple who appeared to have been killed for a sexual offence. There was underwear hanging on a tree nearby. I ran back to the camp, in terror, leaving my mattock behind me. Comrade Khann knew it was missing, but he didn't know it was my fault.

When any New People from our village arrived at the camp, it was like receiving a letter from home. We learnt something had gone wrong. Most of the leaders, and many of the Old People, had disappeared. Comrade Huon and his family vanished overnight. The new Khmer Rouge were from the south-west region. They accused the old leaders of starving the people and of massacres. But they themselves were tougher than anything we had yet come across.

TWENTY-FOUR
To the bamboo jungle

A new decision was announced. A group of fifty young men was to be taken to the jungle to work with the soldiers cutting bamboo for the fishing co-operative. I was chosen to be part of it. We were supposed to be able-bodied men, a description that didn't fit me at all. I thought Comrade Khann was merely trying to dispose of me, and I was terrified at the thought of working with soldiers. It might be like what we had seen of the Re-education Centre.

I was surprised to see they had laid on trucks for our journey, which took about sixteen hours, with frequent stops. We went through the deserted city of Pursat, whose ruined buildings were covered with moss and fungi, and picked up supplies from the communal food store. The place was stuffed with rice, some of the sacks had been stamped with Chinese lettering and were presumably marked for export. There was no one around except the soldiers. I looked at the coconut palms, which were laden with fruit, and wondered why on earth nobody had picked it. The city park was covered in weeds.

As we turned off Route Five we passed a convoy of ox carts laden with rice making its way towards the mountains. The road was bumpy. Night fell and I dozed off. We hadn't eaten all day. In the early hours of the morning we arrived in Learch, at the junction of the Pursat and Preah Neang Oray rivers. We lit fires, cooked our food and tried to get what sleep we could. With a single flick of my hand I could have killed at least twenty mosquitoes.

Next morning we set off on foot into the Cardamom mountains. Either side of the track was thickly planted with sweet cassava. Some looked as if it should have been harvested long ago. There was dew on the vegetation, and I washed my face in it. Deer were calling through the mist. We passed through alternating areas of thick forest and cassava fields. The stilted huts in the fields were empty and there was no one on the track. After half a day's walk we reached an area of thick bamboo by the bank of the Oray river. Here we made our camp.

It was very beautiful. Upstream were rapids and a waterfall. The river was about nine metres wide, with deep banks overhung with roots. On the far bank the bamboo was in flower, and I remembered my parents telling me that when the bamboo was in flower it meant there would be a famine. They said that when the flowers produced seeds you could boil and eat them, but that it took at least two years for the flower to seed. I thought, too, about the story of the Thais throwing coins into the thicket, and I could see why the Cambodians would have had to cut the stems down in order to get at the coins. The thicket was tightly packed and had sharp thorns from top to bottom of the stem.

We each had to cut thirty pieces a day, at least six metres long. We were given a *parang* each and told not to cut the thickets nearest the camp. We had to hack a path into the jungle. I made a kind of ramp out of a branch, climbed up to the top of a thicket and began stripping off the thorns, working downwards. We were barefoot and for the first week we suffered terribly from cuts. Soon our clothes were in tatters.

We began to suffer from malaria, cholera and diarrhoea. When people died, the soldiers burnt their bodies and used the ash as fertilizer on the vegetable patch where they grew cucumbers and cabbages, which we then ate. There were ten soldiers in our group. Comrade Chhoeun was in his thirties, the rest were no more than fifteen. They had one gun between them. They never came with us to cut the bamboo, so some people were tempted to escape.

However, the first people who tried were caught and brought before the evening meeting. Comrade Chhoeun made a speech in which he told us the Angkar was everywhere. The only place there was no Angkar was under the ground. These people had tried to escape the Angkar. In a few minutes they would have their wish.

The prisoners watched the comrades in silence. Then they were dragged off into the jungle. When the soldiers came back they were carrying bloodstained sticks and *parang*s. Nobody else tried to escape.

We took the bamboo by raft, a hundred sticks at a time, down the river to Learch. It was suspected that people were using these trips as an opportunity to steal sweet cassava from the abandoned fields along the way, so when it was the turn of my co-operative to make the journey a soldier was detailed to come with us. Each of us made his own raft, and on the day we set out the river was high.

The view was fantastic with overhanging trees. Kingfishers dived for their food. Large lizards fled from the bank at our approach. I looked down into the clear waters at the shoals of fish. They made me hungry. I took off my stinking clothes and washed them from the raft. There were ten of us in our flotilla – I was towards the back. On the first raft were my friend Phath, who shared my mosquito net because he didn't have one, and the soldier. To pass the time, people hummed the revolutionary songs they so despised, and tapped out a rhythm with bamboo.

We all had our rations with us, and cans like paint tins to cook them in. I shouted to the soldier for permission to eat. We had brought firewood but the soldier told us we would have to cook on board the rafts. We had to be at Learch by dusk.

I cut a piece of bamboo about thirty centimetres long, chopped it in half and laid it so as to make a raised platform and protect the raft. Then I took out my home-made tinderbox, which was a segment of bamboo filled with kapok. To get a spark, I used china against iron, but the kapok was damp and it took me half an hour to make fire. I supported the pot in exactly the way my father had done on the first trip to the estate. A friend punted up alongside to cadge a light. My pot contained a little rice, bamboo shoots and green edibles. People were making the most of the occasion, over-taking each other and begging tobacco from the soldier. We all had our fires going, and we were trying to pass the cheroots from raft to raft.

The current became stronger, and the raft started moving faster than I had expected. I'd been concentrating on the food, and thinking how much better it would be if I only had a little fish. Now I turned round and saw rapids ahead. I took my pole and went forward to steer. There were rocks in the water. I was approaching the white foam and I was steering from the wrong end. I'd never done this kind of thing before.

I tried to keep the raft away from the rapids, but it swung round, sending the pot and the cooking fire into the river. I was too weak. I couldn't control the thing. The raft slammed against the rocks. I steadied myself with the pole, but the ties had broken and I sank straight down through the bamboo. It happened extremely fast, and I struggled to swim away from the sharp bamboo. There was another raft coming up behind me, also in difficulties. It was too late, and the bamboo gashed my right hip.

I'd never even swum before. I couldn't move my leg. So I floated downstream until the current brought me to the bank, some 450 metres down. I caught hold of a creeper and steadied myself, and as I did so the thought struck me: I had lost the bamboo, the property of the Angkar. How was I going to explain it to the leader of the camp? He would be able to accuse me of anything he liked.

It turned out that three other rafts had been lost, but although we were all injured none of us had drowned. We were washed up on the opposite side of the river to Learch. I'd not only lost my raft and my meal, but also my clothes, which had been spread out to dry, my spoon, my tinderbox and my *parang*. All I had left were my shorts and *kramar*, which I tied around my waist. Luckily, Phath had taken the tarpaulin and the mosquito net, and he had got through the rapids. Luckily, too, my companions had managed to save a *parang*. There was no track. We had to hack our way through the jungle, limping along, wondering how we would explain ourselves.

They were waiting for us at Learch. It was around midnight, and they ferried us across to the village. It was lucky that we had been accompanied by a soldier, though he was in as much trouble as we were. When we returned to the camp, Comrade Chhoeun warned us that next time we would not be forgiven.

Supplies had been arriving once every ten days at Learch, from where we collected them. But now the truck had been requisitioned by the military. There were to be no more supplies. When our food ran out, the soldiers in the camp were in the same boat as us. As we went to cut the bamboo, we searched the jungle for fungi, leaves, shoots and wild tubers. Quite a few people died from eating the wrong thing.

Incredibly enough, the soldiers made no attempt to harvest the sweet cassava. It had been planted by other soldiers, but there may have been some reason why it was unwise to touch it. As the wild vegetation grew scarce, the New People went out every night to steal the cassava. Phath, who was still sharing my mosquito net, went out a couple of times before asking me whether I wanted to accompany him. I had sworn that I would never do anything against the Angkar again, but hunger won the argument.

When we got to the field, there were three men already working there. We hid until they had gone. There were fireflies, and there were noises in the undergrowth. We were waiting our turn. Probably the wild boar were waiting their turn to steal. When we got the cassava we ate some of it raw, and buried the rest in a marked spot for later use. That night the raw cassava kept me awake.

Still no rations came, and foraging was added to our official duties. We found snakes and leaves and wild tubers. Once again people died from trying the wrong mushrooms. The soldiers were foraging too, but nobody asked them why they didn't dig up the cassava. Then Comrade Chhoeun went off to Pursat to find out what was going on. His authority was delegated to one of the boys.

A message arrived at our mosquito net that someone wanted to see Phath. He went off and shortly afterwards I could hear him being beaten up. I could guess what he'd been accused of, and I began to wonder what he might say under torture. The next day when Comrade Chhoeun returned we could hear Phath screaming again, louder than ever. We had just got back from work, and I had no idea how long this had been going on.

At the evening meeting, Comrade Chhoeun told us that the rations were coming. With great difficulty he had found a truck and some food and it was on its way. He went on for quite a long time saying that the food was on its way, and that there would be less of it in the future. While this was happening Phath was brought before the meeting, limping and pale. Comrade Chhoeun told us he had been seen digging cassava and had confessed to having done so twice before. At this point I wondered what else he had confessed.

The next stage was unusual. Comrade Chhoeun asked the meeting whether we wanted Phath disposed of. Not a hand was raised. Then he asked how many people wanted him kept but made to work extra hard. After a brief pause, the soldier who had been on the disastrous raft trip asked for permission to speak.

He made a stirring speech, with strong gestures and a powerful voice. He said that Phath had been an excellent worker, he had never gone off sick since we had been in the jungle and that he had always strictly obeyed the rules of the Angkar. This was exactly the kind of person the Angkar needed. 'If he doesn't mend his ways,' said the soldier, 'the banana is already in our hands. We can squash it, we can eat it any time we want. It's as easy as eating a banana to have him put away.' It was a great speech. The piece about squashing the banana had been vigorously acted out, and we applauded with real enthusiasm. Comrade Chhoeun looked put out. He tried to interrupt the applause, but we wouldn't let him. This was the first time any of the soldiers had publicly backed our side, and it meant a great deal to us.

Phath was released and nothing more was said about the matter. Except that as he went to sleep that night he whispered, 'Don't worry – I didn't tell them anything.'

TWENTY-FIVE
Down from Rattan mountain

The manner of the soldiers changed very rapidly. They looked anxious. They sat away from the camp, earnestly discussing something. We didn't know what. They had admitted there had been a failure over the rations – and such an admission was something new. On the other hand they said it was our fault for not working hard enough. Previously they had been very precise over our work quotas. But now they no longer bothered to count the bamboo as we brought it in. Their minds were not on our work.

A third of our group had died, and replacements came, including a friend of mine from the co-operative. As we worked in the bamboo thickets we were able to take breaks and chat. You could hear footsteps several metres away. If anybody seemed to be coming we sang revolutionary songs and swung our *parang*s at the nearest bit of bamboo.

My friend, Eng, had a lot of news. Things had got worse. A lot of Khmer Rouge had come up from the south-west region and seemed to have ousted the comrades in the north. Many of the old leaders had been executed. Others had fled, and their families had been wiped out – including the babies. Security had been tightened. Spies not more than twelve years old had been planted everywhere. The paddy-dikes we had built had been destroyed because the new leaders said they were in the wrong place. And the last dam had been left unfinished. Comrade Huon had fled with his whole family and formed a resistance group against the new arrivals. They lived somewhere near the Tonle Sap and they kept raiding the co-operative for food. The Khmer Rouge were as savage with each other as they had been with us. Two captured members of the resistance forces had been executed and their heads stuck on poles at the end of the village.

The New People, said Eng, were petrified. A whole group of them had arrived from Svay Rieng, the region on the border with Vietnam. For some reason this group was being treated extremely badly. They were segregated from everybody else and they were killed on the slightest provocation. Most of the units I had known had been sent up to the highland areas, and the stores with them. The Khmer Rouge are falling apart now, he said.

Every night, somewhere in the jungle, we could hear trucks passing. At dawn they returned. You could hear the difference between the two noises, the laden trucks struggling uphill, and then returning light. But it was hard for me to guess what was happening. I didn't even know where I was on the map.

Comrade Chhoeun told us we had almost enough bamboo now. (It never occurred to me at the time, but presumably they had lost control of the fishing commune to the resistance forces.) A party of ten of us was instructed to go to Rattan mountain, to cut rattan. We needed baskets for the workers on a new dam on Tuk Puss mountain – Boiling Water mountain.

I was always suspicious when a few of us were taken away from the work-field. Worse, we were told we would have to fend for ourselves on the journey because rations were so short. I was in despair. I thought we would never survive.

Along the narrow track through the jungle, we looked out for anything edible and at midday we were given time off to look for tubers and bamboo shoots. But we were leaving the best bamboo area, and as the path grew steeper the trees grew thicker and there was nothing on the forest floor except dead leaves. There were no streams, and when we grew thirsty the two soldiers accompanying us cut a kind of creeper. Water dripped from the cut, and we held the creepers to our mouths. Or we drank the liquid from the pitcher plants, which tasted urinous and was full of dead insects. The soldiers had no rations either, but they were good at finding wild sugarcane, tubers and small fruit. We passed several abandoned camps where the charcoal burners had been. The ground beneath us changed from clay to sand to rock. The large trees had great, spreading, spaghetti-like root systems. Where they had fallen over they left large bare patches of rock beneath them.

At dusk, we pitched our camp at the foot of Rattan mountain. There was a green stream, whose water mixed in our cooking pots with various green shoots we had found made a very green supper indeed. At the evening meeting, the team leader told us we would have to leave very early the next morning; we were to stick together for fear of getting lost, and for fear of meeting the forces who guarded the Thai border. We hadn't realized we were near the border.

As I was sharpening my *parang* the next morning, a strange-looking man appeared out of the mist. He was immensely muscular, with a tattooed chest, long hair tied in a pony-tail with a red ribbon, and very long earlobes. He wore a black uniform and a rattan bracelet. He had a bow in his hand and a bamboo quiver full of arrows. I'd heard about the Khmer Loeu, the mountain tribes, but I'd never met one. He had a deep, gruff voice but he used the same language as the Khmer Rouge. He was to be our guide.

He climbed Rattan mountain with extraordinary agility, as if he had suction pads on his hands and feet. We followed with difficulty, and as the mist dispersed we saw monkeys, black and pink hoopoes, woodpeckers, paradise fly-catchers with long white tails, and there were tiny blue and yellow birds about the size of your thumb. There were hornbills in the treetops. The trees were hung with ferns and brightly coloured orchids. Leeches came at us over mushrooms the size of dinner plates. I would have picked the mushrooms, had they not been black and yellow.

We heard the waterfall a long way off, and when we got there the scene was astonishing. The stream fell about sixty metres, and there were rainbows in the spray. The pool was shallow and carved out of solid, smooth rock. Behind the fall was a curtain of moss and fern. We sat down and sharpened our *parang*s in the cold water.

The Khmer Loeu told us we would increase our chances of finding rattan by fanning out over the mountain. We had to get at least fifteen lengths each, then we were to meet up again by the waterfall. Our group consisted of four people – there were no soldiers with us. As we climbed up through the jungle, we found that all the plants were covered in tiny thorns. I had two pieces of bark with me, which I threw on the ground with each pace forward to protect my bare feet. As we went, we shouted every five minutes to stay in contact with the other groups. Sometimes we confused messages with echoes.

Rattan is a creeper which grows along big trees or on the floor of the jungle. It is covered in long needles. If you get one in your skin it's easily broken off, and you have to dig it out with a larger thorn. It can grow up to forty-five metres long. We found a good patch of it, and began by clearing the lengths growing on the forest floor. Then we attacked those on the trees, but they were hard to pull down.

I climbed a tree in order to cut the rattan from the top. It took a long time and when I got to the top, I found some fruit, hard like quince and with a bitter-sweet taste. It was difficult to chew as I'd lost several teeth but I was convinced it was not poisonous. Monkeys had been at it. I picked all that the monkeys had left, wrapped them in my *kramar* and slung them over my shoulder. There were four or five stems of rattan to be cut down. When I had finished, I shared some of the fruit with my companions. It was quite a little party, and we had forgotten to keep shouting to the other groups.

Now I called out. Nobody replied. We all shouted. The echoes rang around. We began to grow anxious. We weren't at all sure how to get back to the waterfall. We kept listening for it, but the wind confused us.

One of my friends said, 'If we don't know how to get back, and we're lost, why don't we all escape to Thailand? It can't be far.'

I objected. From what I'd learnt from Eng, anybody who fled would have his whole family wiped out. But two of our company had no family left anyway. One of them said it would be better to die from a single bullet through the chest than to be tortured and starved to death.

The more they talked about it, the angrier these two became. And when we said goodbye to them they were crying.

They set off in the direction of Thailand, as they thought. We wished them good luck. But now we were scared because we'd have to explain when we got back what had happened to our companions. We stripped the rattan of its thorns, pulling the lengths between two saplings, and tying up our bundles of fifteen each. We set off back to the waterfall, shouting to the other groups, but making no contact. After an hour we found we had come full circle and were back where we had eaten the fruit.

We tried again. It was getting towards dusk. Bats came out, owls began to hunt, and there was a high-pitched whining of beetles. Finally, we came on a track that looked as if something had been pulled along it. We didn't know whether to turn left or right. We followed it and came to the place where they'd cut the rattan. Immediately we turned round and hurried back towards the waterfall. When we could hear the water, and the voices of the other groups, we began shouting as if we'd just lost our companions.

The Khmer Rouge were waiting for us, and when we told them we had been separated from our companions they looked very anxious. We said we'd split into two groups in order to get the rattan, and somehow they had got lost. We lay on the smooth rocks by the pool, waiting for the others. Now the team leader was panicking. He knew that if he came back with two men missing he would get it in the neck. I offered the remainder of the fruit around. The team leader asked if I had any more, and when I had to refuse him, he turned away as if it was a put-down.

The waterfall after dark looked fantastic. The rainbows had gone. The mist and spray gave a soft focus to the whole scene. I lay on my back and watched the moon rise. The bats and insects swarmed overhead.

The group leader was pacing up and down the rocks. I thought it was quite likely he would be executed when we got back. He asked the Khmer Loeu what he should do. But we had waited so long, and still the missing men had not returned. It was time to get back to our bivouacs.

When we did so – which was quite difficult in the dark – I set about preparing another slimy green dinner. The team leader came up to me and asked again about the missing men. He handed me a small polythene bag of tobacco, and a cheroot which he had rolled.

'Comrade Meth,' he said, in a shrivelled voice, 'if there's anything you can remember about them before they left, come and tell us.' He paused and looked in the pot. 'By the way, have you eaten yet?' he said. 'We've got a lot of cassava. Come and eat with us.'

I wondered where they had got the cassava from.

Over supper he asked me if I knew anything about the relatives of the two men. I told him they'd all died of disease last year. I was going rather beyond what I knew. He pleaded for more information but I had none.

When I got back to my bivouac, there was a strong smell of rank weeds. I couldn't think what it was until I found my cooking pot. The soup had reduced to a repulsive purée.

I couldn't sleep. I took out my new tinderbox and tried to make fire. The tobacco was very welcome, and when I got a cheroot going my thoughts drifted. I found myself unexpectedly happy about my three little brothers' deaths, because I realized that if they were still alive it would be unbearable to watch them struggling through the famine. They had escaped. Whether my two colleagues had escaped I didn't know.

I wondered why the Khmer Rouge were fighting each other, and why their manner had changed so suddenly. I thought of all that I had been through, astonished that I was still alive.

We got back to the camp the next day. The morning after, the two soldiers who had accompanied us were discovered to have gone missing. Comrade Chhoeun told us the news and said that they wouldn't get far from the Angkar. 'The Angkar,' he said, 'has a thousand eyes, like a pineapple. Nobody can escape it.'

The next bit of his speech was most surprising. 'Tomorrow,' he said, 'this work camp will be dispersed. Your co-operative leaders want you back for the harvest. Friends and comrades, thank you all very much for your co-operation here. I shall never forget your hard work. I will report it to the highest echelons of the Angkar.'

He had said 'Thank you.' It was inexplicable.

The soldier who had saved Phath's life asked a question. 'What about the bamboo and rattan we have collected? Are we going to bring it along with us?'

Comrade Chhoeun told us to pile the bamboo on the river bank. As for the rattan, if we wanted to take some with us to our co-operatives, we would be welcome to do so.

It took us all day to pile the bamboo. I thought, nobody's going to collect it – it'll stay here for ever; they'd never wanted it. They'd just been keeping us occupied between the rice seasons. Apart from the Ream Kun dam, none of our other projects had come to anything either. Everything had been left unfinished, and some of the work had already been undone.

There was no meeting that night. We built a bonfire by each hut. We were excited to be going home. People took the bamboo and began whittling chopsticks for their families. Others made toy baskets as presents. They made walking sticks. They carved spoons. Phath was sitting alone. He had nobody to give anything to. He kept chopping up bamboo and burning it on his own little fire. He looked as if he didn't want to talk to anyone.

Comrade Chhoeun had one more surprise for us. At a brief meeting the next morning, he thanked us once again and told us we were to find our own way back. He told us we could take some rattan if we wanted it. Then the Khmer Rouge picked up their shoulder bags and walked off into the jungle in the direction of Rattan mountain. We watched them, speechless. We looked at each other. Then back at the disappearing figures.

They didn't turn around. They didn't wave goodbye. They just strode out of our lives. And I heard a little voice whisper in my ear: Hey, come back, you bastards; don't leave me here in the middle of nowhere; get me back to where you took me from!

TWENTY-SIX
The boy who killed his family

Everyone started talking at once. They'd left us without passes, so how were we going to get from one co-operative to the next? We could be accused of spying. They might think we belonged to the resistance forces. It was years since we had had anything like an identity document, and we absolutely depended on the Khmer Rouge to vouch for our status.

There were four people from my co-operative, and we decided we must forge a pass. But we'd never seen what one looked like. We went into the abandoned headquarters. There was a pile of burnt papers in the middle of the room, but fortunately I found the charred remains of a document authorizing a Khmer Rouge to go down to Prey Svay for rations. There was a stub of pencil stuck under the roof, and there was a piece of paper which had been screwed up and shoved into the thatch. We smoothed it out and I sharpened the pencil with my *parang*.

It felt very odd holding a pencil. It seemed far too thin for my hand. I would have been more at home with a spade between the fingers. Very slowly I wrote:

PASS

The holders of this pass, Comrade Meth, Comrade Phath, Comrade Eng and Comrade Tha, are permitted to return to co-operative 102, having finished their tasks in the bamboo camp in the Learch region. The above four comrades have permission to stay temporarily at any co-operative along the way. They are to be helped with directions and food, as far as you are able.

From the leader of the bamboo camp
Learch village,
Comrade Chhoeun

We gathered our few belongings and left.

Others in the team lived much nearer, and they had already gone. When we reached the first co-operative, number 506, we went straight into the headquarters. 'I don't understand,' said the leader, 'why *our* people from the bamboo camp haven't got a pass like you.'

'Well, Uncle,' I replied, quickly, 'our co-operative is further away. We had to ask Comrade Chhoeun.'

He believed me. The pass seemed to work.

At 802, the leader looked confused. He had never heard of the bamboo camp. He accused us of belonging to the resistance forces. We thought we were finished, but at that moment members of this co-operative arrived from the bamboo camp. I saw the guy I'd been with on Rattan mountain. 'Comrade,' I said to him, 'did you get the pass you asked Comrade Chhoeun to write for you?'

He understood. 'No,' he said, 'Comrade Chhoeun said our co-operative was so near we didn't need one.'

We breathed again. We were allowed to stay in the village. But we didn't sleep that night as we were convinced that we would be taken away. And indeed we saw other people being marched out of the silent village.

Eng's and my sisters were working at Tuk Puss mountain. We reached there the next evening, and we were back among our own people. They were in a terrible state. They stank worse than I did, and the teenagers were no more than skeletons. We got some food at last, and then went to the leader's hut. Everyone seemed scared of something, but they didn't tell us what. That evening, when we were billeted with the single male unit, all the company leaders, Comrade Khann among them, came up and asked us if we had seen any fighting along the way from the jungle.

I thought they must mean fighting between the Khmer Rouge groups.

It wasn't clear why Tuk Puss mountain, Boiling Water mountain, had been so named. There was no water, and not much mountain. It was, however, extremely hot. The ground had been scrubland and was now charred black. The wind stirred the ashes. It was a most desolate sight. The labourers' shacks were made of leaves. Water was rationed. You were allowed, once every ten days, to walk around three kilometres for an after-dinner wash. And this was the place they had chosen for another reservoir.

When I realized that Bopha and Sisopha were somewhere around, I wished I could stay with them. But by now the pass I had shown committed me to going back to the co-operative. I met Bopha briefly on the dam. She looked desperately thin and pale, and she told me she hadn't had a period for several months. I'd managed to steal a piece of cassava, and I gave this to her before hurrying on with my group.

Eng and Tha and I had all seen our sisters, and they were all desperately unhealthy. Phath, who had also stolen some cassava but had no one to give it to, kicked it along the sandy track. We were sad. He was sad and angry.

Prey Svay, which we had last seen as a busy village, was now deserted. We went from hut to hut, looking for the headquarters to show our pass. The body of an old man lay in the sun. He had recently been shot. We walked on. There was a tall column of smoke in the distance: they must have been fighting, but we hadn't heard anything.

At the far end of the village was a group of soldiers, fully armed. Before they could challenge us, we went up to them and presented our pass. They scrutinized it and asked if we had eaten yet. They directed us to the army canteen.

About twenty soldiers were eating at a long table. Each had a gun propped against his knee. They ate quickly, always on the alert, but they weren't interested in us. They were combat troops with something more important on their minds. They left as soon as they had finished their meal.

We took their places at the table, and a woman cleared the plates away. I noticed that the army ate off china. The woman came back with a vast bowl of steaming hot rice and a plate of fried pork. 'Help yourself,' she said, 'eat as much as you can.' And we did. It was wonderful, after three years of eating out of your hat, to hear the chink of spoons against crockery.

The woman came back, sweating with the heat of the kitchen, to take our plates. 'You won't be able to cross Route Five,' she said, 'the other side is occupied by the Vietnamese.'

We looked at each other.

'You see that smoke over there,' she said, pointing through the window and wiping her brow with the back of her hand, 'they've burnt the rice store. 'You'll have to stay the night here.'

She went back into the kitchen. None of us said anything. There had been no whisper of a Vietnamese invasion. I wondered how on earth they had got this far. And then a horrible thought occurred to me. I remembered how Meng had been given an enormous meal before being killed. Maybe we were prisoners. Maybe they were just about to put us to death.

Another group of soldiers came in. They talked between mouthfuls. I heard one say, 'I saw them running.'

'Why didn't you get them?'

'I wanted to let them get closer, but they didn't.'

One of them was a boy of thirteen or so. He said his foxhole had been too deep and he'd had to climb up his gun to get out. Another one had broken his spade, the ground was so hard. He was given a US-army folding spade. When they were almost finished, one of them said he would show us to our hut.

He slung his gun on his shoulder and we followed him across an open field. Then he pointed to a hut and said, 'OK, that's it. Go and sleep there.' It wasn't far but it seemed a long way. I thought he was going to mow us all down.

When we got into the hut, we didn't set up our nets. We were all very suspicious and afraid. We couldn't believe the Vietnamese had got this far, and we couldn't understand why we still hadn't heard any fighting. Why was nobody coming near the hut? We might get stuck between two front lines. What had happened to the inhabitants of the village?

Eng and Tha and I were in favour of going back to Tuk Puss. We were afraid that if we crossed the lines we would say goodbye to our sisters for good. But Phath told us not to be so stupid. If we tried to leave a military base, we might be accused of spying. They might follow us to Tuk Puss. But we were afraid to stay where we were. They might just kill us, or we might get caught up in the fighting.

Phath said, 'Look at it this way. Suppose what she said was true, and the Vietnamese are on the other side of Route Five. Why don't we surrender to them? Then we'll be free.'

Eng said, 'What if the Vietnamese think we're spies?'

Phath said, 'Just look at us. We're skeletons. They'll know we're innocent.'

We knew we were leaving our families behind, but we thought the only way to survive was to cross the lines. We waited till midnight. The base was absolutely quiet. We picked up our bundles and our *parang*s. Phath was more determined than ever. 'Let's agree,' he said, 'that if anything happens, we'll defend each other.' My heart thumped. We agreed, and crept out of the hut.

*Parang*s in hand, shoulders hunched, we ran along the base of the dike towards Route Five. Nothing was on the road. We dashed across and into a paddyfield full of tall rice. We were not far from the co-operative, but if we went straight there we might get shot. So we waited in the field, sitting back to back, scared the Khmer Rouge might be out looking for us.

At dawn we realized we were on our land. We had worked this field before. We walked to the co-operative, where a boy I knew jumped down from a tree and told us to halt. To our surprise there were no Vietnamese around. The boy told us the situation was bad, but we didn't ask him what he meant. He told us to hand over our *parang*s and wait while he reported to the co-operative leader.

A few minutes later we followed the boy to the village. The fields needed urgent harvesting. The birds were taking the crop and the wind was knocking it flat. I wondered where everyone was. Perhaps they had all died.

The Khmer Rouge were sitting at the edge of the village, all of them armed. They were all new faces except for one, a stout boy of fourteen, formerly one of the reconnaissance team. He was cooking for the soldiers. I handed the pass to the leader. He called over a man I recognized as one of the New People. He appeared to have been promoted.

'Who the hell is Comrade Chhoeun?' asked the leader.

'I don't know,' said the man. 'When these people were sent to cut bamboo, I wasn't around. Anyway, Comrade Huon was very secretive. He never told anybody anything.'

'Are you sure these people are from here?'

'Yes, comrade.'

'Well, I'll hold you responsible if anything goes wrong.'

The new leader in the single male unit had about fifty men in his group. The rest were up at Tuk Puss. Old People and New People harvested the rice side by side. There was a lot of muttering in the field, particularly from the Old People, against the new comrades from the south-west region. The rice was being sent straight to the highlands.

Meetings were reduced, and the Angkar was no longer mentioned. They talked instead about the Revolutionary Party. By day the soldiers guarded in the fields, afraid that the resistance forces would snatch us away. At night we didn't sleep in the village but in the fields. Security was very tight.

Eng had been right. Several of the Old People had fled to the Tonle Sap, and operations were being conducted against them. One day as we were harvesting the rice, we heard screams. A member of the resistance had been caught. He was brought back on a pole, like a pig to the slaughterhouse. Behind him came his son, Comrade Thol, the boy whom I had seen cooking for the soldiers. He had a thorny stick in his hand, with which he was whipping his father as they went. The father squealed in agony. His uniform was drenched with blood. They made their way towards the headquarters.

News soon spread that Comrade Thol had killed his whole family – his father first. His mother watched while he slit his throat. Then Comrade Thol killed his six-month-old sister. Finally he killed his mother.

He was rewarded with an AK–47, of which he was very proud. He came round the fields to show it off. And he had a sharp eye for mistakes. A boy from the Old People stepped on some paddy by mistake. Comrade Thol beckoned him away. A woman, also from the Old People, broke a sickle. Comrade Thol observed the incident. She never came back. A boy called Chhay who had a brother in the co-operative left Tuk Puss without a permit to come down and join his brother. When he arrived, Comrade Thol was asked to identify him. He refused to know anything about Chhay. The brother was working with us, weeping in the fields. He could do nothing to save Chhay, or he would be Comrade Thol's next victim.

Comrade Thol could have stared the fruit off a tree. He was a hero of the new Khmer Rouge.

TWENTY-SEVEN
Blacksmiths and bicycles

I became a blacksmith. Three of us had to pedal a fan to heat the charcoal in a clay furnace. We melted down old engines in a clay retort, poured the liquid metal into moulds and produced ploughs. The work was dangerous — we had bare hands and feet. But we were careful and had no accidents. The rations were better than anywhere else — we had to be in good shape to work, so they gave us plenty of rice, fish and dried meat. We worked in the mornings. In the afternoons we were given a net and sent to the Ream Kun reservoir to fish. The three of us used to make bonfires by the dam and eat the best of the catch before going back.

The worst job was distilling alcohol from plastic objects like containers or tarpaulins. The plastic was put in a metal ammunition case. A tiny hole was drilled in the top and a metal tube inserted, which led to a bottle. The case was sealed with clay and heated in the furnace. As the plastic melted it produced a vapour which condensed in the bottle. Minute quantities of liquid were produced in this way and used in lamps. One day the container exploded: two Khmer Rouge were injured and one killed outright, but our leaders continued to be very proud of this invention.

There were no meetings after dinner so we had more time to sleep. We went to bed at eight and woke at seven. It was great. But one night we were woken by several blasts. Nobody knew what was going on.

In the morning I was detailed to go with a team to Maung Russei, in the company of one soldier. We were given a cart and a pair of oxen. Our job was to collect scrap metal from the threshing mills, which they were dismantling. Before we reached the town, there was a small bridge. Now it was broken. Several buildings had been blasted and the area infirmary was demolished. I wondered where the patients had gone.

The soldier with us said that everything had been destroyed by the Vietnamese the night before. It was the first time the Khmer Rouge from our co-operative had mentioned the Vietnamese, and I didn't believe the soldier's story. As I was gathering scrap metal, the soldiers were doing some hurried digging behind the infirmary. I thought the Khmer Rouge had probably blown up the bridge themselves, to stop the Vietnamese advance, and killed off the people in the infirmary.

But I now believed that the Vietnamese were around. A couple of days later, the leader's radio was removed. All children and unhealthy teenagers were sent to Tuk Puss. The harvest was still not in. The forge was closed down, and we were told to bring along everything we could by bike.

But we had first to build our own bicycles. We went all round the empty huts of the co-operative, collecting broken bits and pieces left over from the days of Lon Nol. The contents of the Old People's houses were very interesting. Each had at least one sack of rice, good clothes they had got from us, sugar, salt, tape-recorders. Some had enormous stores of tinned food – US rations. It looked as if they had been preparing for some great event.

I found five old bicycles out of which I managed to construct one that worked. We made bamboo panniers to fit on the back, and now had five bikes in our team. The first day we took chickens; the second, chickens and eggs. On the third day, we made the journey on foot because we were driving the cattle. We had strict instructions not to lose any cattle or we would pay for it, but along the way one of the cows collapsed. It was about to give birth; we waited awhile. It was very difficult to keep the herd in one place: they were always trying to run away.

When the calf was born it was obviously going to be too weak for the journey. The soldier in our team decided to slit its throat, and give the meat to the commune canteen but as he cut it up, the workers in the fields around dropped their sickles and rushed up to beg for meat. When he refused to give them any, they just grabbed at the meat and ate it raw. The soldier was unarmed. He couldn't do anything about it. In next to no time the meat had all gone. The people returned to their sickles and went on with the harvest. The soldier looked really frightened. Whether he thought he would be found out for losing the calf, or whether it was the new experience of being disobeyed, I do not know.

He disappeared before the next trip. The new team leader said he wasn't coming with us that day because he had too much to do at the co-operative. As nobody had ever checked up on us, we didn't bother to ask for a pass. This time we were taking supplies of palm sugar. It was in the form of a thick treacle, almost as stiff as tar.

The way between the co-operative and Tuk Puss involved crossing the dried fields, pushing the loads over several dikes, and negotiating a sandy track by a reservoir, where it was impossible to ride and difficult to push a heavily laden bike. We got through the sand and up on to the dam. We were riding again when a boy ran out from behind a bush and aimed a gun at us. He told us to put our hands up, leave our stuff where it was, and walk forwards.

'We're in big trouble now,' said one of my friends.

We did as we were told, and were taken to a hut.

'Why did you cross our line?' asked the Khmer Rouge commander.

'We are taking palm sugar from our co-operative to Tuk Puss mountain,' I replied.

'Do you have any passes? Who is your leader?'

'He's not with us today. He has to sort out the rest of the stuff in the co-operative. He forgot to give us our passes.'

'Have you seen any Vietnamese troops along the way?'

'No, comrade,' said one of us. 'If there had been, we wouldn't have been able to get here.'

'Do you realize you crossed enemy lines when you passed Prey Svay? We had a skirmish with them about an hour ago.'

I wondered why I hadn't heard fighting.

'You must be spies,' said the commander. 'You have been sent to investigate our positions.'

'No, comrade, we are not,' I said. 'If we were, we would not have biked along the dam in full view. We are from co-operative 102.'

'You'll have to stay here with us until we find out who you are.'

I thought I was finished. I still couldn't understand how there'd been fighting and we hadn't heard a thing. The soldiers didn't look as though they'd been fighting. Their uniforms were neat and new. I could smell the fresh cloth. Their *kramar*s were new. Everything they had seemed to be new. And they were panicking. They seemed genuinely to believe that the Vietnamese had taken over Prey Svay.

I looked at my companions. They were as scared as I was. We

were told to go and sit under a tree. Then two soldiers went over to our bikes and checked the flasks. They poured the sugar out all over the ground. If it was too thick, they put sticks in and stirred it. They'd gone completely mad. Half the time they were looking out across the fields, expecting the Vietnamese to appear at any moment. Then they were back pouring the thick treacle over their feet and their trousers. The flies started going for them. They gave me one flask that they'd stirred. The rest they began to throw in all directions. In any other circumstances it would have been funny. Did they think we'd been hiding guns in the treacle?

Around sunset I heard the Khmer Rouge commander telling his men to retreat to the hills. He said the Vietnamese were going to attack tonight. Quite why he said this in front of us if we were spies, I don't know. What's more, nobody had brought him this news. He just decided that that was what was going to happen.

The soldiers set off in single file, taking us with them. As we were going up into the hills I could see groups of civilians with their bundles moving down towards Prey Svay. At midnight we arrived at a dam. All the way I had thought we would be shot at any moment. A guard was set to watch us. Nobody slept that night. The Khmer Rouge were talking within earshot but I was too terrified to pay attention to what they were saying.

At dawn we set off again. The soldiers were saying to each other that they were going to Phnom Dongrek. If so, they were going in the wrong direction. But the Dongrek mountains were a famous hideout for guerrillas.

Around mid-morning I finally saw the leader of Tuk Puss labour camp. I told him our problem and he spoke with the commander and secured our release. It was good of him to do this, because I realized from the direction he later went that he was on the run.

My companions and I split up immediately and went in search of our relatives. As I approached Tuk Puss, I saw the New People were raiding the fields for cassava, sweetcorn, plantain and unripe pumpkins. They were filling sacks and taking stuff to their huts. The Khmer Rouge paid no attention to this. They looked nervous, and were gathering at their headquarters, ready to go. They were armed to the teeth.

All the soldiers were going up the mountains. All the New People were coming down. Many had arrived at Tuk Puss, and were building bivouacs in the fields. They lit bonfires to roast cassava. They were fetching water. They seemed suddenly happy and afraid of nothing, although they were starved and the Khmer Rouge were still all around. It was as if one half of society had suddenly become invisible to the other, as if we inhabited different dimensions.

I went into Tuk Puss camp, and wandered from hut to hut in search of my sisters. There was no sign of life. The widows' unit, the widowers', the single males', the single females', the married quarters, the Khmer Rouge headquarters, the reconnaissance team hut – there was nothing in them, nothing at all. There wasn't a single garment lying around. There wasn't a broken spoon, there wasn't a sandal. If they'd taken a vacuum cleaner to the place they couldn't have done better.

In the canteen, there *was* something. The water jars had been smashed. The vast rice cauldrons made of melted down engines had been overturned, and the flies were at work on the thick crust of old food. The fire-pit was still warm. In the infirmary there was nothing, but in the nurses' quarters there was a piece of mirror. I looked at myself. This was a new experience. My cheeks were sunken. My skin was swarthy. I made some funny faces. My teeth were disgusting. The front ones, which the reconnaissance team had broken, were black and decayed. I couldn't get my face to work properly. If I tried to smile, it looked as if I was weeping. I threw the mirror away.

It was clear that the inhabitants of Tuk Puss labour camp never wanted to set foot in the place again. That was why they were out camping in the fields. The sun was setting and the line of soldiers was still winding up the mountain. There were wounded men, carried on hammocks. People were supporting their comrades. I still couldn't understand why I hadn't heard a single shot.

I went round the field looking for my sisters and trying to find somebody I knew to beg some food from. It was all very quiet. People lay in their bivouacs, puffing tobacco. Someone was threshing rice with a spade handle. Children were husking it in their hats. People were mending sacks and organizing themselves for survival.

I peered into a bivouac and saw Comrade Ran. I'd already heard that she'd married one of the Old People in the fishing commune. He looked scared when I appeared. She was thinner than she used to be and must have gone through something bad: her breasts had shrunk and her hair was cut like a man's.

'Comrade Ran,' I said, sitting down in the bivouac and nearly knocking over the pole, 'have you seen my sisters?'

They'd strewn dead leaves over the floor, and the tarpaulin was in a corner. That was their bed. Their pillow was an American rice sack, half filled. I thought she was pleased to see me, although she was upset. Her husband was stirring some rice porridge.

'Yes,' she said, 'I saw Bopha yesterday sometime in the camp, but I'm afraid I don't know about Sisopha. Have you eaten yet?'

'No, I haven't,' I said, 'I've been held by the comrade soldiers.' I was still choosing my words carefully. Her husband laid out the food for all of us. They'd got enamel plates and they had five spoons. At the end of the meal, during which her husband said nothing while I recounted all the recent events, I asked if I could keep my spoon. She would have given me some rice if her husband hadn't been there. I went off and slept in the open.

While I was dithering around the next morning, a friend slapped me on the shoulder and said, 'Hey, Someth, what the fuck are you doing here? Still fond of the Khmer Rouge? Come on, let's go. Our dreams have come true.' We joined the vast crowd coming down from the mountains.

We came to the Seventeenth of April Canal, named after the day of the liberation of Phnom Penh. Thousands of lives had been spent on this scheme. Now we camped beside it. It was like a party. Everyone shared their food. They'd brought the commune animals, which we were happy to eat. You could hear people shouting out, 'Anyone not got any roast pork? There's some over here. Hurry up, it's burning.' Some had plates. Some still had their hats. They called out for salt, and someone would raise his hand and beckon them over. I watched a man giving instructions to a cook not to overdo the beef.

And then they started singing.

The next day I went on towards Prey Svay. I felt wretched about my sisters and my inability to find them among the crowd, but I was drawn along in the general movement. As we got to Route Five, we reached the battlefield. Tonnes of rice had been burnt and were still smouldering. Dozens of dead Khmer Rouge lay in the fields. Uniforms were strewn everywhere, abandoned. I thought of the Lon Nol soldiers, on 17 April, how they ran past our house and people gave them clothes. We couldn't do that now. Not for anybody. I wondered who had set fire to the rice. That was *our* rice. You shouldn't set fire to rice.

Everyone, as they arrived at the scene, stood still and gazed at the mounds and mounds of burning rice. We just could not believe that somebody had done something like that. We always thought we had been through the worst, but every day produced some new atrocity.

A sudden movement caught my eye. I turned round to face a line of guns. Ho Chi Minh sandals. But olive uniforms. It was the Vietnamese.

PART THREE
The path to exile

TWENTY-EIGHT
Revenge

One of the soldiers shouted something at us. The woman beside me said we'd been told to drop everything and put our hands in the air. We all froze. Then came an order to divide up – women on one side of the road, men on the other. As we moved away from the women, we whispered to them that if things got nasty we would pretend that we were married to them. The soldiers came along, frisking the men first, and asking whether any of us was Khmer Rouge. I think they could have told from our skinny bodies that we were no such thing. At any rate they didn't seem very concerned, and they hardly checked the women. The interpreter had a strong Kampuchea Krom accent.

We had chanced upon a small mobile artillery unit. It seemed quite a relaxed affair. Some soldiers were sleeping in hammocks, with their guns propped at their side. Others were butchering a cow and cooking their evening meal beside the trucks. In the fields Cambodian children were gleaning the last of the harvest. When they had found no Khmer Rouge among us, the soldiers told us we could camp nearby, but not too close to the base.

I lay down in the field with my back against the paddy-dike. I couldn't believe how easily the Khmer Rouge had been defeated. They had vanished in a puff of smoke. People were still pouring down from the hills, and camping all around us. I was worried about my sisters, and began to search from tent to tent.

As darkness began to fall, a group of Old People and Khmer Rouge arrived, unarmed and in simple peasant clothes. They walked with their heads down, in fear of recognition, and made their camp as far from the crowd as they could. They sat together as they used to when they were supervising us in the field, but now their necks seemed to have shrunk and they were hiding their faces.

One of them knew my sisters well. It was Comrade Thol, the one

239

who had killed his own family. I went up and tapped him on the shoulder. He jumped. 'Have you seen Sisopha?' I asked.

Thol's voice shook, and he stuttered, 'I saw Sisopha and Bopha leaving Tuk Puss with a bullock cart, on the way to Maung Russei.'

'Thol,' I said, 'are you sure you've seen them?' This was the first time I'd interrogated a member of the reconnaissance team. His face was pale.

'Yes, I'm sure,' he said. 'They weren't taken up the mountain with the other comrades.' The others said nothing. Their heads retracted like turtles. We were only a few hundred metres from the Vietnamese. 'Believe me,' said Comrade Thol, pleading for his life, 'they weren't taken up the mountain. They were going to Maung Russei.'

'Good,' I said, and walked away.

I was wondering what would happen next. People were lighting the sandals they had found abandoned in the fields. The Vietnamese had thrown away the intestines of the cow, and the Cambodians were cleaning them. There was a smell of singeing hide. Others were preparing rice. The faces around the fires looked happy enough.

'Are there any Khmer Rouge around here?' asked a voice from Kampuchea Krom.

'I haven't seen any,' I said. I wasn't interested in the Khmer Rouge. I was just thinking about my family. The Cambodian speaker was surrounded by soldiers.

'Are you alone here?' he asked. 'Where's the rest of your relatives?'

I told him there were only three left apart from me. I thought they were somewhere in Maung Russei, and I hoped that I could join them there. He told me I would need a pass at the checkpoints, and I could get it the next day.

By now the whole field smelt of burning rubber from the sandal bonfires. The cow had been entirely consumed. There were some full stomachs. People sang pop songs from the Lon Nol period, and as their freedom became more familiar – as they began to believe in it – they started to think about revenge.

They were talking about the most hated people from their area, the canteen chief, leader of the reconnaissance team, the co-operative leader. A man would say, 'If I find him, you'll see what my anger is like.'

His friend would say, 'I'll give you a hand.' But people didn't want any help. They wanted the satisfaction of settling the scores on their own.

'How are you going to do it?'

'I'm going to chop him like a log.'

'Too easy. You should think of something worse. . .'

And so they began to think of something worse, like tying him to a tree and chopping up his flesh for the crows, or the kind of thing the Khmer Rouge had boasted about – the liver trick.

It would have been kinder of me, perhaps, to have reported Comrade Thol's presence to the Vietnamese. The next day I saw several of the old leaders from my area tied up and blindfolded in the camp, when I went to get my pass. Then I set out, in great excitement, along Route Five.

A young woman ran across my path, pursued by a group of men armed with *parang*s, axes and sticks. She ran quite a good distance before she fell to the ground, screaming, 'No, it wasn't me, I was told to do it. Please don't kill me. Please don't kill me.' The word 'please' was back in fashion.

It took them five seconds to kill her and cut off her head. The man with the axe held it up by the hair. He yelled into her face, 'I've got you now. Why did you starve me and my children? I'll get your husband next.' He took the head with him and went off with the group.

Although I'd seen hundreds of corpses in the last few years, this was the first time I'd actually witnessed anyone being killed. The Vietnamese stood by and did nothing.

At Maung Russei many people I knew were camping along the edge of the road. There was Comrade Ran, wearing a sarong now, sitting in the back of a cart, her face obscured by her *kramar*. Her husband looked more nervous than ever. Comrade Ran told him to stop the cart. She said my sisters had gone towards Wat Svay that morning, and that they were looking for me. Then she jumped back on the cart and handed me a plastic bag of tobacco. 'I'm sorry about everything,' she said.

Wat Svay was only half a day's walk from Maung Russei, but the road was cut and the soldiers wouldn't let anyone pass. There was a pond by the road, and those who had been refused permission decided to camp there. I found several friends from the bamboo jungle, including Phath, the boy who had been tortured for stealing cassava. We made a bivouac together and talked about past and future.

I now learnt that Phath had been a high-school student; he was a nephew of General Thapana Nging, a member of the cabinet. He was the only survivor from a family of thirteen.

We sat by the pond and I unwrapped Comrade Ran's tobacco for the first time. To my astonishment there were two packets of cigarette papers. She must have hoarded them for the whole Khmer Rouge regime, and what's more they were in perfect condition. Phath helped himself. We sat and smoked. After a while he said, 'If I find that bastard Chhoeun – ' from the bamboo jungle ' – I'm going to chop him in pieces.'

'Revenge isn't going to solve your problems,' I said.

'At least it'll stop my nightmares,' he replied, turning a deep red. 'When they tortured me, did they ever think for a moment that I was a Cambodian too? *Did they?*' He was pointing at my face. 'Come on – answer me!'

We sat there in silence. I noticed his cigarette was burning down to his fingertips. 'Come on,' I said, 'have some more tobacco, and then let's think about something to eat for tonight.'

Phath had been a close friend of mine. Otherwise I wouldn't have dared to disagree with him in this mood. I remember too that when he was caught stealing cassava he never said that I'd been with him. Now he had nothing and no one left. Nothing but a couple of green mangoes. I had rice. We scrounged some salt and began to make our meal.

During the next few days the fields around the pool became crowded. People cooked and sang and ate and cooked again and ate some more and slept and ate. They couldn't believe their luck at having survived. They beat out a rhythm on their cooking pots and danced in circles. They talked about their missing relatives, and they talked about revenge. It was mainly the men who were obsessed with revenge. They spent hours elaborating on the things they were going to do. But for my part, for some reason, I had no interest in it.

Now my rice was almost finished, and we all had to think about where the next food was coming from. At night we celebrated. By day we formed into groups to look for the Khmer Rouge food stocks. Phath knew of some in the fighting zone. Someone else had worked in one rather nearer. About fifty of us set off for it.

We walked back through my old co-operative. We passed the cassava field where I had been caught, and the grave that I had dug for Chhith. It was overgrown with tall weeds and creepers, but I could still see him clearly, before my eyes, as he had been when I buried him. The village was empty. Broken ox carts were strewn around.

The food stocks were hidden in a large cave on the bank of the Maung river. The man who had led us warned about booby traps. We followed him in, stepping in his footprints. I filled a sack as quickly as I could and rushed outside. Two or three others came out after me. Then the cave exploded with rice. It hit me like shrapnel. I checked for wounds but found none. Three men had been killed and several wounded. It was dark now and we decided to spend the night in the field. We did everything we could for the wounded men, but three more of them bled to death that night. We ripped the shirts off the dead men to make bandages for the others. One of the wounded kept saying, 'Don't leave me here. Take me with you. I don't want to die at the beginning of the peace.' We reassured him as best we could.

We were stopped on the way back. The Vietnamese thought the wounded men must be soldiers. But we pushed a woman to the front and she explained what had happened. We were told not to leave Maung Russei again without permission.

The crowd around the pond was mostly women, so many of the men having died. We had found *parang*s, and in the days that followed people sharpened them up and carved the handles. They took them on their shoulders everywhere they went, in case they met one of their old tormentors. Phath used to set off in the morning with a *parang* and a little bag of rice. He went regularly to the little market that had grown up down the road, hoping to meet Comrade Chhoeun. One day he thought he'd spotted him from behind. He ran up, saw his mistake and said, 'Sorry!' The man laughed. He had a *parang* as well. 'Don't be silly, I'm not *him*,' he said. He knew exactly what was on Phath's mind.

We had eaten so much rice we were getting bored with it. Some of the cattle had roamed loose and were grazing in the place where the fishing commune had been. We went in a group, past the useless Ream Kun dam, the Re-education Centre and the mass graves. The Vietnamese now occupied the Centre. I thought again of Mealea and my father.

The next day our hunting camp was alarmed to hear revolutionary songs. We fled into the bushes thinking it must be the Khmer Rouge.

Some boys came up, and looked at our tents in alarm. 'It must be them,' said one, 'let's go.' And they began to run.

'Hold on,' said a friend of mine, 'we were only hiding because we thought you were Khmer Rouge as well. Why are you singing those stupid songs?'

'In case we met the Khmer Rouge,' said the boys, and we all came out of the bushes, laughing. The boys had come from Kompong Kau, and one of them had known Orphea. But he was uncertain where she was.

We spent a day rounding up cattle, but that evening nobody wanted to kill the pig. None of us was used to butchery. In the end Phath said, 'OK, I'll do it.' And he slit its throat quite proficiently. We ate well that night. Then we all rushed to our mosquito nets, just as the widowers used to do, except that that night we'd all had so much pork fat it sounded as if the frogs were inside the mosquito nets.

As we passed Ream Kun dam on the way back, people were fishing the reservoir with nets. And a small crowd had gathered around the body of Comrade Thol. He had been dismembered, and people were talking to his head, spitting at it and telling it that this was the 'reward for murdering your parents'.

Phath had found a calf. I had a cow, and when we got back to Maung Russei, he kept saying he'd kill his and I'd kill mine. We both had to share the duties and now it was my turn to kill. I tied the cow to a tree, pushed its chin upward, closed my eyes and slit its throat. I was terrified that I wouldn't succeed. The cow would break loose, with a wound in its throat, and it would be mad at me. But I succeeded on the first go.

As we began cutting our animals, people rushed up with little drawstring purses in their hands and asked to exchange some jewellery for meat. For a leg joint I got a gold Buddha necklace and a pair of sapphire earrings. For a fillet steak weighing about two

244

kilos I got a sheet of gold the size of a postcard. People were offering large sapphires, bracelets, rings. Phath, who was planning to go back to Phnom Penh as soon as possible, sold the whole of his calf. He got a great bagful of treasure. But I stopped selling after I'd acquired enough salt to preserve what I'd got.

The village began to come to life now. The original inhabitants rebuilt their houses. They put curtains in the windows and locks on the doors, fenced in the gardens and planted flowers. The Re-education Centre was pulled down. People were beginning to leave for Phnom Penh, with home-made carts to carry their provisions. As yet there was no law and order, and as yet there were not many crimes, revenge excepted.

One day, on a rice-foraging trip, I saw the co-leader of the Tuk Puss mountain work-field, who was wanted by several of our group. He was sitting quietly on a rice sack, staring at the ground, apparently miles away. Three men came up behind him, and before he had even time to turn, his head came clean off his body and rolled at his feet, so that just for a split second it looked as if he was sitting there contemplating his own head.

Apart from foraging for rice, there were three ways of making your living. Those who didn't want to leave the village, for fear of meeting the Khmer Rouge, worked in the market or made palm sugar or toddy. Then there were the fishermen, who went in groups for safety. And then there were the gold-diggers, who wandered round the outskirts of the village searching for corpses and graves. Most Cambodians had gold-capped teeth, so these men became known as the millionaires. With astonishing speed – this all happened in a matter of three weeks – the gold-diggers had motorbikes, brand new Hondas which they had bought along the border. They had amazing watches, gold chains round their necks, shirts open to the waist, Thai cigarettes. But they still had Ho Chi Minh sandals. Footwear was not a priority among the smugglers.

The smugglers quickly worked out a relay from Thailand to Sisophon, to Battambang and down to where we were and beyond. So the price of goods built up all along the way. Gold was the currency. It came in sheets. If you wanted to pay for something small you snipped a bit off with scissors. People didn't yet have scales. When they cut up the gold from the old regime they discovered for the first time that it was impure – there was a core of some kind of heavy metal powder. But the gold was just sucked out in the direction of Thailand.

In its place came sarongs and jeans, cloth, proper milled rice, cosmetics, tinned foods, fruit, cigarettes and alcohol. All this had happened before I had managed to make contact with my sisters. Then one day someone said, 'Hey Someth, I bumped into your sister half an hour ago. She's looking for you somewhere over there.' Without stopping to thank him I rushed off in the direction he indicated. And there I saw Bopha, sitting dejectedly at the roadside with two companions. I gave a shout. We ran towards each other and burst into tears.

TWENTY-NINE
Weddings

When Bopha told me how she had heard where I was only two days before, I suddenly felt guilty. The road to Wat Svay had been open more than a week. Since then I'd been wandering around Maung Russei, worrying about my sisters but not going to look for them. I don't know why this was. Perhaps I was in a state of shock.

That evening one of the gold-diggers held a wedding party. Bopha and her friends came with me. A cow and a pig had been slaughtered, and the food was laid out on bamboo benches under a stilted house. The groom wore jeans and a new white shirt, a complicated watch and a gold bracelet. The bride had a new sarong and blouse, something like nine necklaces of varying sizes (I thought she was going to break her neck), and several rings. The only thing that reminded you of the last regime was their Ho Chi Minh sandals.

There were three tape-recorders playing identical music, and there were piles of torch batteries on hand. There were pump action kerosene lamps from Thailand, and you could see the dust being raised by the dancers. Home-made drums and two-string violins provided the traditional music, but there was no *achar* or monk. Vietnamese soldiers joined in (maybe they'd helped out with gasoline), dancing with their guns slung over their shoulders. The girls flirted with them and taught them *ram vong*, the round dance. There were about 300 guests. They arrived singly and left in pairs after eating and drinking toddy and smuggled spirits. Wives dropped in and dragged their husbands away. Elsewhere in the village there were smaller parties, lit by petrol lamps or Ho Chi Minh sandals. There was an improvised stringed instrument, made by digging a hole in the ground and covering it with a metal sheet. A bridge was placed on the metal, and two nylon cords stretched over it. The sound was like a double bass. Girls and boys sang to tin cymbals, and there was dancing through the night.

The road to Wat Svay was lined with little stalls. There were bicycle repair shops, watch menders, soup stalls, buckets of live fish, toddy shops with bottles of cloudy liquid, cake stalls and most of all the tailor shops, selling sarongs, blouses, and jeans. Some of them had sewing machines, rusty from disuse. There were sandal stalls with piles of old tyres. There were wheelwrights, and general blacksmiths making *parang*s and axes. Convoys of carts arrived from the region of the Tonle Sap, carrying rice and fish, and there were *cyclos* and motorbikes piled with contraband.

Sisopha and Bopha had made a little shed under the mango tree just by the pagoda. There were monks in smuggled robes. The altar was decorated with silver paper, and people were at their evening prayers. There was incense. There were candles. People had put up spirit houses by their sheds.

I couldn't believe how much Sisopha had changed for the better. She was healthy and her complexion had returned to its normal pale colour. She had met two brothers called Than and Khun. Khun was a very bright little boy, always smiling and ready for a chat. Than was extremely shy with me. I didn't realize at first why he was quite so shy. In those days he never seemed to smile. He was the kind of person of whom we would say, 'If he smiles, there'll be a tremendous thunderstorm tonight.' I remembered him from Tuk Puss work-field, where he had been a company leader. The other leaders thought he worked just a bit too hard. He kept himself to himself.

The reason why Than felt shy of me was that I was the head of the family, and he had an important question to ask.

I set out to find Orphea, who was living in a village called Thmar Kaul, the other side of Battambang. My sisters had packed some rice and dried meat in banana leaves. I walked part of the way, and hitched lifts on the ox carts. As we approached Battambang I noticed groups of Cambodian soldiers manning the checkpoints. They were partisans, armed by the Vietnamese. Usually there was one gun between three soldiers. They had Hanoi-issue uniforms, but no helmets. Their main function seemed to be that of receiving bribes from the smugglers. Also on the roadside people now had gold balances. The weights varied from stall to stall.

The bridge across the Sangké river was intact and guarded by

Vietnamese. The river was in spate, and children were swimming across holding banana trunks for floats. Battambang itself appeared not to have suffered too much. The market looked like something from before the war. There was even a place where you could hire electric guitars and sound systems for parties. There was a cooked food section, with grilled catfish and satay chicken. There were barber stalls and street dentists (doing a good trade – everyone had bad teeth now). The schools were occupied by the Vietnamese troops and the other modern buildings by the partisans' families. The only thing that wasn't functioning was the cinema. There was even a public transport system of Honda *cyclos*.

These markets continued all the way to Thmar Kaul, a beautiful village spread along a tributary of the Tonle Sap. It had big stilted houses roofed with tiles and surrounded by flourishing fruit trees. Its inhabitants looked cheerful and healthy. They had full stores of rice. I had never been here before, and I went from house to house asking for Orphea and her friend.

It was late afternoon. Women were husking rice or mending clothes while their husbands chopped wood for the cooking fires. Children ran around pulling wooden toys. Nobody knew Orphea, and when they asked me for a description I found it hard. It was a year since I had seen her, and I didn't know how much her looks would have changed through malnutrition. As it grew dark I wondered where I could spend the night. Kerosene lamps were being lit, and families were at dinner.

At the end of the village I saw a woman sitting on her steps, enjoying the cool of the evening. I stopped at her gate and asked my questions. She wanted to know everything – where my sister had worked, how I had been separated from her and so on. When she heard that she had been a nurse in Kompong Kau, she grew uneasy and asked why I was looking for this girl. I repeated that I was looking for my sister, and began to describe what had happened to the rest of the family. Finally the woman seemed to relent and said that her daughter too had worked in Kompong Kau infirmary. The daughter came out. I told her Orphea's name. The daughter jumped with surprise saying, 'She's my best friend. She's in the kitchen cooking supper.'

Out came Orphea, and to my delight I realized that the description I had been giving was completely wrong. She had grown into a beautiful young woman.

Back in Wat Svay we made improvements to the hut, staked out a little land and planted sweetcorn and vegetables. Sisopha was trading rice cakes for gold or rice. Orphea and Bopha went harvesting in the abandoned fields. One way or another we scraped along.

Than now plucked up courage to ask Sisopha to ask me to ask Bopha if she would marry him. I think this was one of Sisopha's matches. At any rate, she was in favour, and I was in favour if Bopha was in favour. I asked Bopha. She was in favour but what she said was, 'I don't mind, it's up to you, brother.' That meant yes. So I told Sisopha to tell Than, and Sisopha, being a little shy on this occasion, told Than's brother's wife to tell Than's brother to tell Than. Than was told. The next day his family came round, in the traditional way, to discuss the arrangements. Than was too shy to come with them. Bopha sat shyly in the corner of the hut. I was feeling shy, as this was the first occasion on which I had acted as head of the family. I just wished I could get out and dig the vegetable patch.

Than began to help me with the vegetables. He was a model worker. If you didn't tell him to stop he would work till he dropped. Whenever he bought himself a snack in the market he would bring one back for me, leave it without a word on the fence, dig for a while, and then say, 'That's yours, brother.' We had a few conversations. His mother had died when he was young, and his father had been executed by the Khmer Rouge during the war.

Two days before the wedding, Than's family arrived with their ox carts and camped around our two huts. They brought rice, fruit, herbs and smuggled spices. They brought sarongs for Bopha. Than's brother killed a cow, and we all helped prepare the traditional banquet. There were going to be fifty people. A tape-recorder, generator and loudspeaker had been hired from Battambang. There were musicians in Than's family. The monks and *achar* had been invited. The night before the wedding, the teenagers from the village came to dance.

I was annoyed not to be able to get any sleep. A convoy was leaving the next morning to go into the hills in search of sweet cassavas. I would have to go with it. I'd already given my gold to Sisopha, and I had nothing for Bopha's wedding present. The opportunity was not to be missed, and I had borrowed the ox cart from Than's family.

At six o'clock, as the wedding music began, I said goodbye to the family, taking a supply of the wedding food with me. It took us a day and a night to negotiate the sandy track to the cassava fields, and another day to dig and load the cart. I saw some ripe papayas, and thought that would make a good gift. There were about thirty of us in the convoy. We worked quietly and in fear of the Khmer Rouge. At night we arranged the wagons in a protective circle, tying up the cattle inside, and lighting small fires against the mosquitoes. We slept early, our *parang*s at our sides, and were off as soon as the light permitted.

Two Khmer Rouge appeared from nowhere and stopped the convoy. We were all convinced that we would be forced to go off with them. But the Khmer Rouge were frightened too, and they began by asking if there were any militiamen among us. They were very polite, and their uniforms were ragged and filthy. They looked like the guys who had first entered Phnom Penh. They came from cart to cart, begging for food. Their eyes were drawn to my papayas, which I thought it best to give them. Then they allowed us to go, thanking us first, to our amazement. We moved off as fast as we could. I'd noticed that the soldiers had no magazines in their guns, but nobody knew whether there were others of them in hiding. The load of cassava fetched a handful of jewellery, so I was able to give Bopha her present.

An extension to our hut had been fixed up for Than and Bopha, and Than had extended the vegetable patch and cleared a blocked well. He was very good with his hands, and very adept at finding food. We went to the flooded forest together to trap birds. Choosing a nest carefully, Than made a note of the exact spot on the nest where the bird landed. Here he placed a noose made of fishing twine, which was attached to a twig, and to a strip of inner tube. When the bird hit the right spot, the tail triggered the noose.

We caught a lot of birds this way – egrets, pelicans and herons. We took the eggs and the young, and loaded everything on to the cart. Than was in his element, humming away as he set up his hammock between the trees. We roasted an egret each and boiled a few eggs. Then the mosquitoes moved in and we called it a day.

On the way back Than saw a python track. We followed it and

found the snake curled up under a large dead log. My first instinct was to grab my *parang* and cut the python's head off, but Than told me it would knock me down before I even touched it. He quickly cut two forked branches a short distance away. Then he said, 'We have to get it to move. When it does so, you stick your fork on its tail and I'll take the head. Then we have to pull both ends. The quicker we do it, the safer we'll be.'

He rustled the grass with his fork. The python started to move. It was huge, three metres long and as thick as my thigh. Its skin was beautiful, the scales a bright metallic blue, edged with shiny green and yellow. We pounced, caught the snake and pulled it as in a tug-of-war. I heard a crack. 'We've done it!' said Than, wiping the sweat off his brow happily. The snake was almost immobile. We tied it in a sack, and Than sat on it all the way home.

At Wat Svay we traded some of the birds for gold. Than's brother set about killing the python. He mixed some tobacco leaves with powdered lime and water, and forced the liquid into its mouth. 'If you don't do that,' he said, 'the rest of the body goes on wriggling even after you've cut the head off. It could still knock you over. This is a good method I learnt a few years ago.' The python struggled a little and died. Than's brother made a spicy stew with coconut milk and lemon-grass. We sold the skin to the smugglers on their way to Thailand.

THIRTY
Escape

In the early days of the Vietnamese occupation, there was no political organization at all. We sorted out our own lives and let them get on with mopping up the Khmer Rouge. There was no law enforcement, but at that stage there wasn't much crime. We were so glad to be rid of the last regime that our relations with the new one were friendly enough, even if it was the invading force we had always dreaded. People joined up as militiamen. The Vietnamese would check their credentials with their neighbours, to make sure they were not re-arming the Khmer Rouge. The militiamen were given food for pay, and received handsome bribes from the smugglers.

I hardly paid any attention at first to what was going on. We were asked to attend meetings at Wat Svay about once every ten days. Most people didn't bother. When I dropped in on one out of curiosity, a Vietnamese speaker was praising, through an interpreter, the achievement of his troops. They had saved us from the wicked Pol Pot regime, which had starved us and slaughtered us while sending all our rice to China. The intention now was to create a new united Indo-China, a union of free allies.

I wasn't sure that all the rice had gone to China. It seemed just to have been stored away and now we were finding it and stuffing our faces with it. I wondered why the Khmer Rouge had built up such large stocks. It seemed to me that they didn't believe their regime was going to last for ever. They were going down a road which would lead either to war, or to some kind of rebellion. The stocks were part of a contingency plan. That was the only way I could explain them to myself.

So for a while people lived as if there was no tomorrow. Then the Vietnamese took over the rice that was left, and put it into com-munal stores for redistribution to the people. The boundaries of the fields had been destroyed by the Khmer Rouge, so the farmers who had survived could not simply reclaim their old land. Nothing had yet been decided about the system of rice production, and anyway people were fed up with agriculture. We all took to trade. Obviously this could only last as long as the gold lasted. The Thais were amazed at the amount of gold that was coming out of Cambodia. 'Where do you *get* it all from?' they asked a friend of mine, a smuggler.

'Oh,' he said, 'we've got gold trees in our country. We just pick it and put it in our pockets.'

We were formed into groups, each with a leader, to organize the rice distribution. The leaders went to the production team for their rations. But the production team was thoroughly corrupt. They filched rice from the communal store and sold it at high prices on the open market. The smugglers got richer. The militiamen were very happy. The rest of society got poorer very suddenly. People were going without food again. A large proportion of the rice on the market came from Thailand, which meant that it was very expensive.

And now crime became a problem. Robberies took place almost every night, and some of the robbers had pistols. People bought guns from deserting Vietnamese soldiers. The revenge killings resumed, and two or three times a week you would come across a fresh corpse. The starving Khmer Rouge came down from the hills to the villages, where people were still waiting for them. Celebrations continued every night, and these often ended in quarrels and murder.

The road was open as far as Phnom Penh, and convoys of Vietnamese soldiers were frequently seen on their way there. The trucks were carrying fridges, electric fans, televisions, new furniture which the soldiers had somehow got from Battambang. Civilians also travelled to the capital, but many were said to have been robbed or raped on the way. There were armed gangs along the road. The Vietnamese started to offer lifts on the convoys in return for several grams of gold. Some people managed to scrape together the right amount. We couldn't. So it was too dangerous to go to Phnom Penh.

On the other hand, we couldn't stay in Wat Svay. Food was running out, and the prospect of starvation was too much to face again. I mistrusted the Vietnamese as my father had taught me to from infancy. I didn't believe for a moment that they would leave Cambodia now they had occupied it. To return to Phnom Penh would be to live under their rule. They were our traditional enemies.

The only alternative was the Khmer Sereikar camp, the Freedom Khmers. They were just by the border with Thailand, and they were fighting both the Vietnamese and the Khmer Rouge. These people worked with the smugglers, and were given food by the Red Cross and the aid agencies. In my mind I had a picture of a clean and well-organized camp. It was said that the camp authorities would help you make a living by smuggling across the Thai border.

I was very depressed about my family's future, and began keeping a journal to dispel my depression. As the money and food began to run out, I talked with my sisters about what we were going to do. Sisopha was in favour of returning to Phnom Penh, but it seemed too difficult. In the end, we chose the camp.

Than, Bopha and Khun went first. A week later I set off in the morning with the smugglers. At each of the checkpoints along the way we had to give the Vietnamese some gold. We shared the costs among the twelve of us. That night we camped in an open field, setting a guard to watch out for gangsters. We had no guns, only *parang*s. In fact, people slept very little but three of us always kept watch.

The next day, the nearer we got to Svay Sisophon the more stalls there were along the road, and for the first time we began to see people trading in Thai money. There were more soldiers around – mostly Vietnamese. They were playing football or volleyball in the fields, and wandering hand in hand with Cambodian girls.

Sisophon was unlike anything I'd ever seen before. The houses were stacked with merchandise, prosperous and solid. Fat-bellied tradesmen with thick gold chains around their necks sat behind their displays of goods. It was the centre of the gold economy, and everybody knew what he was doing. The tradesmen had balances in glass cases. The smugglers had their own balances. Even the Vietnamese had balances, so that they could settle the arguments which frequently broke out. The tradesmen held the gold in gas jets, heating it till it was red hot, then letting it cool. If it discoloured as it cooled it wasn't pure. All gold had to be cut before it was accepted, to make sure there was no core of base metal. The most elaborate bracelets were being chopped up in this way. There were little children who waited for the traders to go, then searched where they had been cutting the gold for the tiniest specks of dust. And the point was that all Cambodia's gold was leaving the country. It was being sucked out into Thailand, as if by an enormous vacuum cleaner.

There were other currencies as well: there was an old kind of coinage which we called trough money, dating from pre-colonial days and shaped like a toy pig trough, some of it elaborately decorated; when it was sawn in half, the silver was absolutely white and pure. The traders were hammering them into different shapes, testing their malleability.

Then there were the jewel dealers, usually women. Not far from here, in Pailin, there was a sapphire mine and many Cambodians were experts in valuing jewels. The women had low-cut blouses and nice big bosoms to distract the customers. The stalls were simple low tables, about a metre square. Nothing was on display. They paid for the jewels in gold or *baht*, Thai money.

Antiquities formed another source of wealth. There were Buddhas from every period, stone heads of statues, *appsara* (bronze dancing girls), ivory carvings, jade, every portable treasure you could think of. Sisophon lay at the junction between roads coming from Phnom Penh and Siem Reap, the area of Angkor Wat, the ancient capital.

If you didn't dare go as far as the Khmer Sereikar camp, you did your business here. Absolutely everything was available in the market. But the prices at the camp, which was known as Camp 007, were fifty per cent lower, and if you ventured as far as Thailand, things were cheaper still. The smugglers in my group conferred. Some of them wanted to trade here and return. Those who wanted to continue agreed to meet at the level crossing before dusk.

I didn't wander around too much. I was scared of being picked up by the soldiers. The problem with getting to the camp was that the Vietnamese had mined the track, and quite often mortared it. They were making the journey very dangerous for the smugglers, and very profitable for everyone around, including themselves. The greater the danger, the greater the mark-up, the greater the bribe.

We met up as darkness fell, and waited for the best moment. The clouds grew thick. It was going to rain very soon. That's good, said the experts among the smugglers, the patrols don't come out when it's like this. We heard the sound of shelling from the direction of the camp. We waited for the lightning. Those who had Thai money wrapped it tightly in polythene. People took off their sandals and tied them to their belts. We would be going through water. If you had a purse, you hung it from your neck and tied it securely so that it wouldn't bump around. Those who had motorbikes no longer risked them on this stage of the journey: there was a special lock-up in Sisophon where they could leave them. The place issued tickets with plastic covers, and these were now being carefully secured in purses. Others rolled up their bags as tightly as possible and tied them to their backs. The lightning began. The thunder came closer. When the rain began to pour, the smugglers said, 'Now's the time.'

I put out my cigarette. I'd been smoking furiously all evening. By now there were about fifty of us, including women and children who had decided to live in the camp. We went in single file, wading down into the flooded field and followed the railway track for a few yards. The water was waist high, and fathers had to carry their children on their shoulders.

We turned right across the field. The ground gradually rose and we were squelching through mud. Before us lay a large dam built by the Khmer Rouge. We rested for a while, because we were told we would have to go over the dam very quickly. There were gunshots. Some guard or other was firing into the night. In twos and threes we crawled up the side of the dam, checked to see that all was clear, rushed across and down the other side. Some people were in quite a good mood – they rolled down the dam like professional soldiers. The children were extremely good and didn't make a sound.

Now we were going over bamboo scrub. Many of the bushes had been cut, leaving sharp ends, and it was hard on our bare feet. We were in single file again, treading in each other's footsteps. As conditions got worse, people began using torches to avoid the bamboo. The people behind hissed, 'Do you want to give us all away to the patrols? Put it out!'

I wandered slightly from the track, and was pulled immediately back into line. 'You idiot,' said a voice, 'd'you want to blow your head off? I wouldn't care if you were alone but I don't want to die with you.' He flashed his torch at a pile of dead leaves two or three metres away. 'It's a mine.'

'How do you know that?' I asked. 'This is the first time I've been smuggling.'

'Oh, I see,' he said. 'We were taught by the Khmer Sereikar in the New Camp. They come here every two or three days and check the track and bury any bodies they find.'

The rain was still pouring a couple of hours later, when an explosion at the front of the line made us all fall to the ground like dominoes. One man had stepped on a mine and been killed. Three were badly injured and groaning. We went on past them. Nobody took much notice of the incident – it seemed normal to them. I used to hear the smugglers saying that explosions were a kind of dance rhythm in their lives.

Just before dawn we came on a large group of refugees, also in single file, walking from the direction of Siem Reap. The two columns joined together. Now we had many more children. The refugees had all their household goods with them. We were going through scrubland where the smugglers told us we were likely to be shelled. They had a method of counting from the firing of the gun to the explosion of the first shell. After that, when you heard the gun fire, you counted again to the same number and fell flat. In this way you could run between the shells. But there was nowhere to hide. It was too dangerous to leave the track. But people did leave it as the shells began to fall. They hit the mines and were blown into pieces. There were fragments of flesh and clothes everywhere – in the trees, hanging from the bushes. We moved forward, counted, fell flat, waited and moved forward again. The explosions seemed to come gradually towards the track, and the whistle of the shells was right over our heads. I fell down again. A couple of hundred metres ahead of me a family was destroyed by a shell. When I reached the spot, I saw four dead people, and a little girl screaming in agony. She had lost half of an arm and a leg. Everyone was walking past her. I decided this time to help. I took her, bleeding, in my arms.

When the sun was over our heads the shelling stopped. 'Ah,' said the smugglers, 'they've stopped for lunch. We're safe. We'll get the goods in another hour.'

We began to run across the field towards the thick jungle. I was covered in blood, and the child was gasping. Beyond the trees lay an open field, and there in the distance stood a group of men with M-16s. They were wearing the uniform of Lon Nol soldiers. And there was something else very surprising about them when I got up close. They had on face powder, lipstick and false eyelashes. These were the Khmer Sereikar.

THIRTY-ONE
Smuggling and dancing

The Khmer Sereikar showed no interest in the dying girl. They wanted to know whether there were any militiamen among us, and whether we had any Cambodian antiquities in our possession. These were to be confiscated. The people behind me started concealing their valuables in pots of fermented food which they were carrying specially for the purpose. I asked for directions to the infirmary and rushed into the camp. Everyone was disgusted by the blood on my clothes.

A German medical worker, the first Westerner I had met in years, took the child from me. Her voice was fading and her eyes rolling back. She was calling for her parents. I said she was my sister. The German girl took her into the hospital tent, and I sat down on the bench outside. The blood began to attract the flies. The woman came out with some hospital pyjamas for me and told me I could wash at the tank nearby. By the time I had got the blood off and returned, the child had died. The girl asked through an interpreter what I wanted done with the body of my sister. So I told her the truth of the matter.

I wandered round the camp in a daze. The huts were laid out in rows, flimsy constructions of tarpaulin. In front of each was a display of goods for sale, including French bread, doughnuts and biscuits. People were walking past with two or three watches on either wrist. You could buy eels and pigs and sexy underwear. The paths were muddy and the conditions primitive, but the women were well dressed and happy. They wore make-up. They'd plucked their eyebrows. The heavy whiff of Thai perfume combined with the mud and excrement made me feel quite sick.

Pushing their way through the crowd came the Khmer Sereikar soldiers in their para uniforms. Some of them wore the insignia of the old Lon Nol army, and they dressed the same way, with scarves full of Buddhist charms around their necks. They had reflecting sunglasses. The muscular ones wore their shirts unbuttoned and showed off their magic tattoos. They had cowboy hats, and their pistol belts were worn aslant their hips. They walked with a slow swagger, like heroes, a black cigarette in the corner of the mouth. They stuck their bayonets into the tops of their American boots.

I set up a bivouac under a tree and sat down outside. My neighbours were all girls. They were washing, cooking rice and plucking each other's eyebrows. I could smell fried pork and garlic. The girls took a look in my direction and giggled. Perhaps they found my hospital clothes funny. I asked them what they did for a living.

'We go to the Thai village and buy things to sell to the smugglers.'

'Do you buy in gold?' I asked. They looked surprised at my ignorance and stopped plucking their eyebrows.

'No, in *baht*,' said one, 'you know – Thai money.' The girl who had been washing came over, sat down and lit up a Samit, producing the lighter from her brassiere.

'So where do you get the *baht* from in the first place?'

'You change your gold with the camp authorities,' said the smoker. She had long, painted, red nails. She smiled, 'If you want me to take you there you're very welcome.'

'It's too late now,' said another girl. 'The office will be closed.'

I took out my cigarettes and asked for the lighter. It was still warm, and smelt of perfume. 'Thanks,' I said. 'The trouble is I need money to buy something to eat. I haven't had anything for the last twenty-four hours. I'm starving.'

The girls looked at each other. The one who had been doing the cooking joined us. She was nice and plump. 'That's all right,' she said, 'you can join us. We've got plenty of food.' Then she coughed, turned to the girl with long nails and said, 'Don't blow that smoke in my face.' She was certainly the plumpest of the girls. I wondered what sort of girls they were.

Nice lean pork with garlic and lemon-grass. And iced water afterwards. Iced water! Another first in five years. Over the meal I told them my story, and that I was looking for my sisters and my brother-in-law. The girl with the long nails choked on the iced water.

'Are you married?' asked the cook. She wasn't just the plumpest. She was the prettiest.

'No, I'm not,' I said, sensing a blush coming.

'So who do you mean by your brother-in-law?' she probed. I kept my eyes on my plate.

'The man who married one of my sisters.'

'I see,' she said, and she passed me the metal bowl of iced water. 'Have some water.' I looked into her eyes as I took the bowl, and understood exactly what was going on.

I spent three or four days with the girls, and in that time the cook taught me all the Thai I needed to become a smuggler.

The poorest people in the camp were those who dug wells. Their livelihood was dependent on the weather. If it rained, they ate the leftovers. If it was dry, they had satay beef. The middle classes were those who worked for the aid agencies. They were paid in rations. The smugglers were the aristocrats, although their lives were always at risk. They were threatened by gangsters, Khmer Sereikar and Thai soldiers.

Than, when I met him in the market, was already a smuggler. Bopha and Khun were manning the stall in front of the hut. They didn't have much, just a couple of cartons of cigarettes, some bags of Crab tobacco, Five Goat batteries, and watermelons. Khun had a Snoopy T-shirt, inscribed 'I am the best'. Than had a watch and Bopha had a new gold chain. Their journey had been worse than mine. It had taken longer, they had been shelled and Khun had wept the whole way, from the pain in his feet. Sisopha and Orphea had better luck. The only risk had come from the mines. Now we were together again in one hut.

The smugglers wore training shoes for ease of running. I hid my money in my socks on the inside ankle, and placed a packet of cigarettes on the outside, to distract anyone doing a body search. I had jeans and a T-shirt, and fifty *baht* about me. I slept lightly, and when footsteps came past the hut I knew that the smugglers were setting out. I joined the group, most of them men, and as we left the camp we were stopped by the Khmer Sereikar. They used to beat you up if they caught you and you had nothing for a bribe. I was the last in the line.

'Where's your pass?' said the soldier.

'How much?'

'Twenty *baht* a head.'

So I would only have thirty to buy contraband. A dollar and a half.

I ran to catch up with the smugglers and we reached the border in half an hour. We sat down in a jute field since it was still too dark to go on. This was the worst part of the trip because there were often gangsters among the jute. People told me what to do in the village. The main thing was to get in as quickly as possible, bang on the doors, ask the Thais what kind of things they had, pay for the stuff and flee. If you spent more than half an hour you were likely to meet the soldiers, and then anything could happen. The smugglers had to stay as close as possible in the village in case they met gangsters. If the gangsters had no guns, the smugglers swore that they would help each other repel them. But they normally had guns.

The time had come. We ran across the raised road and the next field, reached the village and began banging on the doors. On my first attempt, I roused a very fat man in shorts, who was angry and half asleep. He had nothing. The second man had only sweets and doughnuts. I handed over the money and fled as I was told. That trip earned me twenty *baht* profit. After a few days of trading I had enough to buy the items most in demand by the Sisophon smugglers: torch batteries, tobacco and polyester cloth. Blue was the colour they favoured.

Everyone in the Thai village was involved in smuggling, and there was even a little soup stall to sell us breakfast. The really expert smugglers, who knew in advance which houses they were to visit and who therefore had a few minutes to spare, would have a bowl of soup and a coffee. The owner of the stall was half Chinese. He charged well over the odds for his soup. Sometimes before the customers had finished, one of us would shout out, 'Soldiers!' It might be true. It might be a joke. The effect was that the customers would down spoons and run for their lives. The soup vendor didn't much care. Suppose this happened once or twice a week, he was still well covered by a mark-up of 500 per cent.

The convoys of soldiers arrived every day between six and seven in the morning. Getting caught by them was no joke. I remember finding one man who had been beaten up by them. His legs had been broken and his skull cracked. We took him to the camp infirmary, who sent him off to hospital. Later his family were informed that he had died.

By now I was dealing regularly with one man. I went one morning with 500 *baht* and asked him for fifty metres of cloth. He agreed to supply it the next day, and I left the money with him. I had some more cash spare, so I took a couple of watermelons with me and was returning through the jute field when I bumped into three gangsters. At first, in the mist, I mistook them for smugglers, but as I drew near them they stepped to either side of the path, pulled out their flick knives and ordered me to stop. They were wearing tight jeans, and flowered shirts tied at the waist.

For a split second I thought of fighting them. The melons were conveniently tied with jute, and I thought if I threw one to the left, one to the right and kicked the guy in the middle, I might just do it. But then one of the gangsters moved behind me, and I thought better of it. I dropped the watermelons as ordered. They told me to give them all the money I had. I handed over my cash. They asked for more. I told them I had nothing more. They ordered me to strip. I threw them my clothes, one by one. I paused before taking off my shorts. They checked even the waistband, but found nothing. Then one of them said something like, 'You arsehole, you're a poor smuggler.' He kicked me in the backside, smashed one of the water-melons, and they all disappeared into the mist.

I put on my clothes and was just about to reach the border, when I heard the cry, 'Soldiers!' There were gunshots. There were three army trucks on the road. The Thai soldiers poured out in all directions to chase the smugglers, who kicked up a tremendous cloud of dust as they ran. I nipped across the border and hid behind the dike, fearing I would be shot. Footsteps came towards me and one of the smugglers ran right over my back. He was carrying a very heavy burden, a yoke with two buckets of water. As he trod on my back, he slipped. The buckets spilt their contents of water and watermelons. We both laughed. We often joked about these incidents when we had got over the border, looking back at the soldiers and laughing at the way they ran.

Now there was a shout from the jute field. A woman was screaming for help. My companion and I stopped laughing. Silence fell. When we put our heads over the paddy-dike again, we could see the soldiers loading the smugglers they had caught on to the trucks. Then three or four soldiers came out of the jute field and drove off with the rest.

The woman, when we saw her, was staggering naked in the direction of the camp. You could see the impression the bark of the tree had made against her back. There were bite marks on her shoulders. Someone had given her a *kramar* to wrap round her waist. Another man took off his shirt and she put it on, looking at the ground and whimpering.

The next time I saw her she was in the uniform of the Khmer Sereikar. She had given up smuggling.

I could see that Camp 007 was not run for the benefit of the refugees. It was like Phnom Penh on a small scale, corrupt from top to toe. The Khmer Sereikar lied about the number of refugees on their list in order to get more aid, just as the Lon Nol officers had lied about the phantom soldiers. Almost half of the aid received was sold to the smugglers. The soldiers' families got the profits. The camp authorities controlled the gold exchange at an extortionate rate, and punished anyone who traded gold for *baht* by confiscation of their goods.

The only useful thing the Khmer Sereikar did was to accompany the smugglers to the Thai village, in order to protect them from the gangsters. But this service had to be paid for. While we bought our goods, the soldiers sat in the soup shop and kept watch for the Thai army. But they weren't going to fight with the Thais.

Every night in the camp the authorities put on a concert of taped music, selling tickets at two *baht* a head. These events were sold out. It seemed ridiculous to me, the way people were living – terror during the day, romantic music at night. They appeared to have no interest in what was happening in the rest of Cambodia. They were obsessed with a trade that had no future and with fun. But behind this indifference to their surroundings, they knew that they would never be able to get away from their nightmares. All they could do was enjoy themselves as best they could. For my own part, when I thought about the future of my family, it scared me. I felt as if I was coming from nowhere and going nowhere.

One day a smuggler was shot in the village by the man with whom he was trading. The news scared everyone. Sisopha suggested I should get a job with the medical teams in the camp. It had never occurred to me that speaking English and French, I could be of some use. I realized that I was still living as if under the Khmer

Rouge, pretending to have no education. I went back to the German girl at the infirmary, and asked if I could help. She took me on and I began to interpret for the team.

An attack was expected from Phnom Chat, the Khmer Rouge camp. We were told to dig shelters. Soon after, I was returning from breakfast in the market when gunfire broke out. Some people jumped into their foxholes, but others who had a large amount of merchandise on display preferred to stay by their stalls. I rushed home and we waited till the gunfire stopped. People stuck their Buddhas in their mouths and waited nervously. When I got to the infirmary the wounded were already arriving. There had been about a hundred casualties.

The Vietnamese had moved their artillery forward, and the shelling was quite close to the camp. Refugees were arriving in large numbers from Phnom Penh. They told us that people were being arrested as Khmer Sereikar agents, and that those who claimed to have a background in higher education were being sent to Ho Chi Minh City for political training. Malnutrition had returned. The rice stocks had been taken to Vietnam, and people were dependent on the stuff that was being smuggled from Thailand. It sounded a very bad idea to go back to Phnom Penh, and yet Camp 007 was becoming more dangerous every day. The United Nations High Commission for Refugees had begun building a large camp inside Thailand and we were asked if we wanted to go. But we were afraid of the Thais, and we didn't know whether we would be able to come back, once we had left the country.

Sisopha was talking to some of the new arrivals when she realized that they were old friends with whom she had trained in the Royal Ballet, all those years ago. They decided to form a classical dance troupe here in the camp. The Khmer Sereikar liked the idea, and a long shed was put at our disposal. It was in the military base, next door to the place where the soldiers went for their magic tattoos. Before long we had about forty people training as dancers and musicians. I became secretary to the troupe, Sisopha and Bopha danced and Orphea sang.

We began performing one night a week to large crowds, and during the day we often gave impromptu shows for foreigners, from whom we begged the materials for costumes. When our skills had developed the Thais invited us to the military base. The soldiers seemed to enjoy it. We were beginning to become celebrities in the camp, and all kinds of favours came our way.

When the next attack was expected the Khmer Sereikar took us to spend the night in the military camp. We packed up all our belongings and moved behind the protective fence. They showed us the escape route we should use in case they were defeated. We couldn't sleep that night, although nothing happened. In the morning we were told that the report had been false and the danger was over.

The camp had returned to normal. A couple of trucks had arrived from Thailand, bringing bamboo for the construction of a new infirmary. Just as the Thais were unloading the bamboo, there was a sound of gunfire from the north-east. The workers dropped their loads, jumped back into the trucks and drove off as fast as they could. The firing came closer and we ran to our hut. This time the traders abandoned their merchandise and jumped into the foxholes. People looted the stalls as they ran, and knocked each other over in the rush. As they passed the food stalls, they reached out and stuffed banana fritters into their mouths. In the hut, all my family had taken to the foxholes, and now we began to hear the popping sound and explosions of the rifle grenades. The Khmer Sereikar were running away.

The area around us was suddenly deserted, apart from the families cowering in their holes. Merchandise was scattered everywhere. The wind blew the underwear along the street. A basket of eggs had been overturned, and the crowd had run over them. A bundle of five live chickens, tied together by their legs, was jerking around. People had shed their flipflops as they ran.

A grenade fell about twenty-five metres away. The dirt fell on the plastic sheeting of our roof. We had nothing to protect us from above. A second grenade landed much nearer. We heard an old woman, a relative of Than's, scream for a moment and then die. I told my family to move out under a tree. As soon as we got there, and lay down behind a dead tree trunk, the third grenade destroyed our hut.

And now we saw the Khmer Rouge, coming along one street away with their trousers rolled to their knees as they had been when they took Phnom Penh, their *kramar*s tied around their heads, and rolled-up hammocks slung from their waists. They strode along, paying no attention to the people in the foxholes, but looking for the Khmer Sereikar.

As I watched their faces set for killing, my body shrank. It seemed to curl like a query mark. The Khmer Rouge were not a nightmare. They were real. They were there. I feared them more than anything in the world, and I hated them. I hated the way they thought, the way they spoke, even the way they were walking made me hate them. I hated the way they hated us, and tortured us, and broke us, starved us and humiliated us. I'd only hated one person before in my life – and that was my first teacher at school, the sadist with his collection of canes and jak-fruit skins.

The first lessons of my education were all about punishment. We learnt that if a boy did wrong in this world he would be punished in the next. But this was not the next world. This was *this* world. The food in hell was maggots instead of rice. But we'd already eaten maggots. Demons were supposed to saw the stomachs of those who tampered with a boundary stone. But we knew all about that. We knew all about the tree of iron spikes, the red-hot platform, the pan of boiling oil. People were turned into crows in the next world. But we had seen people turn into crows in this world. That was what Mealea had seen – people turn into crows, crows turn into demons. There was no next world. There was nothing left to happen in it.

Hell was the threat that a monk used against a tiny child, or a king against his people. But the monks and the kings and the threat had disappeared, and of those last five years only the hell remained.

I watched the Khmer Rouge stride along the path. We were between the lines, all of us were between the lines. The Khmer Sereikar, with their magic scarves, their reflecting glasses, their cowboy hats and their pockets full of money, were behind us, standing with their backs against the Thai border, waiting for permission to cross.

The Khmer Rouge came past. It would have been easy to shoot them, and for the first time in my life I really wanted to. My family lay beside me – Sisopha, Bopha, Orphea, Than and Khun. I had to get them out.

The next day we left Cambodia for good.

THIRTY-TWO
Dancing for the Khmer Rouge

Khao-i-Dang refugee camp, with its broad straight roads of red gravel and its checkerboard design, was a little Phnom Penh. When I arrived there with the dance troupe in early 1980, it had a population of more than 100,000. The huts were made of bamboo, with palm-leaf walls and blue plastic sheeting for roofs. They were neatly built and laid out. There was always enough to eat. Hygiene was reasonable and the medical facilities were good. By the time I left it seven months later I was bored stiff, deeply frightened, and couldn't wait to see the back of it.

The city was overwhelmingly unemployed. You could work for the aid agencies, or on the construction of huts, or in the administrative offices – for the whole place was divided into sections along the lines of the Phnom Penh *quartiers*. For this work you would be paid in extra rations. But nobody really needed extra rations. You could try to sell them to the smugglers in 007, but you ran a high risk of being taken to the rocky terrain at the foot of Khao-i-Dang mountain and shot by the Thai soldiers.

By day the safety of the refugees was guaranteed by the presence of the foreigners. But at night it was different. The Thais came round in plain clothes with pistols confiscating contraband. The soldiers had already taken much of our property on arrival – tape-recorders, gold and jewellery, and any dangerous-looking knife. The night-time searches removed any goods that were on display. These would then be sold back to the better connected of the refugees. The tankers arrived every day with water, and their drivers brought cigarettes and cloth. We paid for this with *baht*. Gold was being kept against our hoped-for arrival in a third country.

Sometimes there was a market. Sometimes there wasn't. The Thai authorities were always trying to close it down. There were tailor shops, but these were secret. There was a coffee shop and you could even get alcohol, but again all this was illegal. Little girls sold cigarettes and sweets, but they never displayed more than five packets on a tray. When the market was open, there were cooked-food stalls selling food smuggled in by the soldiers' families, and this was welcome as we very soon got fed up with a diet of sardines and rice. People made noodles from their extra rice, and sold these to the soup stalls. Sometimes you could even find bread. There were card games in half of the huts, and people gambled with everything they had. There were discreet little brothels, attracting trade by word of mouth.

The most conspicuous buildings in this strange kind of city were the pagoda and the church. You went to the church in the morning, hoping that your attendance there would speed your departure to America. Cambodians had never been Christians before. Now they were eagerly bringing home Cambodian bibles, which made excellent cigarette papers. In the evening, doubling their bets, they prayed in the pagoda, which had a handful of monks and nuns and an *achar*. And again everyone prayed to get out as soon as possible.

What we called the main post office was a little hut with three noticeboards outside. If a letter came for you, your name would be posted here. Here too were the lists of people due to leave for the transit camps, the first stage of their journey abroad. This was the most crowded part of the city, apart from the World Food Programme Centre. You didn't send your letters out through this office, you gave them to any aid worker. Everyone with relatives abroad bombarded them with letters and requests for help. They wrote to anyone they knew.

Most people wanted to go to the States, second choice was France. Then came the countries we knew nothing about, but which had a reputation for taking people: New Zealand, Australia, Belgium, Canada. A Cambodian US citizen arrived from California offering to get people out in return for a certain sum of gold. He loaded up the gold, made a list of fifty customers, left and was never seen again. There were always rumours of ways of getting out. The Chinese had a reputation for doing this best, with the help of the Chinese community in Bangkok. The Vietnamese soldiers who had deserted were the ones with least hope.

There was a rumour that former officers would be taken immediately to the USA. Bopha, who had become pregnant and could therefore no longer dance, had taken a job in the section office, where people came to fill in their tracing cards. She showed me a list, in which practically everybody was claiming to be an officer and to have been trained by the CIA. Then we heard that the French would take all the intellectuals, and suddenly people had two tracing cards. They were no longer officers. They were teachers, professors, qualified engineers . . .

Finally, it was people who had worked for foreign agencies. The stories changed again. The more tracing cards there were, the more rations arrived. So the section leader was on to a good thing on the phantom soldier principle.

There were phantom orphans. The orphanage got the best rations, tinned chicken curry, for instance. Parents sent their children to live there, partly for the food and partly in the hope that they would be adopted. Once the child was in the States, the parents hoped to stage a dramatic and touching reunion. I reckoned about forty per cent of the orphans fell into this category. One of the women running the orphanage in my section had a large number of non-existent names on the list. One day there was a check up and she came rushing round the camp, begging for children so that she could make up the numbers. In the evening the orphanage tended to be rather deserted as the children were with their parents.

There were so many people in the camp it was not surprising that I should meet some old friends. Three or four of the photographers and some of the others who frequented the Groaning Table had survived the regime and were now being processed for departure. They were all very changed and not just physically – I looked at one of them and said, 'You've lost your teeth.' 'You've lost your teeth too,' he replied. All the happiness in their dispositions had been knocked out of them. They had dry smiles, and their jokes were hard and cynical.

And I met a man I had worked with on the Ream Kun dam. Although he'd been a group leader (and had regularly gone sick – he was not a hard worker), I'd always thought he must have had some education. I'd been right, but he was astonished to find that I'd been anything other than a stupid peasant. 'You kept that very well hidden,' he said, and we laughed. Either of us could have betrayed the other. But now he was without any family and without a contact in the West.

We spent a lot of time together, wandering aimlessly around the camp. And it wasn't hard to recognize the odd Khmer Rouge. I knew by the way they walked. They pretended to look at the ground, but their eyes were darting around. They were taking in everything. They looked just like the reconnaissance team in the work-field. And you could tell by the yellow edge of their *kramar*s. Some of them were still obsessed with pens, which they wore in their top pockets as a badge of rank.

Although the Khmer Rouge lived in fear, they knew that the danger had diminished. The *parang*s had been confiscated, and, besides, if anyone killed them, he might jeopardize his chances of going to the States.

But there was one day when a couple of hundred Khmer Rouge, all neatly uniformed, were brought to the gates. Little boys who had been playing there rushed through the camp with the news. People picked up their yokes and went down to the gates to welcome them. The Khmer Rouge had been evacuated from one of the camps on the border. As the crowd began to gather around them, they looked extremely nervous. People were saying, 'If I find the leader of my reconnaissance team I'm going to beat him to death.'

But the camp police, who were drawn from the refugees, although they had no weapons or uniforms, provided an escort, and the crowd kept back. The Khmer Rouge were taken to the orphanages, which were fenced in, and stayed only a night in the camp. If the camp authorities had thought that they could mix us up in this way, they were wrong. The next day the group was taken to Sakeo, an exclusively Khmer Rouge camp well away from the border.

The position of the Khmer Rouge had completely changed. Before, they had been considered the enemies of Americans and Thais alike. But now that the Vietnamese were controlling most of Cambodia, any enemy of the Vietnamese was a friend of the Thais. So the Khmer Rouge, as they were pushed out of their strongholds, were taken to Sakeo to recover. (Later on, they were encouraged and equipped to return to Cambodia, where they once again grew in strength. When I think about how the Thais have used Cambodians to destroy Cambodia, I am reminded of my father's story about them throwing the coins into the thicket at Lung Vek.)

Our classical dance troupe was one of three in Khao-i-Dang. We were all fierce rivals. There was an idea that we might be able to dance our way to a third country, preferably France, where Sihanouk's daughter, the legendary Bopha Devi, was living. People thought that she was just waiting for a troupe to turn up. Then she would train us all properly and take us on a world tour. Clearly, a lot depended on being considered the best in the camp.

An announcement was made that members of all three groups would be taken to perform in Sakeo. We were curious to see how the Khmer Rouge lived nowadays. Sisopha, Orphea, Than and I were among those chosen from our group. As our coach drove into the Khmer Rouge camp, we found the comrades lined up on either side of the road, men on the right, women on the left, smiling and clapping their hands to order. They looked as if they had been forced out to welcome some extremely unpleasant foreign head of state. A few of the dancers leant out of the coach and waved at them like film stars. I couldn't help laughing. It was so clear that our hosts loathed us.

They'd laid on a wonderful spread. There was tinned beef and chicken curry, a massive bowl of steaming rice, bananas cooked with coconut milk and sugar, and an oil drum full of bottles of soft drinks (Coca-Cola, Fanta and Sprite) and ice. A buffet. We were to help ourselves, Western-style. As I picked up my spoon I noticed that it was scratched with its owner's initials – a sign that it belonged to somebody really important. And they'd still got their US-military spoons. They hadn't thrown anything away.

There was much excitement in the changing room, as the buffet was consumed and the actors made up. We were stars. The girls really lingered over their make-up, and I had to hurry them up. 'Don't worry about that eyebrow,' I said, 'the Khmer Rouge have never seen anything like it before. Just get on stage.'

The traditional opening number was called the Wishing Dance. Orphea was singing to this effect: We are the dancers from the royal palace; we wish you health, prosperity and happiness. As Orphea and her companions sang these words, Sisopha and the other women were kneeling on the stage, swaying elegantly from side to side, with bowls of confetti in their hands. When the words stopped, they rose to their feet, tiptoed towards the Khmer Rouge and daintily flicked the confetti in their direction.

There were excited whispers when they came backstage. 'They seemed to like it!' said Sisopha. Then it was time for Than and me. We were standing in opposite wings. On cue, we put on our monkey masks, I made a signal to Than and we swaggered forth, piss-elegant and ready to fight, our wooden swords held high. We passed each other, I stamped my foot and we cartwheeled back to our original positions where we knelt down, placed our swords on the ground, and made the monkey's sign of respect to the audience. As I bent back the fingers of my left hand to do so, I could see the Khmer Rouge properly through the mask, in their neat rows, every *kramar* identically arranged around the neck. The men and women were separated by a gangway of at least three metres.

They looked distinctly worried. Nobody could tell what the monkey's sign of respect to the audience meant. It was a dance which had never been seen outside the palace before. Only courtiers and official visitors would have known it. In the monkey dance the white monkey is the king. Than, being the slimmer of us, took the role. I was the black monkey, who rebelled against the monkey law. We cartwheeled around and fought. Than had a magic sword. I didn't. We stabbed each other. I climbed on Than's knee and tried to plunge my weapon into his head. He struggled free. Then it was Than's turn. One foot on my left knee, one on my right shoulder. I struggled in vain. The blade went home. Now I was wounded and weak. Than jumped off and grabbed me by the shoulders. We struggled a while and then I died offstage.

When we came out to pay our respects, we would normally have removed our masks. But Than had a horror of being recognized by the Khmer Rouge. I looked into the audience again. They were slow-clapping. They had hated it. Maybe it was the story. Maybe they felt the black monkey should have won. If so, I'm sorry. That was the last time I let them down.

A month or so later, we were taken off to be processed.

THIRTY-THREE
Visas

I was nervous as the coaches left the gates of Khao-i-Dang. Perhaps it was all a trick. We had heard about an occasion when the Thais took a group of refugees up into the Dongrek Mountains and forced them over a cliff into Cambodia. Many had been killed. We were all thinking the same thing. But then we noticed the convoy of coaches was led and followed by the cars of the Red Cross.

After a few minutes the convoy stopped in the middle of nowhere. Out from behind the bushes came dozens of children with baskets of cakes and fruit. Everything had been beautifully prepared. Bopha had a craving for anything sour. We bought mangoes, water apples, guavas and rambai. Khun had a plastic bag of iced syrup with a straw. I thought of the bus I had taken on the journey to the estate all those years ago. Husbands and wives were shouting instructions at each other, and children were clamouring for treats. As in the old days, it was the wives who were looking after the money. The little vendors clung to the side of the bus, shouting their prices.

The refugees began clapping and singing. We sang the old folk songs, and those who couldn't remember the words hummed along. Aranyaprathet came and went, and the old smugglers pointed out the shops where they had collected their merchandise. The place was bristling with television aerials and motorbikes. The water lorries passed us on their way to the camp. At the checkpoint beside the road we saw Thai smugglers being stopped by the police, their motorbikes laden with goods.

Then for a brief moment we saw Sakeo and the Khmer Rouge. The camp was quiet. Black pyjamas were hanging to dry. People were filling buckets at the water tank. Somebody in the coach wondered out loud whether the Khmer Rouge would be going to a third country as well, but he was told they would be sent back to Cambodia soon. They would be sent back refreshed and re-equipped.

The people in the coach couldn't care less about the Khmer Rouge now. They were thinking about Chunburi, where they knew that conditions were better and they would be able to trade. No more sardines! And then there was the Third Country. Some people had relatives in France. They were already writing them letters. There was a Honda employee on his way to Japan. One girl, who had worked with the nurses, had found her way to Belgium. But most of all people wanted to go to the States.

'Now, Mr May,' said the American interviewer, 'you say here that you used to work for the correspondent of the *Washington Post*. Your English must be OK. I don't think you need an interpreter. Are you *sure* that you are younger than your sister . . .' and here he checked his file, '. . . May Sisopha?'

'Yes, sir,' I replied respectfully, 'she really is older than me.' The problem was that I had lost my looks. My teeth were in a terrible mess and when I looked in the mirror what I saw was an old man. I wasn't surprised that the guy didn't believe me.

'Are you *sure*', he continued, 'that Ram Than and Ram Khun are brothers?' It's true they don't look alike. Than was dark from working in the fields. Khun was a little boy. Dancing had been his first job.

'Yes, sir, they are brothers,' I said. Then he asked me when Than and Bopha had got married, and I seemed to convince him that we had all been together for about a year. He sent us out, demanding that Than stay behind for further questions.

This really worried us. Than is extremely shy, and as far as I know he had never been interviewed before. We sat down in front of the Joint Voluntary Agencies building. It was one o'clock and the heat was intense. Around us, everyone had put on their best clothes for the interview and the women were carefully made up. Those who had already lied in their interviews were trying to make the rest of their families learn the stories they had told. Many of the families were composites – they had taken in single people along the way and were passing them off as brothers. Some were pretending to be related to people abroad. Others had bought tracing cards for gold in Khao-i-Dang: they had to remember a lot of things –

their names, their dates of birth, the rest of the family details, a description of their house, all of it invented. There were also Thai girls of Cambodian origin who had come along to the camp to see if they could get to America.

Men who'd had successful interviews wanted to celebrate, and they would slip through the barbed wire to the noodle shop outside. When any soldiers came they had to rush back before they were caught, leaving half-finished drinks and ripping their shirts on the fence. These men could have eaten in a back room, but they preferred the front of the noodle shop where the hookers were.

Chunburi was not very closely guarded. There was a small market along the perimeter fence. At night the prostitutes came in, and some of the refugees bribed the soldiers to take them to nightclubs in Bangkok. I wouldn't have minded doing that myself – the basic bribe was ten dollars – but I'd given what money I had to the care of my sisters so it was going to be a bit difficult to explain.

Some of the girls in the camp were earning a little on the side. Jeeps arrived for them in the evening, and brought them back early in the morning. Soon they had nice clothes and hi-fis. It was in Chunburi that the adultery craze really got into full swing, and there were blazing rows among the women. The task of the interviewers was made even more difficult by the fact that some heads of family tried to ditch their wives and introduce their girlfriends under the wife's name. There were terrific scenes in the interviewing room.

Now Than emerged from his interrogation and Khun was called in directly. Than had been asked to describe his house before the war – how many rooms it had and what kind of trees there were around it, lots of details. We wondered how on earth Khun, being so young, was going to remember any of it. Ten minutes later I was called back in.

The interviewer was by now convinced that Than and Khun were brothers. 'However,' he said, 'I still do not believe that you are younger than your sister.'

'Well, sir,' I said, 'I don't know how to convince you. I really am younger than her. I – '

'*Get out!*' exploded the interviewer at the next table, and he threw a file across the room. He was talking to a young couple. 'Don't try to fool me. I know all the names of the commanders of the Republican Army, and I've never heard that name before.' Then he turned to the interpreter and said, 'Could you please tell them to get out of my sight?'

The interpreter translated the order. The husband said, 'But he really *was* my commander.'

'I'm sorry for this,' said the interpreter gently, 'but it's better for you to leave as he said. Otherwise your file will be stamped in red and then you'll never get out. Believe me.'

'What the hell are you saying to them?' interrupted the interviewer. 'Your job here is to translate what I say and no more than that. Understand?'

'Oh, yes, that's all I've done,' replied the interpreter. The couple left dejected.

'Hey, Mr May,' said my interviewer, 'let's get back to business. You're lucky to be with me. If you'd been with him the same thing could have happened to you. Now, think of a year you prefer, just one or two years older than your sister, and I'll change it for you. If you don't, believe me, you won't pass the next interview.'

'Could you let me think about it for a few hours?' I said.

The other couple had been telling the truth, and I was being asked to lie about my age. As I discussed the matter with my family, I felt a surge of anger at the Americans. If they hadn't interfered with our country in the first place, I thought, we wouldn't be in this mess now. We added two years to my age, and I returned to the interview room.

'Great,' said the interviewer when I told him of my new date of birth, 'everything is fine now. You'll have the next interview in a couple of days. Good luck.'

I thanked him very much.

'By the way,' he said, 'my interpreter is leaving for Canada tomorrow. What are you doing, apart from waiting for interviews?'

I was doing nothing.

'Your English is reasonable but it needs practice. Would you like to interpret for me?'

I was delighted. The pay was ten *baht* a day, enough for two packets of cigarettes. So I began working for Mike, a kind and considerate man. There was always a Coke at my elbow, and sometimes there was fruit.

On the second day of work we had a strange couple with

northern accents who claimed to have lived in Phnom Penh. Mike sent the wife out and asked the husband for details of the house. When the wife's turn came, the conversation went like this:

MIKE: How many rooms are there in your house?
ME: There are five rooms in your house?
WIFE: There are five rooms in my house.
ME: She said there are five rooms in her house.
MIKE: What kind of trees are there in the courtyard?
ME: There is a jak-fruit in the courtyard?
WIFE: Jak-fruit.

And so on, with the wife pretending to think, and me raising my voice at the end of each sentence to make it sound like a question. But this was the only dishonest case we had.

The worst interview was with the Immigration and Naturalization Service, who if you made a mistake could easily tear up your file before your eyes and send you back to Khao-i-Dang. The interviewer came from the embassy in a chauffeur-driven car. He looked extremely grand, and we felt he despised us. Once he had stamped our files, Accepted, he gave me a hard look. 'Mr May,' he said, 'you worked for the *Washington Post*. Did you know that the *Washington Post* were working for the Khmer Rouge?'

I thought he was accusing me of being an agent, and my face must have shown it because when I left the room I saw from the corner of my eye that he was laughing at me.

The last great hurdle was the medical examination. Bopha was more than eight months pregnant. Other pregnant women had been kept back until the birth of the baby. We knew that if the child was born in the States it would be an American citizen. But we needed blood-tests and X-rays and immunization. My sisters put their heads together and decided that Orphea looked so like Bopha she could stand in for her. Poor Orphea. She had eight blood-tests and two injections before we were transferred.

Now, to our excitement, our names came up for transfer to Lumpini camp. We saw just a little of Bangkok along the way – the first sight of a capital city in five years. And in an air-conditioned coach. We noticed the enormous streets with pedestrian bridges. I wondered if people ever fell off them into the road. There were supermarkets, which I'd never seen before. The sudden mass of traffic and the blaring horns reminded me of what Phnom Penh used to be like – only this was more so. For a moment, I thought, perhaps Phnom Penh is like this. I wished we had done the route by night, it would have been more beautiful.

At the gates of Lumpini I saw from an old notice that this was the municipal prison. My heart sank to my boots, or, as we say in Cambodian, my liver suddenly dropped out. But the inside was reassuring – it was crowded with Vietnamese, Cambodians, Laotians and Mong tribesmen. Every family seemed to have a stereo of some kind, and the noise of pop music from competing people was overwhelming. The Thais had allowed traders inside, and people were swapping gold for *baht*. There was a coffee shop selling alcohol too, and families toasted their imminent departure in brandy, sitting on the filthy ground.

We had to stay awake all night because we were told that if we missed our names on the list we would have to remain here. There was nowhere to sleep; in fact, it was hard enough to find a place to put your baggage. People shouted their addresses at each other so they could keep in touch in their new homes. When people were called out, their friends rushed up to take over their sleeping space. Fights broke out. A Laotian who had gone to the Vietnamese men's washroom got beaten up. The police came in and took the participants away. Everyone was yelling to their kids to stay together or they might be delayed for months. Those who didn't know any Thai were trying to learn the numbers of their tracing cards.

We stayed awake. Than and Khun had by now learnt how to read and write all of our names. They kept a regular check on the noticeboard. My sisters kept together, comforting Bopha, who looked as if she'd swallowed a time-bomb. At any moment she might go off. And if she did it here . . . I didn't like to think about it.

All that night, all the next day, all the next evening we waited. At midnight Than came rushing through the crowd with a piece of paper in his hand. He had copied my name and number from the list, just to be certain. We gathered our stuff together. The loud-speaker called us to the gate. Bopha managed to smile and get to her feet. She was on a slow fuse.

The two guards on the gate were as drunk as fish. They swayed to and fro, telling us to take our places along the pathway. But when we sat down, they cackled with laughter and told us to go to the other side of the path. And when we'd been there for a few minutes, and Bopha was just beginning to relax, they sent us back to the previous position. The guards were having a wonderful time. They lurched up to us and told us to sing — not a slow song, nothing romantic, it had to have some rhythm. They wanted each nation to give them a song.

One of the Cambodians got up nervously. He obviously hated what he was doing, but, like all of us, he knew that these guys could pretend we weren't on the list. He chose a song nobody liked very much. It was Sihanouk's 'In the Night'. Normally this is a really romantic song, but the singer made it last no more than a few seconds. He garbled the words, skipped verses and sat down furiously. But the drunker of the two guards was enjoying himself. He danced to the music and called on us to clap the rhythm. All the time, he lit cigarettes, took a couple of puffs and stamped them out ostentatiously.

The Laotian when he sang sounded just as if he was talking. I don't know what it meant, but it was melodious enough and it drew applause from his people. The guard was disappointed. He wanted something he could swing to. A Vietnamese got up and sang for all he was worth. It seemed to last five minutes. It had rhythm and backing. It earned the singer a cigarette. Then for a final number all the peoples of Indo-China were asked to sing in chorus. We all sang different songs and we sounded like frogs.

The drunker guard collapsed. When the buses finally arrived at dawn, his companion shook us each by the hand. He told me he wished he was going with us. But even when we got on the plane we were not convinced we would get out of Thailand. People were saying, 'They can take us off even now.' They watched the doors nervously. I read the seat-belt instructions and translated them for my family.

Sisopha said to Bopha, 'Don't make it too tight.'

Bopha said, 'It's really kicking now.'

Epilogue

Of the fourteen people who left Phnom Penh in the evacuation, only four survived. But my family, at the time of writing, has nine members. Orphea is studying computing at the University of Maryland. Her ambition is to work in a bank in data processing. Sisopha and Bopha work as chambermaids in a Holiday Inn near Washington DC. Sisopha has married Cisco, who comes from El Salvador, and they have a child called Sotra. Khun is at Alexandria high school. He wants to become a pilot. Than worked first as a nurseryman and is now an assistant cook in a Washington restaurant. Thavy, the daughter of Bopha and Than, recently began at infant school.

Thavy timed her birth pretty accurately. It was three days after our arrival in Washington, when we were staying at the Buddhist Temple on 16th St NW. We were sharing a room with two Vietnamese and four Laotians, refugees like ourselves. I was the only one who had much English. The television was on, with the volume turned down. We were watching 'I Love Lucy', and listening, simultaneously, to Vietnamese and Laotian pop music on two cassette players. Bopha had been uncomfortable on the flight and had been suffering pains for the last two days. Suddenly Sisopha called out for me to do something. The pains were serious now.

I rushed down to the temple coinbox. I'd been told the emergency number but in my panic I got it wrong. A recorded message told me to phone the operator. 'Quick, I need an ambulance,' I said.

'Hello,' said the operator, 'say that again. What can I do for you?'

'An ambulance, I want an ambulance.'

'What do you need an ambulance for?'

'My sister has a stomach-ache,' I said, twice over. There was some surprise at the other end of the line. 'She has a stomach-ache. I think she's going to have a baby.'

Finally the operator understood. She laughed. She said very slowly, 'If she is going to have a baby it's not called stomach-ache it's called labour pains.' By now my panic was complete. She reminded me I had to give her the address. With great difficulty I found the I–94 form I had been given in Bangkok and located the address on the form.

Upstairs, Bopha was gasping with pain, being comforted by Than and her sisters. Sisopha was in control. My mother had trained her well, and she had witnessed the births of my little brothers. She told Khun and myself to meet the ambulance outside. Khun waited on 16th, I kept a look-out on Kennedy Street. The ambulancemen came smiling. 'Is this the one with the stomach-ache?' they asked. They brought up their gear to the attic.

It took a long time to interpret the question, 'What time did the waters break?' because (a) I didn't understand what it referred to, and (b) I was shy with my sisters. Finally we got the answer. Bopha's secretiveness had continued to the last moment and the waters had broken two hours ago. Now the ambulancemen moved very fast. They asked me to come with them to interpret. At the last moment Than asked if he might come too.

In all the events I have described so far, I don't remember having been in such a panic as on that evening. I don't know why. When Phnom Penh was rocketed, or Camp 007 was shelled, other people panicked. I didn't. Life under the Khmer Rouge was constant fear, but panic would have been fatal. Perhaps the answer is that it was my turn to panic. I'd earned the right. Bopha was simply in agony. Than was comforting her as a husband should. The ambulancemen were fixing a saline drip. There was nothing for me to do. I sat there looking at the extractor fan in the roof and I just panicked.

The siren went. The ambulance moved off. The ambulanceman asked which hospital we were going to. I thought, Which hospital? Which *hospital*? *Which* hospital? The extractor fan looked like a neat piece of work. I hadn't seen one of them for a long time. The ambulanceman was nice. Strong-looking. Really muscular. He'd taken out a notepad. 'OK,' he said, 'what's her doctor's name?'

'My doctor's name?'

'*Her* doctor's name,' he said, leaning forward and laughing.

'He's in Bangkok!' I exclaimed. It sounded like the wrong thing to say.

'Now,' he said slowly, 'which hospital do you want to go to?' This time I thought of the right answer. 'I don't know,' I said.

He went up to the driver and told him to go to DC General. Then he sat down beside me. Bopha was screaming. 'Where have you come from?'

'Cambodia.'

'How long have you been here?'

'Three days.'

He sounded surprised. 'How did she get through the flight?'

I didn't know. She had looked pretty uncomfortable, picking at her steak and chips. But a lot of people had been uncomfortable. As we took off from Bangkok, a farmer behind me had said, 'Look, our feet are off the ground. What'll we do if something happens? If it was the sea we could swim. But we don't have wings!' There was vomiting all over the craft. But the chips were delicious and there were . . . brussels sprouts? And beautiful little portions of jelly, and butter wrapped in golden foil, which we slipped into our bags.

In San Francisco Bay, I remember the notice telling people not to pick the shellfish from the shore as some of it was poisonous. And then the shouts from the showers, as we discovered hot water. It was amazing. We were put two to a room. There were neatly made beds, sheets and blankets. There were wardrobes and mirrors and writing tables. There were bedside lights. There was wallpaper. I'd never seen anything like it.

The refugees were very keen on style. At every stage in our journey we had been given Western clothes, training shoes in Bangkok, and jeans, and sunglasses. People had enormous sports jackets, which went right down to their knees. We put on as many shirts as we possessed. We couldn't believe how cold it was. By now everyone had a comb, and we were experimenting in recreating the hairstyles of the 1960s. The young men had picked up hair cream, and there were partings all over the place. They'd given up banana-leaf cheroots and were smoking long thin More cigarettes. It was chic to display the packet in your vest pocket. We admired the sports cars on the belt-way and told each other which brand we would be buying when we'd made our fortunes. I was astonished at the way the roads climbed over each other. When I looked at the skyscrapers I thought how exhausting the stairs must be. And where were all the bicycles?

Now we were among the businessmen on the flight to Washington. *Their* jackets fitted. So did their shoes. There were blonde women in fur coats, beautifully made up and with *café-au-lait* legs. On a second glance I realized they were wearing some kind of long thin sock. I wondered about these. They seemed to be reading slimming magazines, and when the plane began to descend they made themselves up all over again.

We'd all been worried that Bopha might give birth mid-flight. She kept very quiet, and now that we were landing I wondered how on earth I was going to recognize our sponsors. The steward told me to hold up my Intergovernmental Commission on Emigration bag which had my name on it. I took him at his word. I walked all the way along the corridor holding the bag in the air. People looked at me very oddly. It seemed to take about two years before we reached the barrier. To my surprise, our sponsors from the Buddhist Social Services were Vietnamese . . .

The ambulanceman reached forward and adjusted the flow of the drip. All attention was focused on Bopha who was screaming. She gasped at the contractions. The ambulance came to a halt.

It took till midnight to deliver the baby. The doctors asked me to interpret, so I watched the whole business. I was horrified at the sight of the forceps. They looked like some instrument of torture. Than waited outside smoking Winstons. When I told him it was a girl he cheered up tremendously. The nurse asked for a name. I asked Than. Than asked me. I said I didn't know. Than didn't know either. Bopha was in no fit state to be asked. I suggested Thavy. Than said Thavy sounded great. I said, are you sure? Than said, yes. The doctors told us to go home, and that would have been that. Excepting we didn't have any money.

We didn't have *any* money – not in our pockets, not at the temple. I told the nurse. She said, take the bus. I said I didn't have any money. She said, take a taxi, pay at the other end. I said I didn't have any money at the other end. The nurse was in a bad mood. I was in a bad mood. The nurse took out a map and showed me how to get to the bus stop. I said, can I take the map with me? The nurse said it was the only one she had. The nurse was the fattest woman I had ever seen in my life. She was unimaginably huge. She waddled off, to return with a photocopy of the map and two tokens.

I was in a panic again. Another of the problems, in retrospect, was that I didn't yet have glasses. We walked along, stopping under lamp-posts to check the map. Than had just been learning the Roman alphabet, and he tried out this new knowledge on the street signs. Then he would ask how far it was. 'Shut up,' I said, 'just let me concentrate.' And I turned the map around again. I hadn't read a map for years. It was very cold. I'd been warned it was going to be cold, but I hadn't dreamt it would be this cold. We jogged from lamp-post to lamp-post, stopping to peer at the map.

While I was trying to work out the way forward, Than was keeping a mental record of the way back. My panic was that we'd never find the temple again. His panic was that he'd never relocate the hospital – and he hadn't yet seen Thavy. His jungle training must have been very good because he did find his way back on his own soon after.

The bus driver looked at the tokens and shook his head. Where on earth had we got them from? he asked, chewing. I told him our story. He said we'd have to pay. I told him we had no money. He drew in his breath. OK, he said, come in. As I showed him where we wanted to go, he looked briefly over his shoulder at the map. 'I *know*,' he laughed. I sat down right behind him just in case.

Washington, I could see, was beautiful at night. So many of the houses seemed to have flashing neon signs, some of them showing dancing women. I wondered why so many people were out so late at night. There were so many girls in short skirts. I thought they must be freezing. And they seemed to know a great number of people. Cars stopped for them, and they chatted away like anything. And then a very distant memory – something to do with bananas and oranges – flickered in the back of my mind.

The bus seemed to wind around town. Then I saw the sign for 16th Street, but I didn't know which direction we were supposed to be going in. I pulled out the map again, and panic hit me full in the face. After the alphabetical streets come all the complicated names. We stood on tiptoe, trying to make out the signs. But the driver was going too fast. I put the map in my pocket and began looking for something I could recognize. The trouble was, a lot of it was just park. On the left side, it wasn't a town, it was a bloody forest. On the right, the houses looked identical.

The bus stopped, and the driver said, 'OK, you two. This is your stop. Or do you want to go to Silver Spring?'

Than said, 'Oh yes, here's the tennis court.'

I was grateful to the driver, because at that time in my life I had no idea where on earth I was.